CINEMATIC

Flashes

CINEPHILIA AND CLASSICAL HOLLYWOOD

CINEMATIC

Flashes

RASHNA WADIA RICHARDS

INDIANA UNIVERSITY PRESS   *Bloomington & Indianapolis*

This book is a publication of

INDIANA UNIVERSITY PRESS
601 North Morton Street
Bloomington, Indiana 47404–3797 USA

iupress.indiana.edu

Telephone orders 800-842-6796
Fax orders 812-855-7931

∞ The paper used in this publication
meets the minimum requirements of
the American National Standard for
Information Sciences – Permanence of
Paper for Printed Library Materials, ANSI
Z39.48–1992.

Manufactured in the
United States of America

Library of Congress
Cataloging-in-Publication Data

Richards, Rashna Wadia, [date]
    Cinematic flashes : cinephilia and
classical Hollywood / Rashna Wadia
Richards.
    p. cm.
    Includes bibliographical references
and index.
    ISBN 978-0-253-00688-2 (cloth :
alk. paper) – ISBN 978-0-253-00692-9
(pbk. : alk. paper) – ISBN 978-0-
253-00700-1 (e-book) 1. Motion
pictures – United States – History –
20th century. 2. Hollywood (Los
Angeles, Calif.) – History – 20th
century. I. Title.
    PN1993.5.U6R495 2012
    791.430973 – dc23

                              2012026048

1 2 3 4 5   18 17 16 15 14 13

FOR JASON

Contents

Acknowledgments ix

· INTRODUCTION: Inventing
Cinephiliac Historiography *1*

1 SONIC BOOMS: 1929 and the Sensational
Transition to Sound *33*

2 SHOW STOPPERS: 1937 and the Chance
Encounter with Chiffons *77*

3 SIGNATURE CRIMES: 1946 and the Strange
Case of the Lost Scene (as Well as the Stranger
Case of the Missing Auteur) *113*

4 APOCALYPTIC ANTENNAE: 1954
and the End of Storytelling *161*

· CONCLUSION: The Cinephiliac Return *211*

Notes *221*

Bibliography *243*

Index *257*

Acknowledgments

This book was conceived in Robert B. Ray's seminar on experimental film criticism at the University of Florida in the fall of 2001. Robert introduced me to the concept of cinephilia and guided critically my many inchoate ideas. This book would not exist without his support and wise counsel, and I am truly grateful for his enduring influence on my work and my life. I also benefited immensely from the guidance and encouragement offered by Nora Alter, Susan Hegeman, and Greg Ulmer. They challenged me to think historically and helped refine my arguments considerably. In the English department at UF, I was thrilled to find a stimulating and demanding intellectual environment where I could hone my ideas and prepare for life as a teacher-scholar.

After graduate school, many mentors and friends have helped this project along. Among those who offered helpful feedback at conferences, responded to email inquiries, read my work, and provided encouragement at just the right moments, I want to thank especially Chris Holmlund, David T. Johnson, Christian Keathley, Christopher D. Morris, James Naremore, and Drake Stutesman. I am profoundly indebted to the two anonymous reviewers who read my manuscript for Indiana University Press. Their insightful comments and thoughtful suggestions have made this book much stronger, and I am extremely grateful to them.

Having encouraging colleagues and amazing students has made the process of revising and completing this book much easier. Members of the English department at Rhodes College have been terrific mentors and wonderful friends. I am lucky to work every day with Mark Behr, Gordon Bigelow, Marshall Boswell, Jenny Brady, Lori Garner,

Judy Haas, Mike Leslie, Scott Newstok, Leslie Petty, Seth Rudy, Brian Shaffer – and especially, Rebecca Finlayson. Outside my department, I am thrilled to have Jeanne Lopiparo, Laura Loth, and Evie Perry as my buddies. My students (too many to name) at Rhodes College and SUNY Brockport deserve special thanks for their passionate and thoughtful engagement with the movies. I am indebted especially to students in my seminars on film noir and fifties American cinema at Rhodes, where we tested the viability of cinephiliac historiography as a research method with tremendous success.

I am grateful to Jane Behnken and Raina Nadine Polivka, my editors at Indiana University Press, for their confidence in this project. I also thank June Silay, my project manager, and Candace McNulty, my copy-editor, who helped bring this book to life. I really value the institutional support I have received for research and travel over the years. In particular, thanks go to the University of Florida for awarding me the Alumni Fellowship from 2001 to 2005 and to Rhodes College for giving me a Faculty Development Endowment grant in 2009. My research has been greatly aided by the knowledgeable staff at the Margaret Herrick Library in Beverly Hills, California. Portions of this project were presented at conferences organized by the Society for Cinema and Media Studies and the Literature/Film Association, and I am thankful for the intellectual stimulation offered by those forums. I am also grateful to Kristi McKim for inviting me to present my work at Hendrix College; that enormously invigorating research trip was exactly what I needed while completing this book. An earlier version of chapter 2 was published in *Framework: The Journal of Cinema and Media* (48.2; 2007), and I thank Wayne State University Press for use of that material.

Finally, I would like to recognize my friends and family for their countless kindnesses. Sangreal and Eric Smith have offered their life-long friendship, and I am fortunate to have them as my closest allies. My parents, Aban and Yazdi Wadia, nurtured my love for the movies, especially old Hollywood movies, and I am forever and deeply grateful that they encouraged me to follow my passion, even when it led me so far away from them. My parents-in-law, Patti and Mike Richards, have been generous and encouraging; they have regaled me with stories of the studio era (Joseph Breen happens to be my great-grandfather-in-law), and I really appreciate being able to make their home my home base in Southern California. Eustis Richards's gentle canine sensibilities have brought me immense joy. Writing at my desk day after day would be far more tedious without his occasional nudging, yawning (yes, he yawns when he's excited!), and general goofy antics. Ultimately, I am most grateful to my husband, Jason Richards, who has watched every movie and read every word in this project multiple times. I dedicate this book to him; without his love and partnership, this long, strange trip would not have been imaginable or worthwhile. I am really glad I asked him in to watch Chaplin's *Modern Times* all those years ago.

CINEMATIC

Flashes

The things that have gone out of fashion have become
inexhaustible containers of memories.

WALTER BENJAMIN, *Arcades Project,* "J [Baudelaire]"

Is there a *theory* that can make use of the *concept* of contingency?

NIKLAS LUHMANN, *Observations on Modernity*

Introduction

Inventing Cinephiliac Historiography

IN A MOMENT

Her Hollywood debut is a fleeting farewell. Esther Blodgett (Judy Garland) is to wave a melancholy goodbye from a mock-up train window. On set various technicians prepare for the shot by gearing up the artificial lights, wind, snow, and steam. After Esther is quickly wrapped into a burly fur coat, the camera begins to roll. Then, there is a glitch. What is meant to be a memorable shot of a handkerchief trembling in the wind as the train leaves the station reveals a face. During the shoot, Judy Garland's bewildered visage inadvertently peeks through the window, a disruption that cannot be afforded at this point in the narrative. The moment is cut; the shot will have to be redone.

During a second take, we see what is necessary to keep the plot rolling: just a solitary hand, waving adieu. Made at a time when the studio system had already begun its slow but ceaseless crumble, it is understandable why George Cukor's *A Star Is Born* (1954) struggles with goodbye. Fortuitously, the next shot is better choreographed, so it carries the narrative along. But there is something about this other goodbye that always overwhelms me. Whereas the first take is clearly designed to be memorable, the second take has a startling irresistibility. In comparison to the former's poetic exterior shot of a frozen train window, enhanced by a glimpse of the troubled star's sorrowful face (Figure 0.1), this frame is highly cluttered and yet almost mundane (Figure 0.2). Next to the unglamorous inner workings of the studio system that take up more than half the frame, I am always struck by Judy Garland's discombobulated

1

0.1. *A Star Is Born* (dir. George Cukor, 1954).

body, estranged from her own hand waving goodbye by the frame of the mock-up train. I can never quite explain its emotional potency, but I am always startled by the unexpected pleasure of this excessive moment.

Looking back on classical Hollywood today, what can we say about such momentary audiovisual pleasures? Are these moments merely dazzling disruptions, to be dismissed as interesting but insignificant? Can we do more than collect them, catalog them, and cherish their entrancing interruptions? The Impressionists called such ineffable moments *photogénie,* reveling in the camera's ability to render mundane objects or gestures suddenly enigmatic. Jean Epstein likened *photogénie* to "a spark that appears in fits and starts," noticed in fleeting flashes, like Sessue Hayakawa walking out of a room in William C. DeMille's *The Honor of His House* (1918).[1] For Epstein, "a few instances offer the magnificent sight of his harmony in movement. He crosses a room quite naturally, his torso held at a slight angle. He hands his gloves to a servant. Opens a door. Then, having gone out, closes it."[2] The focus here is entirely on cinematic details. *Photogénie* is in Hayakawa's glide across the room, in his tilted torso and his gloves, and it "sweeps the scenario aside."[3] The Surrealists also favored such uncanny moments that could unexpectedly reveal, as André Breton suggested, "an almost forbidden world of sudden parallels, petrifying coincidences."[4] Indeed, for the Surrealists, the narrative situation was never as appealing as the poetic pull of cinema's alluring interruptions. As René Crevel argued, what is most compelling

0.2. *A Star Is Born* (dir. George Cukor, 1954).

is "a single minute's lyricism, the detail of a face, the surprise of a gesture," because its enchantment is "capable of making us forget all sorts of wretched stories."[5] In film theory, such striking moments have belonged to the tradition of cinephilia, practiced most ardently by a generation of post–World War II French critics enamored with American narrative cinema. Classical cinephilia was an attempt to capture in writing the thrill of cinema's peculiar details, curious gestures, and idiosyncratic traces, found particularly euphoric when encountered in standard studio films. As the next section will show, cinephilia fell into disrepute by the late 1960s, when audiovisual pleasure was discredited. Influenced by structuralism and psychoanalysis as well as a politically charged intellectual milieu, film theory came to regard cinephilia as an obsessively personal relationship with the screen rather than a theoretically rigorous approach to cinema. Since then, cinephilia has been mostly aligned with an uncritical buffism, condemned alongside the guilty pleasures of scopophilia, voyeurism, and fetishism.

Can cinephilia be more than that? After all, isn't the contemporary cinephile in the same predicament as Esther Blodgett, awkwardly attached to striking details, unable to say goodbye (to cinephilia) even after the studio system's machinery has been exposed? Is there a way to return to cinephilia's pleasures, while also offering a rigorous critique of the cinematic apparatus? To paraphrase Niklas Luhmann's question cited in the epigraph, is there a *critical methodology* that can make use of the *experience* of cinephilia? In a dialogue with Noel King, Paul Wille-men identifies cinephilia with surplus, contending that it hints at "some-thing which resists, which escapes existing networks of critical discourse and theoretical frameworks."[6] *Cinematic Flashes* activates this surplus signification of cinephilia by using moments of intense yet inscrutable audiovisual pleasure for an alternative way of writing film history. The moments I am interested in threaten to disrupt the linear structures of the narratives that contain them. Rather than advancing the plot, they distract attention from it. In short, they signify in excess. These moments are drawn primarily from classical Hollywood cinema, where excess seems counterintuitive. Film historians have long portrayed classical Hollywood as a unified body of work or a standardized system with an unwavering style. The studio system is defined by its rigid classi-cism, unyielding commercialism, and relentless narrative momentum. The moments I am interested in interrupt that onward drive and offer, as Mary Ann Doane suggests, "an escape from systematicity."[7] They are not the defining cinematic moments that are intended to be crucial and memorable – like the rebellious promise to survive from Scarlett O'Hara (Vivien Leigh) in Victor Fleming's *Gone with the Wind* (1939) or the shower sequence in Alfred Hitchcock's *Psycho* (1960). Instead, they are affective; they appear unexpectedly. They make the viewer feel as though she is seeing, almost inadvertently, something more than what is required by the narrative onscreen. That is, the moments I am interested in exceed the classical paradigm, in otherwise standard scenes or films, and offer momentary delight. By using such moments of inexplicable audiovisual pleasure as alternative points of entry into the studio system, this book transforms the spark of cinephilia into a practice of materialist film historiography.

I take my cue for this alternative form of history from Walter Ben-jamin, whose work informs this book both thematically and method-ologically. Writing at a time when the dependable linearity of history was being shattered, Benjamin sought to recuperate the fragmentary experi-ence of the modern age through an unorthodox form of historiography that would itself be fragmentary. Later in this chapter, I will present a comprehensive sketch of Benjamin's theory of historical materialism and how it might offer a model for cinephiliac historiography. Here, let me identify the argument in general. By now, the perception of modernity as a jolt triggered by the emergence of the modern city and its corollaries of mechanization, traffic, and crowds is fairly familiar. Like Georg Simmel and Siegfried Kracauer, Benjamin imagines modernity in terms of "a series of shocks and collisions" that could make "nervous impulses flow through [people] in rapid succession, like the energy from a battery."[8] But Benjamin is most concerned with the effect of these shocks on the practice of historiography. For him, modernity destroyed the ability to believe in history as a series of exceptional events linked by causal connections. No longer could a historian write history by straightforwardly comprehending the past as it really was. Rather, the past could "be seized only as an image which flashes up at the instant when it can be recognized and is never seen again."[9] In place of traditional historicism, Benjamin prefers a materialist historiography that renounces the epic element of history. Instead of grand, summative narratives, the materialist historian seeks fragmentary moments of the past that flash up in order "to blast open the continuum of history."[10] As Benjamin puts it in the unfinished *Arcades Project,* a work that tries to model this alternative historiography, "In the fields with which we are concerned, knowledge comes only in lightning flashes. The text is the long roll of thunder that follows."[11] This book treats cinephiliac moments like lightning flashes that fulgurate, sometimes in the margins of the cinematic frame, exceeding their narrative contexts and offering unusual modes of accessing the cultural history of classical Hollywood. Instead of the standard narrative about the studio system's standardization, *Cinematic Flashes* offers an interdisciplinary, episodic history of the era, enabling us to rethink classical Hollywood as an uncanny network of incongruities, coincidences, and contingencies.

RETURNING TO CINEPHILIA

Introducing a collection of pieces on cinephilia in a recent "In Focus" section of *Cinema Journal,* Mark Betz suggests that "in the last decade the tide has turned for cinephilia."[12] After being relegated to the margins for a long time, cinephilia has experienced a rebirth in film studies. The last few years have witnessed renewed enthusiasm for this once-frenzied discourse. Mary Ann Doane attributes this resurgence to the digital era's ostensible threat to the very existence of the medium that gave rise to cinephilia. Ciné-love, she observes, appears to have been resurrected "to delineate more precisely the contours of an object at the moment of its historical demise."[13] Doane's argument certainly makes sense if we trace the contemporary engagement with cinephilia back to Susan Sontag's dirge, at the centennial marking the invention of cinema, for what was arguably the most dynamic and influential art form of the twentieth century.[14] Tracing the "life cycle" of cinema's first one hundred years, Sontag argued that the medium once regarded as "quintessentially modern; distinctively accessible; poetic and mysterious and erotic and moral – all at the same time" has now become "a decadent art."[15] Why? Because what was once a vibrant medium of cultural expression has now fallen prey to hyperindustrialization. Back then, "you fell in love not just with actors but with cinema itself."[16] Back then, before the age of television and then digitization, cinema had sweeping social and intellectual force. Back then, cinephiles believed that "the movies encapsulated everything – and they did. It was both the book of art and the book of life."[17]

The *then* Sontag refers to is the roughly two-decade period, from the end of World War II until the political shift ushered in by May 1968, during which cinephilia was at the peak of its popularity. As a cinematic discourse, cinephilia became especially popular among a generation of postwar French critics captivated by American narrative cinema, which poured into France after the Liberation. Practiced at such journals as *Positif, Présence du Cinéma,* and most especially at *Cahiers du Cinéma* during what is now regarded as its classical phase, cinephilia was a fetishistic mode of spectatorship privileging the fleeting elements in a cinematic frame that could explode into moments of revelation.[18] By the 1950s, it was fueled by an intense nostalgia for the slowly disintegrating Hollywood studio system and an equally intense desire to experiment with filmmaking techniques, which ultimately developed into the French Nouvelle Vague. Classical cinephiles were drawn to Hollywood cinema because in its rigidly standardized mode of representation, they discovered moments of excess that could be fetishized and, as Roger Cardinal puts it, given "wholly 'unreasonable' priority or value."[19] Like Jean-Luc Godard's obsessive depiction of Eve Brent framed through the barrel of a gun in Samuel Fuller's *Forty Guns* (1957), a scene he would recreate with a rolled-up poster in *Breathless* (1960). Cinephiliac discourse was driven by detailed descriptions of such capricious moments. Consider François Truffaut's account of a moment from Howard Hawks's *Scarface* (1932):

> The most striking scene in the movie is unquestionably Boris Karloff's death. He squats down to throw a ball in a game of ninepins and doesn't get up; a rifle shot prostrates him. The camera follows the ball he's thrown as it knocks down all the pins except one that keeps spinning until it finally falls over, the exact symbol of Karloff himself, the last survivor of a rival gang that's been wiped out by [Paul] Muni. This isn't literature. It may be dance or poetry. It is certainly cinema.[20]

What Truffaut focuses on is the visual force of the moment. That the last bowling pin symbolizes Karloff as the last survivor in the narrative is only secondary to the pleasure of seeing that last bowling pin finally falling. This isn't analysis. It may be a sketch or a review. It is certainly cinephilia.

Among the *Cahiers* cinephiles, writing about such moments produced a clandestine mythology, which developed into praise for the films' *mise en scène* and subsequently into *la politique des auteurs*. Theirs became a crusade for seeing popular cinema as art and, more importantly, for seeing the director as an artist. Their favored moments offered proof of authorship, which might have gone unnoticed by the average viewer conditioned to be absorbed in the narrative at the expense of its striking details. Auteurism allowed them to rationalize their discourse to a certain degree. Showing consistency of style or theme across a body of work appeared to produce a schema for evaluating directorial talent. Still, cinephiliac discourse could not be fully codified into a theory, because the classical cinephile was interested in preserving the enigmas of cinema. In his review of Otto Preminger's *Angel Face* (1952), Jacques Rivette stands on the threshold of a systematic exploration of the director's oeuvre, but then he backs away:

> I can see very well that this would be the right moment for a predictable elaboration of the theme or the characters. For instance, Jean Simmons's role, and its analogies with or divergences from some of our director's other heroines etc. . . . I can see that very well, but the devil is whispering in my ear, "Is it really important; is that false and criminal purity not the very site of convention and artifice?"[21]

Rivette is not interested in explaining Preminger's work. Having identified Preminger's directorial technique with improvisation, with prefer-
ring "chance discoveries that mean things cannot go according to plan,"
Rivette refuses to find the key that could unlock all its mysteries. Instead,
his review tries to preserve the film's ambiguity.[22] He returns obsessively
not to *Angel Face*'s narrative but to its "particular gestures, attitudes and
reflexes – which are the *raison d'être* of [Preminger's] film, and its real
subject."[23] But these gestures, attitudes, and reflexes remain ultimately
inexplicable. Rivette may gesture toward them, but he cannot (or will
not) fully elucidate their effect on him. Thus, rather than interpretation
and analysis, classical cinephilia focused on experience. It was a kind
of manic spectatorship translated into writing, even though that initial experience remained untranslatable. Classical cinephiles invested
themselves in "a private, idiosyncratic meaning . . . characterized by the
compulsion to share what is unsharable, inarticulable."[24] And cinephilia
remained an intensely personal, eccentric love of cinema, reproduced
eccentrically.

But this kind of writing came under attack by the late 1960s. At *Cahiers,* trouble began brewing in 1963, when the journal replaced the chief
editor's position with an editorial board. What was at stake immediately
was a struggle between classicists and modernists. Younger critics like
Jean-Louis Comolli, Jean Narboni, and Claude Ollier soon joined the
board and brought with them a new political consciousness. They were
interested in new cinemas and were far more receptive to films from
Latin America and other third-world cultures than from Hollywood. By
the latter part of the decade, *Cahiers* was also absorbing the political and
cultural unrest spreading throughout France and much of the world. In
February 1968, protests began over the French government's decision to
replace Henri Langlois as the head of the Cinémathèque Française, the
film archive where Langlois screened an eclectic mix of films and nurtured the young *Cahiers* Turks' cinephilia. Although Langlois's dismissal
was reversed, the protests widened to register comprehensive antipathy
toward the de Gaulle government. They now included students and labor
and led to extensive strikes, shut-ins, and occupations. Revolution was in
the air, and it was at least partly fueled by a growing anti-Americanism.
By the late 60s, U.S. economic expansion, by way of corporate conglom-

erations, and military expansion, most notably in Vietnam, were widely criticized. In this environment, studio Hollywood stood no chance. As James Morrison has shown, after May '68, the *Cahiers* critics "promptly repudiated any lingering allegiance to Hollywood on the grounds that it could only be seen, from that point, as an arm of the American power machine."[25] The task of the critic now became to subvert personal cinematic pleasures and uncover the films' underlying ideologies. As David Kehr points out, "Althusser and Marx replaced Hitchcock and Hawks as *Cahiers* icons."[26] From a political perspective, American cinema came to be seen as representing the bourgeois status quo, and thinking about directors as artists was dismissed as subjective and romantic. Attention thus shifted from the cinematic experience to the cinematic apparatus, and cinephilia was replaced by a theoretically informed and critically rigorous structuralism.

Drawing on semiotic and psychoanalytic theories, Christian Metz inaugurated a more scientific approach to cinema. In place of the quasi-mystical adulation of films, film fragments, and auteurs, film scholarship committed itself, as Dudley Andrew puts it, to understanding "both the textual system that comprises any *film* and the larger systems that make up the *cinema*, regulating its function within economies of the psyche and of society."[27] A classic example of this cine-structuralism is the *Cahiers* editorial collective's analysis of John Ford's *Young Mr. Lincoln* (1939), whose insidious ideological machinations they hoped to uncover by revealing how the film was based on a "double repression – politics and eroticism."[28] There was no more room for an overtly subjective mode of writing or for the love of cinema itself. As cinephiles became increasingly political, they also became exceedingly suspicious of visual pleasure. In fact, in order to expose cinema's structuring absences and repressed meanings, a film critic could no longer have any affection for spectatorial pleasures. As Metz famously declared, "To be a theoretician of the cinema, one should ideally no longer love the cinema and yet still love it: have loved it a lot and only have detached oneself from it by taking it up again from the other end, taking it as the target for the very same scopic drive which had made one love it."[29] Once structuralist criticism took hold, the love of cinema appeared quaint at best and dangerous at worst. Like Metz, Serge Daney argued in "Theorize/

Terrorize" that the critic now had to get away from cinephilia, "to turn cinephilia back against itself, to reverse it like a glove."[30] That is to say, the naive obsession of one's youth had to be abandoned in order to perform serious scholarship.

What began as skepticism about cinephilia quickly bloomed into a desire to destroy it. By the 1970s, structuralism became codified in France as well as in Britain and the United States, and it ushered in a new age of academic film studies. In a recent dialogue with Peter Wollen and Lee Grieveson, Laura Mulvey confirms the transition from cinephilia to film studies at this time: "What begins with cinephilia, with the love of Hollywood, . . . becomes the theoretical study of Hollywood, becomes also a sustained critique of the ideology of Hollywood," a critique that is only possible via "a rejection of your own cinephilia."[31] Such animosity toward cinephilia, a notion we will return to in the conclusion, continued for another three decades. Even during subsequent turns toward historical poetics, cognitive psychology, and cultural studies, cinephiliac discourse largely disappeared. Meanwhile auteurism was co-opted by the film industry, which promoted directors as products after the birth of New Hollywood. Newly christened auteurs from Martin Scorsese to Peter Bogdanovich to Brian De Palma filled their films with quotations from, sometimes homages to, classical Hollywood cinema. Auteurist commentaries or directorial cuts became exceedingly popular. But cinephiliac discourse stayed buried in film studies for almost thirty years.

Cinephilia remained mostly submerged until Susan Sontag's requiem for the fading of cinema. Her elegy was not just for cinema but also for cinephilia. With the balance having shifted definitively in favor of cinema as an industry, Sontag argued, ciné-love could not survive. She lamented the passing of a time when "going to movies, thinking about movies, talking about movies became a passion among university students and other young people."[32] In the age of blockbusters, digitization, and the internet, that passion is now gone. Cinephilia is dead, Sontag noted, because it is no longer possible to imagine film spectatorship in terms of "unique, unrepeatable, magic experiences."[33] By extension, cinema is dead, because it doesn't inspire the kind of reverential awe it once did when cinephilia was in vogue. Sontag's piece was meant to be both a generational lament and a *fin de siècle* rumination. It mourned the loss of a certain style of movies as well as the pleasures of movie-going.

Rather than serving as the final word on a passionate mode of spectatorship, however, Sontag's elegy sparked a resurgence of international interest in cinephilia. In the last decade, numerous reassessments of cinephilia have appeared. It looks as though, after a long stupor, cinephilia has reemerged as a vital and vitalizing force in film studies. Indeed, if the period between 1945 and the late 1960s was the moment of cinephilia, then the last decade has seen something of a resurrection, proving that cinephilia may have been dead, but its ghost has lingered in writing about cinema. Initial reflections came from film critics, many of whom, like Sontag, took up the work of mourning "a lost love," the title of Stanley Kauffmann's piece for *The New Republic,* or lamented the waning of public taste for the "right movies," as David Denby did in *The New Yorker.*[34] Shortly thereafter, film scholars engaged the conversation with a spate of articles, journal issues, edited collections, and monographs on the subject. While some have argued directly with Sontag's premise that cinephilia is dead, others address the issue of what might be at stake in a reconsideration of the love of cinema at this stage. Although the conversation about the reemergence of cinephilia a little over a decade ago may have begun wistfully, considering what it was and mourning or disputing its alleged demise, the focus shifted quickly in some quarters to what it might yet become. In any case, most recent studies of cinephilia have traveled along two axes, either historicizing classical cinephilia or theorizing its transformation in today's global film culture. A few scholars have begun to hint at a third way, which I will outline after addressing each of these moves in turn, not only to assess the contemporary reception of cinephilia in film studies but also to explain where cinephiliac historiography fits in.

1. Historicizing Classical Cinephilia

Among the first to return to a discussion of classical cinephilia is Paul Willemen, who relates it to the Surrealists' celebration of chance, the Catholic discourse of revelation, and the notion of excess. He revisits André Bazin's faith in the ontology of the photographic image, suggesting that what motivated classical cinephilia's interest in sparks of contingency contained within seemingly ordinary moments was the desire to witness a "potential dislocation" by "seeing something beyond what is given to you to see."[35] That "something beyond" is the cinephile's belief that, because of cinema's indexicality, even in the most controlled circumstances, something of the real can appear on the screen inadvertently. That is why classical cinephiles emphasized fleeting cinephiliac moments that exceeded their representational or symbolic functions. But it was not enough to watch these moments or even to catalog them. Writing or, more accurately, "finding formulations to convey something about the intensity of that spark" has always been, according to Willemen, a primary response to cinephilia.[36] That is why cinephiliac discourse was so well suited to magazines like *Cahiers,* where cinephiliac musings found an outlet until the ideological shifts of the late 1960s made them untenable.

Subsequent histories have charted the rise and fall of cinephilia along this terrain established by Willemen. Antoine de Baecque's *La Cinéphilie* fleshes out the history of cinephiliac culture in France from 1944 to 1968 by expanding the context to encompass postwar French society, which encouraged movie-going as well as a broader culture of ciné-clubs and film journals.[37] Cinephilia, according to de Baecque, was not just a love of cinema but also a cultural practice and a way of life. He attributes the birth of the Nouvelle Vague to cinephiliac discourse as well, arguing that its popularity enabled the enthusiastic reception of such unconventional films as Godard's *Breathless* and Alain Resnais's *Last Year at Marienbad* (1961). His narrative ends in 1968, which marked the death of classical cinephilia in part because cinema failed to satisfactorily film the political events of the year. De Baecque's is ultimately a melancholy text about a bygone era and its passions.

Christian Keathley also locates classical cinephilia in this period, but his book is more ambitious because it offers an intellectual history of the idea of cinephilia. Keathley emphasizes a particular aspect of cinephiliac spectatorship, "panoramic perception," or the scanning of the cinematic frame for "marginal details and contingencies" that might increase "the possibility of encounters with cinephiliac moments."[38] He traces its roots back to postwar criticism at *Cahiers,* as many historians do, but he also aligns cinephilia with other disruptive reading/viewing practices, including Jean Epstein's *photogénie,* Marcel Proust's *mémoires involuntaires,* Walter Benjamin's flânerie, and Roland Barthes's "third meaning" or punctum. For Keathley, the cinephiliac moment ends up being "an area of spectatorial experience that resists co-optation by meaning" and therefore "seems to draw its intensity partly from the fact that it cannot be reduced or tamed by interpretation."[39] In place of interpreting cinephiliac moments, he offers the "cinephiliac anecdote," which aims at reinjecting the cinephiliac spirit into film studies. Thus, cinephilia may be dead, but Keathley tries to revive its disruptive energies for doing film criticism today. His approach remains subjective, but the imploration that cinephilia should not be seen simply as a historical object of study is enormously valuable, and cinephiliac historiography takes up that call.

2. *Theorizing Contemporary Cinephilia*

Whereas historians have focused on thinking about what cinephilia was before its demise, there is another group of scholars who rejected outright Sontag's premise that cinephilia was dead. The debate among these critics is not whether cinephilia is viable. Rather, assuming that cinephilia still thrives and has never expired, they are primarily concerned with new forms of ciné-love in the age of new media. The most influential recent work on redefining cinephilia for our time is Jonathan Rosenbaum and Adrian Martin's edited collection, *Movie Mutations,* which consists of five years of correspondence between film scholars and filmmakers, reflecting on, as their subtitle puts it, "the changing face of world cinephilia."[40] Unlike the historical approach's tendency to locate cinephilia in France, Rosenbaum and Martin are interested in delineating a transnational approach to contemporary cinephilia, calling for the study of global communities of cinephiles, whose collaborations can be facilitated by new media technologies as well as international film festivals. Their focus is on employing web-based communities and film festivals as sites for rediscovering cinematic pleasures in independents, the avant-garde, and films from developing national cinemas for the second generation of cinephiles. Contrary to Sontag's claim, the new cinephilia appears to be living up to the spirit, even frenzy, of classical cinephilia. However, despite the anthology's global scope and its attention to film-makers like Raúl Ruiz, Abbas Kiarostami, and Hou Hsiao-hsien, new cinephilia cannot help but slip into its own version of auteurism. More-over, new directors are often recognized because they reaffirm the great masters. Still, the overall notion of seeing new cinephiles as differently and globally connected, and new cinephilia as enabling cross-cultural communication, is highly useful.

Like Rosenbaum and Martin, Marijke de Valck and Malte Hagener present a series of essays that rethink contemporary cinephilia "as an umbrella term for a number of different affective engagements with the moving image."[41] But they also present cinephilia as "a period break and in doing so introduce Cinephilia 2 as a marker for future research."[42] Compared to their classical predecessors, the new generation is differ-ently networked. The essays in this volume explore these differences and the changes in marketing, distribution, and filmmaking that have emerged in response to the new wave of cinephilia. Instead of lamenting the fact that cinephiles no longer frequent movie theaters or local ciné-clubs, younger cinephiles, most of whom are born after the introduction of video recording technology, interface with cinema via new media, with all the benefits of downloading, file swapping, sampling, and even bootlegging.[43] In other words, the new cinephile has become a collec-tor and a trader, a lover and a savvy consumer. At once global and local, new cinephilia flourishes online, where the desire for a gestural outlet that Willemen identifies as essential to classical cinephilia finds a fresh avenue for expression. New cinephilia, it would seem, has embraced new technologies to further democratize the pleasures of cinema.

Growing up in Bombay, India, my own initial interest in cinephilia was fueled by these emerging technologies, at first by the videotape boom of the 1980s and then the rise of cable television and the internet in the 1990s. The coming of video provided access to a whole archive of films that I had only heard about from my father, a self-identified "old Holly-wood buff." For him, videos offered the possibility of owning movies he had grown up with in the 1950s and '60s and had assumed he would never see again. He purchased not only the "classics" but also forgotten films like Boris Ingster's *Stranger on the Third Floor* (1940) and John Sturges's *Last Train from Gun Hill* (1959), which he watched repeatedly after acquiring them. Old, overlooked films became mandatory weekend viewing at our house. My father's obsessive video consumption habits were motivated perhaps by the irrational fear that he might lose these cherished films again. They confirm Truffaut's remark that "when the use of video cassettes becomes widespread and people watch the films they love at home, anyone who owns a copy of *Mr. Arkadin* will be lucky indeed."[44] Truffaut rightly anticipated the revitalizing possibilities for a new generation of movie geeks in the age of video and perhaps the renewal of cinephilia itself. But this renewal, as we have seen, has functioned differently from the earlier generation's practices. While I did go to the movies – at the Eros Theater or the Regal Cinema, both built during the cinema boom of the 1930s, which screened Hollywood and Bollywood releases alike – my most vivid memories of movie-going consist of renting old videos and later DVDs. Rummaging through tiny rental stores, I tried to get my hands on the complete canons of known auteurs like Alfred Hitchcock and Orson Welles and also discovered unknown (to me) directors like Mitchell Leisen and Ida Lupino. Then, more movies became accessible via cable, and I began devouring films that had been heretofore unavailable to most people living outside a few Western metropolises. What I remember noticing in those grainy, usually black-and-white images were seemingly trifling details, like the enormous coffee cup in Edgar G. Ulmer's *Detour* (1945) and Marilyn Monroe being violently shaken on the beach in Fritz Lang's *Clash by Night* (1952). I would watch these films obsessively, rewinding my privileged moments over and over again. Years later, imagine my excitement when I discovered that there was a name for this way of viewing movies and that it could be the focus of serious study. I trace this brief personal history to show where I came in, so to speak, and to confess that my interest in classical Hollywood cinema was shaped by my experience as an accidental cinephile before I became engaged in studying it critically. That experience also motivates the fundamental questions of this book: once we have identified it, what kind of knowledge can we generate using cinephilia? How do we deploy cinephilia as a critical practice?

3. A Third Way

As I mentioned earlier, when cinephilia was initially revived, it was discussed in terms of a lost love. Cinephiliac histories have tended to follow that narrative, returning to cinephilia as a work of mourning for a lost past, a forgotten tradition. On the other hand, scholars who have refused to forfeit the love of cinema to an earlier generation have fought vigorously to demarcate Cinephilia 2, its stakes, and its similarities to mediaphilia at large.[45] For both approaches, what has primarily been at issue is a question of definition. If cinephilia is limited to a historical tradition, what was it? Alternatively, if cinephilia survives and thrives today, what has it become? But those questions are not easily answered, as cinephilia has always been a very slippery concept. "As soon as you look at it more closely," Willemen argues, "it vanishes, like sand between your fingers."[46]

In a beautifully moving piece about his varied preoccupations with cinema, a piece that began as a Serge Daney Memorial Lecture at the Rotterdam International Film Festival in 1998, Peter Wollen runs into similar difficulty when trying to define cinephilia. In his alphabetized entries, C stands for Cinephilia, which by turns appears as "an obsessive infatuation," "a 'sickness,' a malady," and "a desire to remain within the child's view of the world, always outside, always fascinated by a mysterious parental drama, always seeking to master one's anxiety by compulsive repetition."[47] Still, none of these offers a satisfactory explanation for Wollen's watching ten or twenty old films a week in "decrepit, run-down cinemas," or obsessively charting a course through London so he and his friends might watch multiple films back to back without missing the ending of one or the beginning of the next, or euphorically consuming "Hollywood films . . . refracted through French culture" in England.[48] The meaning of cinephilia remains dicey. Later in that essay, Wollen tries to define X, which he compares with *photogénie* and Barthes's punctum. X in cinema, he observes, "stands for an unknown quantity – for the strange fascination that makes us remember a particular shot or a particular camera movement."[49] In other words, X is that moment that eludes complete comprehension and therefore forces our obsessive return to it. Is cinephilia not the name for this irresistible moment that remains elusive as well? If so, the more urgent question for us is: how can we reengage with cinephilia without getting caught up in the ontological bind of the current historical and theoretical approaches?

Stimulus for a third way of thinking about cinephilia comes from an unlikely source. Writing about the ways in which new media technologies have transformed our experience of cinema, Laura Mulvey has recently argued that films need not be tethered to their narratives anymore. Video and digital media have led to new modes of seeing old movies. Viewers are no longer chained to the darkened theater or bound to the inexorable forward momentum of classical storytelling. Consequently, the ability to pause, rewind, and review offers unexpected opportunities. "Return and repetition," Mulvey suggests, "necessarily involve interrupting the flow of film, delaying its progress."[50] These interruptions break down the relentless onward drive of narrative events, providing access to "key moments and meanings . . . that could not have been perceived when hidden under the narrative flow and the movement of film."[51] Unlike the scopophilic delights offered by linear narratives that Mulvey decried and sought to destroy in the 1970s, these cinephiliac interruptions run counter to the flows of narrative development. They do not eroticize the pleasures of looking or reinforce the patriarchal narrative of voyeurism. These interruptions, she notes, can "bring about a 'reinvention' of textual analysis and a new wave of cinephilia."[52] That is why Mulvey is hopeful about using cinematic extracts, located by pursuing cinephiliac spectatorship, for a reinvigorated film analysis. George Toles offers a similar directive to work on film fragments that may lead us "to discover, on closer inspection born of intuition or feeling, how the inconsequential is essential."[53] For him, the rescue of fragments is the new task for cinephilia. Like Mulvey, Toles urges us to isolate moments that appear to signify in excess of their narrative contexts and use them to return to film history from a less frequented direction. That is also why Keathley advocates employing them as "clues perhaps to another history flashing through the cracks of those histories we already know."[54] But how can we use cinephilia for doing film history? A different approach will have to involve opening cinephilia up to multiple vectors, connections, and frameworks. The next section outlines that methodology, via another cinephiliac instance, in order to demonstrate how we might utilize an intense moment that has gone unnoticed in a longer history.

CINEPHILIAC HISTORIOGRAPHY

On a cross-section of an ancient sequoia, a black-gloved hand pauses to mark the passage of a lifetime in a moment. The concentric rings on the felled trunk denote celebrated events of history, as the camera pans left to reveal white loops indicating the conquest of territory, the promulgation of a charter, the birth of a nation. But Madeleine Elster (Kim Novak) is not entranced by this imposing dendrochronology. Her fingers linger over a gap in that grand narrative, where she enigmatically traces her own life and "death." "Somewhere in here I was born," she faintly enunciates, "and there I died," while her trembling hand points at two absent moments on the massive trunk (Figure 0.3). When the camera pulls back to reveal her ghostly visage, she whispers, as if directly to the dead sequoia, "It was only a moment for you. You . . . you took no notice."

This haunting moment from Alfred Hitchcock's *Vertigo* (1958) transfixes me. Although I cannot point out why, its sparse poignancy appears astounding. It is simply a standard Hitchcockian close-up, not as emotive as the following scene, where lovers embrace with waves crashing in the background, or as iconic as the zoom in/track out shot that replicates Scottie's (James Stewart) vertigo in the bell tower later. Its simplicity, however, is deceptive. On that cross-section of an old *Sequoia sempervirens*, monumental events of the last two thousand years leave their mark. But Madeleine's hand drifts to a spot unmarked in that history. That unidentified "moment" marks the life of Carlotta Valdes, a nineteenth-century woman whose life was not grand enough to make it into the official history books. As Pop Liebel (Konstantin Shayne), owner of the independent Argosy bookstore and oral historian, explains to Scottie, Carlotta was just an ordinary woman abandoned by a rich and powerful man after she had their baby. She died roaming the streets, despondently preoccupied by the loss of her beloved child. Scottie seeks out Pop Liebel because this tale, of "the small stuff, you know, people you've never heard of," cannot be found at any library. Madeleine is haunted by that haunted woman, and she returns to places in and around San Francisco that remind her of Carlotta, from the Mission Dolores to the Palace of the Legion of Honor art gallery to Fort Point. Her zealous energy is replicated by Scottie after her death and later by some of *Vertigo*'s most passionate

0.3. *Vertigo* (dir. Alfred Hitchcock, 1958).

viewers, who continue to retrace the sites of Madeleine's and Scottie's wanderings. As Geoffrey O'Brien notes, these cinephiliac pilgrims "seem fated to reenact *Vertigo*'s central gesture – the meticulous but fruitless attempt to re-create a lost object – with regard to the movie itself."[55] In that sense, *Vertigo* might be the ultimate cinephiliac object that remains enigmatic. The moment that Madeleine points to on the dead sequoia, then, might be seen as a *mise en abyme* of cinephilia. Like an ideal cinephiliac moment whose pull is as overwhelming as it is inscrutable, that moment interrupts the systematic flow of history because it does not fit the causal narrative of celebrated events. As Walter Benjamin would put it, it is the kind of moment that can "brush history against the grain."[56] In fact, it represents precisely the kind of nineteenth-century moment that might belong to the *Arcades Project*, a text that sought to uncover an alternative history of Paris by reading its kaleidoscopic, transient diversions and detritus.

Benjamin was preoccupied with the question of history, how to read it and write it, throughout his career. But he was especially engaged with the concept and its methodologies during what is generally regarded as his Parisian production cycle, from around 1927 until his death in 1940. During this time he worked on such pieces as "One-Way Street," "A Short

History of Photography," "The Work of Art in the Age of Mechanical Reproduction," and "Theses on the Philosophy of History," all the while also composing the *Arcades Project,* which was to become an illustrative realization of his philosophy of history. In each of these works, Benjamin attempts to historicize the pivotal change in human experience that occurred as a result of modernity. Traditionally, experience – not only of life but also of art and history – was governed by the logic of causality, and it was transmissible from one generation to the next. But the shift from a traditional, agrarian society to the modern, industrial era brought about a corresponding modification in the ways we understand experience. "Whereas experience was traditionally governed by the principles of continuity," Richard Wolin observes, "making it, at least in theory, something that was always familiar and predictable," modern life could primarily be encountered via a series of shocks – produced by urban life, crowds and automobiles, industrial production, and so on.[57] In place of the continuity of experience, modernity brought about an abrupt break in the form of a "wholesale fragmentation of experience."[58] Unlike many of his contemporaries, however, Benjamin was not distraught over the changes wrought by the advent of modernity. Instead of castigating modernity for destroying our traditional understanding of experience, Vanessa R. Schwartz points out, he wanted to "reimagine history and its study from the vantage point of a world transformed by capitalism, mechanical reproduction, and changing human perception."[59] If modernity had changed the very nature of experience, Benjamin argued, then our relationship to the past and our methods for understanding it would need to change too.

That is why Benjamin's work distinguishes materialist historiography from traditional historicism, breaking with the conventional model of history expressed in terms of linear progress. "Historicism contents itself with establishing a causal connection between various moments in history," Benjamin argues, thereby drawing a straight line from the past to the present.[60] Historical materialism, on the other hand, offers an interruptive model of history, where fleeting images from the past rupture the tedious narration of timeless truths. Traditional historicism's "method is additive; it musters a mass of data to fill the homogenous, empty time," whereas a materialist historian actively seeks out flashes of lightning, those moments that mark the limits of traditional historiography and point the way out of the continuum of history.[61] Accepting the "once upon a time" view of history, traditional historicism "gives the 'eternal' image of the past."[62] But the materialist historian realizes that the past cannot be mastered in that way. History is only accessible in brief moments that fly by, because "the past can be seized only as an image which flashes up at the instant when it can be recognized and is never seen again."[63] In the modern age, if the past can only be read fragmentarily, then the writing of history needs to be infused with such fragments. Benjamin's central insight, as Schwartz puts it, is that "histories would need to be written not only *for* their times but to embody the *forms* of their times."[64] Thus, more than anything, materialist historiography embodies the fragmentary experience of modernity.

What is the method for observing history in fragments? Working with fragments requires a shift from contemplation to distraction. Writing about Eugène Atget's photographs of deserted Parisian streets around the turn of the century, which he compares to the "scenes of crime," Benjamin argues that "they demand a specific kind of approach; free-floating contemplation is not appropriate to them."[65] Atget's photographs appear like fragments snatched out of the jaws of linear history; they cannot be received contemplatively. They can be grasped "much less through rapt attention than by noticing the object in incidental fashion."[66] That is to say, instead of immersing oneself into the historical object of study, historical materialism encourages disengaged or distracted participation. Unlike traditional historians focusing on understanding history as a continuum, materialist historians capture the striking fragments or images or traces as and when they flash up distractedly. At such moments, "thinking suddenly stops in a configuration pregnant with tensions."[67] The materialist historian delights in such tensions, what Benjamin calls "monads," that are extracted from their places in linear history and positioned within alternative contexts. Ultimately, historical materialism's "thinking is always rhizomatic, a becoming encountering a blockage, encountering another becoming."[68] The alternative history that emerges from this process is neither complete nor universal. It develops associatively, using a visual rather than linear logic.

What kinds of material would be suitable for this form of materialist historiography? Unlike other intellectuals of the Frankfurt School, Benjamin was genuinely interested in the cultural products of modern industrial capitalism. He believed that a materialist historian could mine wax museums and city streets, fashion and films, department stores and panoramas, old gas torches and snow globes for an understanding of the past. Where his fellow Marxists saw dangers of enchantment with the stuff of mass culture, which began to proliferate after the mid-nineteenth century, Benjamin perceived the possibility of excavating modernity's phantasmagorias for historiography. In fact, Gerhard Richter points out that his interest in kitschy objects must be seen as "an eminently political gesture . . . because it refuses to accept the condition of insignificance as something natural, exposing it instead as a cultural and political construction that relies on problematic unspoken assumptions."[69] That is why he was particularly intrigued by the forgotten details of mundane, perishable things. For Benjamin, returning to such objects can reveal the forgotten histories locked within them. "To someone looking through piles of old letters," he argues, "a stamp that has long been out of circulation on a torn envelope often says more than a reading of dozens of pages."[70] Although Theodor Adorno criticizes him for being "drawn to the petrified, frozen or obsolete elements of civilization," Benjamin considers a worthless object, like a well-worn stamp, worth more than any major find.[71] That is how, Susan Buck-Morss notes, he breaks "radically with the philosophical canon by searching for truth in the 'garbage heap.'"[72] The *Arcades Project* demonstrates this philosophy by showing how the ephemeral and excessive consumer culture of nineteenth-century Paris tells us more about the past than do grand ideas, celebrated events, or the works of eminent people.

Who would be adept at writing this kind of historical materialism? Since a materialist historiography is substantially different from traditional historicism, Benjamin proposes, marginal figures from the nineteenth century are much more suited to composing such a history. His later work, especially the *Arcades Project,* is peopled with figures who are capable of engaging with precisely those moments that do not fit neatly into sequential histories. The flâneur is the best known of such alter-historian figures. Charles Baudelaire first identified the flâneur as a detached pedestrian who follows a whimsical trail rather than the rules of traffic. Flânerie becomes a capricious method of traversing the modern city, pausing wherever an ordinary object, particularly at the iron- and glass-covered Parisian arcades, catches the eye, in order to discover an entire history out of a single detail – just as Victor Fournel would reconstruct "an entire conversation, an entire existence" out of a word heard in passing.[73] The flâneur's idle, fleeting, and non-utilitarian investment in the glittering merchandise at the arcades parallels the gambler's interest in the bodily sensations offered by the roll of the dice, the ragpicker's pursuit of discarded or outmoded scraps, the detective's scrutiny of the superficial trace, and the storyteller's attention to the slow piling up of details unveiled over various retellings. Ideal for historicizing the nineteenth century, these minor characters–turned–materialist historians exist on the periphery. Or, as Howard Eiland and Kevin McLaughlin point out, Benjamin's alternative historians are "figures in the middle – that is, figures residing within as well as outside the marketplace, between the worlds of money and magic – figures on the threshold."[74] They do not fully participate in the capitalist economy. Nor are they fully detached from it. They are liminal figures who are unwilling to grasp the past in its totality, because they do not stand outside history, observing it objectively. Rather, as Dimitris Vardoulakis notes, "subjectivity is implicated in method."[75] That is to say, their subjectivity informs the methods of materialist historiography. It is noteworthy that Benjamin uses these marginal characters not to evoke historically specific persons but to employ their historical practices – what Schwartz calls each character's "historically specific mode of experiencing the spectacle of the city" – as methodologies for accessing the past from a materialist perspective.[76] In that way, flânerie and its corresponding customs, like gambling, ragpicking, detecting, and storytelling, become exemplary ways of writing alternative histories.

Cinematic Flashes draws on these models both thematically and methodologically in order to translate cinephilia into a practice of materialist historiography. Like the eccentric activities Benjamin identifies, cinephilia is invested in stunning distractions, and it offers a similar kind of fortuitous exhilaration. Cinephiliac moments, as I am treating them, are instances that escape or outshine their narrative contexts. They are thrilling because they appear like raised seams within their plotlines. Unlike moments that are designed to be unforgettable, cinephiliac moments are relatively minor. They offer tiny glimpses of points where the coherent system of representation breaks down. As Doane suggests, cinephilia might be deemed "an investment in the graspability of the asystematic, the contingent."[77] That is why cinephiliac moments may be regarded as moments of cinematic excess, insofar as they surpass their diegetic requirements. To quote Kristin Thompson, in these excessive moments, "the function of the material elements of the film is accomplished, but their perceptual interest is by no means exhausted in the process."[78] It is this inexhaustible element that electrifies the cinephile, who may well be regarded as a descendant of Benjamin's unorthodox historian figures. For the cinephile is similarly drawn to moments that rise up, like lightning flashes, ready to be activated for an alternative discourse. In that sense, cinephilia may be seen as "an alternative spectatorial practice, one that stands in some contrast to the spectatorial posture assumed by dominant cinema."[79] Cinephilia cuts against the linearizing tendency of narrative cinema, highly prevalent in classical Hollywood films, which expect their viewers to focus on the systematic tale and not be diverted by any distracting details. I am especially drawn to such distracting details, as they offer the potential to prompt unanticipated discussions between film history, theory, and visual culture. Classical cinephiles at *Cahiers* were interested in similar moments, although their writing, as we have seen, emphasized only a desire to reproduce the initial encounter with the lightning flash. In the absence of video recording technologies, cinephiliac discourse was necessarily nostalgic, because writing about pleasurable moments was a way of mourning for lost fragments and films. A contemporary cinephile, writing about and yet being so far removed from the studio system, may also be focused on "something that is dead, past, but alive in memory."[80] But my intention here is to move beyond the paralyzing nostalgic impasse of classical cinephilia. While I begin with moments that are indeed dead but alive in memory, my purpose is not simply to reproduce or even to interpret them but to expand upon them. In that sense, I combine the passionate stance of classical cinephilia with the critical rigor of subsequent film criticism in order to use cinephilia as a way of writing film history.

Cinephiliac historiography differs from traditional ways of writing history in the following way: it starts with a moment that leads to a research question that then opens up new cultural, industrial, or technological contexts and ultimately paves the way for fresh theses about the object of study. Rather than opening with a hypothesis about the period being investigated, cinephilia's point of departure is an intriguing fragment or a mesmerizing trace. This means that the cinephile-historian begins with a moment of inexplicable audiovisual pleasure, which is personal. The history that follows is partly a way of accessing and understanding that subjective experience. Because there are no presuppositions made about the initial encounter, cinephiliac histories have the potential to activate various voices, networks, and connections that may not all fit into traditional histories. By way of contrast, consider Richard Maltby's *Hollywood Cinema*, which offers a fairly conventional way of thinking about Hollywood history. In the introduction, he suggests that "this book is as concerned with the idea of Hollywood as it is with individual movies."[81] In fact, I would argue that Maltby's text is far more concerned with the idea of Hollywood, which is explained in terms of its "commercial aesthetic." Thus, the book follows his stated proposition that "the aesthetic systems at work in Hollywood movies cannot sensibly be separated from their underlying commercial ambitions, and that as a cultural institution, Hollywood is best understood by considering the intricacies and contradictions of what I have called its commercial aesthetic."[82] I would not dispute this assertion about Hollywood. However, emphasizing a single argument about any era necessarily implies privileging those moments that fit the overarching thesis and support that narrative. Cinephilia works differently. As Walter Benjamin has suggested, materialist historiography is intrigued more by "the ruffle on a dress than some idea."[83] Such ruffles allow us to investigate history from its particulars rather than from any generalizations. Moreover, they provide access to the dialectical tensions or monads required for an alternative mode of thinking that "involves not only the flow of thoughts, but their arrest as well."[84] Cinephiliac moments are such pregnant pauses that have the potential to develop into unforeseen critical directions. Since cinephiliac historiography begins with specific moments rather than theoretical narratives, it offers "an escape from systematicity – both that of a tightly regulated classical system and that of its vaguely oppres-sive abstract analysis."[85] Indeed, cinephiliac historiography liberates the historian from constructing a singular, inclusive thesis. As the episodic chapters or case studies in this book demonstrate, cinephiliac moments offer varied points of entry into the cinematic and cultural terrain of clas-sical Hollywood. By extracting alluring film fragments from their other-wise ordinary classical narratives, placing them in alternative contexts, and linking them with kindred fragments associatively, cinephiliac his-toriography can uncover multiple histories that might otherwise remain buried under the weight of grand narratives about classical Hollywood.

In chapter 1, "Sonic Booms," the focus is on a moment of crisis in the late 1920s, when the studios are busily scrambling to incorporate sound into their classical narrative style. The industry's account of the arrival of sound, from chaos to standardization, is disputed by media historians, who do not see sound as a revolution and therefore emphasize the calcu-lated corporate decisions about resulting profits rather than confusion or disarray. Both versions of the conversion are accurate. But both of them have missed the sensational effects of the transition to sound. Beginning with a startling gunshot from Jacques Feyder's *The Kiss* (1929), and draw-ing on cinephiliac instants from other early sound experiments, I argue that we can regard the conversion as a gamble. Using the Benjaminian gambler's dependence on tactility, I trace the surprisingly visceral sen-sations of early sound cinema, when classical Hollywood temporarily rediscovers its corporeality as well as its modernity.

In chapter 2, "Show Stoppers," I explore the accidental encounters between Surrealism and the studio system through an eerie fur coat that falls on an unsuspecting working girl's head in Mitchell Leisen's screwball comedy *Easy Living* (1937). The Surrealist world of chance jux-tapositions seems quite distant from the standardized system of studio filmmaking, but glimpses of their implausible association are discov-ered through their ties to haute couture. Employing the Benjaminian ragpicker's reliance on outmoded or neglected articles, I try to imagine what *la mode* reveals about *le mode*, what fashion designing unexpectedly reveals about the method of studio filmmaking. Along the way, fur coats and chiffon dresses from women's films become unexpected mediators between the studio system and avant-garde art, and, for an uncanny moment in 1937, Hollywood looks a lot less like a standardized system than a strange network of accidents and coincidences.

In chapter 3, "Signature Crimes," I investigate the troubled role of the auteur within the studio system. Using the Benjaminian detective's inversion of exteriority and interiority, I demonstrate how we might circumvent the traditional auteurist approach for digging deep for inner meaning by looking at the cinematic surface for clues that might be hiding in plain sight. An unremarkable "signature" moment from Orson Welles's *The Stranger* (1946), where a former Nazi mastermind sketches a swastika on a notepad in a phone booth, becomes the key to rethinking Welles's most un-Wellesian film. In the process, we uncover the unpredictable operations of names and naming, typically so carefully regulated in Hollywood, and, in the context of proto-McCarthyism in the immediate postwar era, see how fakery might be unexpectedly aligned with genre-driven studio cinema.

In chapter 4, "Apocalyptic Antennae," I examine how sci-fi films from the 1950s, usually thought to invoke fear of Communist invasion, in fact explain Hollywood's own eschatological anxieties. The chapter begins with an ominous television broadcast, about gigantic mutant ants heading toward Los Angeles in Gordon Douglas's *Them!* (1954), that amplifies the sense of doom. Hollywood connects itself with sagacious storytelling, in competition with an imprudent media rival, television, which offers nothing more than cold, indifferent information. Following the Benjaminian storyteller's ability to tell and retell tales, and drawing on cinephiliac moments from other sci-fi films, I show how, in representing itself as the endangered species, Hollywood becomes allied with all that is wholesome, masculine, and American – and under threat from the alien Other. That alignment enables us to discover how a seemingly rational industry represents its irrationally excessive antagonism toward its fledgling media rival. Ultimately, it illustrates how quickly the movies adjust to the new popular culture landscape; while the studio system does not survive, Hollywood does, by unpredictably adjusting to a new media universe.

It is usually claimed that film studies was born as an academic discipline in the late 1960s when critics made the transition from cinephilia to a more rigorously defined and theoretically informed field of study. In the final chapter, "The Cinephiliac Return," I turn to an assessment of the return, however partial, implied in the recent resurgence of cinephilia. This epilogic treatment also reflects on the critical value of interruptions.

Cinematic Flashes may appear eclectic. It does not try to develop a cohesive argument about the studio era – and that is precisely the point. Classical Hollywood has long been defined by a standardized film style and a consistent mode of film production. Following André Bazin's lead that Hollywood's success depended on "not only the talent of this or that film-maker, but the genius of the system," most historians have emphasized the American film industry's reliance on a coherent model of classical filmmaking.[86] Initially, this notion of Hollywood as classical cinema was formulated during the post-1968 turn to film theory. Influenced by Althusserian and Lacanian thought, studio films were then characterized by and critiqued for offering the illusion of completeness while masking their processes of production. Borrowing Roland Barthes's opposition of readerly versus writerly texts, studio films were linked to the nineteenth-century realist novel, where "everything holds together," as opposed to writerly texts that are open-ended and ultimately modernist.[87] David Bordwell, Janet Staiger, and Kristin Thompson developed this conception of the studio system by emphasizing how the studios' classical style was perfectly suited for its vertically integrated mode of production and how that combination helped the studios stay profitably in business until around 1960. Their groundbreaking text stressed classicality in relation to "notions of decorum, proportion, formal harmony, respect for tradition, mimesis, self-effacing craftsmanship, and cool control of the perceiver's response," and they offered profitability as the rationale for this type of classicism.[88] Robert B. Ray built on this argument when he observed that the success of Hollywood depended on consistent formal and thematic paradigms. The formal paradigm enabled the "habitual subordination of style to story," and the thematic paradigm offered ideological resolution by drawing on traditional American mythology; together, they created a seemingly homogenous and unchanging formula for box-office success during the studio era (and beyond).[89] Elaborating Bazin's notion of "the genius of the system," Thomas Schatz famously argued that classical Hollywood might best be regarded as "a period when various social, industrial, technological, economic, and aesthetic forces struck a delicate balance."[90] For roughly four decades, from the 1920s until 1960 or so, that delicate balance enabled the industry to thrive. For Schatz, the industry developed "a set of formalized creative practices and constraints, and thus a body of work with a uniform style – a standard way of telling stories, from camera work and cutting to plot structure and thematics."[91] Thus, a narrative about classical Hollywood as an unfailingly rational and standardized system developed in the 1970s and '80s, and it has survived.

Looking back, the majority of historians continue to consider the studio system's operations as being similar to Taylorist and Fordist models of production, with strict division of labor, standardized models, and the systematic regulation of all tasks. Douglas Gomery emphasizes this model, where vertical integration reigns supreme, and profits override all aesthetic decisions; similarly, David Bordwell claims that the system Bazin praised was in fact "a coherent approach to genre, plot, and style that can assimilate a great range of thematic material."[92] Thus, the studio era continues to be noted for its reliable product and predictable system. And classical Hollywood history remains focused on what Maltby calls "the idea of Hollywood."

Without wholly opposing this standardized view of Hollywood history, this book takes a somewhat different approach. *Cinematic Flashes* suggests that alternative practices were always at work within the studio system, and some of them can come into focus by following cinephiliac historiography. If anything, I see classical Hollywood not *just* as a standardized system with an unwavering style, for it was also a disjointed network of accidents, excesses, and coincidences. In order to write the era's history, cinephiliac historiography offers what Miriam Hansen might call "a scaffold, matrix, or web that allows for a wide range of aesthetic effects and experiences," which "require more open-ended, promiscuous, and imaginative types of inquiry."[93] For although the studio system may have been based on rational, classical principles, Hollywood films have not always behaved according to those expectations. As Robert B. Ray has suggested, "for all its commitment to the positivism that Taylor and Ford had perfected, Hollywood was not making model Ts."[94] While the studio system appeared to be a rational institution, its products were not merely functional but also enthralling. Much less has been said by film historians about those alluring moments and the unexpected pleasures they afford. How do we investigate such instants that are "left out, marginalized, or repressed in the totalizing account of classical cinema"?[95] Cinephiliac historiography allows us to explore those moments that exceed the bounds of the standardized system as well as the limits of standard histories. By stepping out of bounds, forgoing a grand narrative logic, and dismissing the desire for interpretive closure, we can uncover alternative views of the studio era. By proceeding episodically, we can see classical Hollywood as a body of films replete with contradictions that cannot be contained by its traditional histories. By rethinking cinephilia as materialist historiography, we can discover a method for writing with moments of excessive yet inexplicable audiovisual pleasure and not just about them. Writing in 1940 "with the resignation of a ghost assigned to a haunted house," F. Scott Fitzgerald had intuited this approach to classical Hollywood. Instead of trying to find a rational narrative, he wrote quirky, brief sketches that illuminated the studio system. Hollywood, Fitzgerald argued, could be understood "only dimly and in flashes."[96] *Cinematic Flashes* pursues those flashes further. In place of a linear history that confirms conventional arguments about classical Hollywood's standardization, it explores four instances where the studio system reveals itself to be excessive, driven by chance, unpredictable, and irrational. If Paris, the capital of the nineteenth century, is revealed in its multiple, marginal traces, then Hollywood, arguably the capital of the twentieth century, may be discovered anew in its cinephiliac flashes as well.

In a strange, convoluted way, the period of motion pictures most dominated by technology and profit considerations also became one of the most creative periods in all film history. ... The silent cinema, progressing steadily, peaked late; the sound cinema, learning from the silent, peaked early.

WILLIAM K. EVERSON, *American Silent Film*

The mechanical marvel that astonished and disturbed viewers at the start of cinema history astonished and disturbed them again thirty years later, and it continued to do so until Hollywood and its audiences learned to adjust to the new films.

ROBERT SPADONI, *Uncanny Bodies*

ONE

Sonic Booms

1929 and the Sensational Transition to Sound

"DID YOU HEAR THE SHOT?"

Although the second gunshot is not heard, its startling boom causes far-reaching upheaval. Convinced that Irene Guarry (Greta Garbo) has shot her husband, but having no concrete evidence to prosecute her, the Lyonnais police scheme to fire another shot and use her unsuspecting visceral response to it to challenge her tale of the night of the murder. After timing their sonic reconstruction for "exactly three-fifteen," two officers go up to Irene's bedroom, where she claims to have slept through the bang of the original gunshot that killed her husband, while a third officer waits in the study downstairs, ready to aurally recreate the sound of the crime. Irene lies on her chaise lounge reading, ignoring with characteristic Garboesque poise the figures who saunter about her room and pretend to gather additional data. She may be curious about their presence, but she remains ostensibly unconcerned. At the prearranged moment, the two detectives fix their gaze on her, while a quick crosscut shows the officer downstairs raising his gun in the air and firing a shot. Unlike the explosion that kills Guarry (Anders Randolf) – that initial shot functions as one of the film's only two sound effects – this second shot remains diegetically unheard. Still, its reverberations register in multiple ways. The silent shot is first marked by the rising note in background music. Then a cut reveals an immensely startled Irene (Figure 1.1). Narratively, her loss of composure at the sound of the simulated gunshot exposes her involvement in Guarry's murder, for which she is charged and nearly convicted. Her defense, that she did not hear the shot

1.1. *The Kiss* (dir. Jacques Feyder, 1929).

that killed her husband the night before, is viscerally disproved. All of France seems to be in uproar over the socialite's trial, which threatens to divulge her innocent liaison with Pierre Lassalle (Lew Ayres), the young son of her husband's business associate, as well as her clandestine affair with André Dubail (Conrad Nagel), her current lawyer. But Irene is acquitted by the testimony of her husband's business partner Lassalle (Holmes Herbert), who discloses that Guarry was "on the verge of bankruptcy" and therefore "utterly depressed." The boom of the initial gunshot is thus attributed to the crash of the stock market. After some visible clamor in the courtroom, Irene is exonerated. And yet, the moment when Irene is physically shaken by sound lingers for me. While the film itself returns comfortably to silence, it remains striking because it is so unnervingly excessive.

Tumult over a single gunshot, and whether or not the protagonist hears it, is not surprising at a time when the industry is experiencing a startling conversion to sound. Jacques Feyder's *The Kiss* (1929) is not unlike other films made during the transition era, like Roy Del Ruth's *The First Auto* (1927), Michael Curtiz's *Noah's Ark* (1928), and John G. Blystone's *Thru Different Eyes* (1929), that focus keenly on the effects of sound. During the conversion years, between 1926 and 1929, when so many films were neither wholly silent nor completely talkies, and when many others were originally "conceived as pure silents," as William K. Everson suggests, and then later "given last-minute doctoring to include long and usually unnecessary [sound] sequences," sound became a central, not incidental, element of the diegesis.[1] In a sense, Irene Guarry's stunned response to the simulated gunshot mirrors Hollywood's own startled reaction to the quick success of Alan Crosland's *The Jazz Singer* (1927) and the ensuing rapid conversion to sound technology.[2]

In Samuel Goldwyn's biography, A. Scott Berg recounts the Los Angeles premiere of Crosland's film, when all of Hollywood's power players, including the Goldwyns and Irving Thalberg, watched in astounded silence. At the end, "thunderous clapping finally brought the houselights up," but Goldwyn's wife Frances Howard recalls seeing "'terror in all their faces' – the fear that 'the game they had been playing for years was finally over.'" Frances would later contemplate writing a murder mystery set in Hollywood, using this premiere night as her novel's opening scene. Perhaps it was never too early to begin worrying about the collapse of the studio system. For Frances, the arrival of sound was "'the most important event in cultural history since Martin Luther nailed his theses on the church door.'" Before that opening night, many in Hollywood had insisted that sound would not dramatically disrupt filmmaking practices. D. W. Griffith claimed that talkies were "impossible" and insisted that they would soon be "abandoned."[3] Irving Thalberg also did not appear rattled when, on his honeymoon with Norma Shearer, reporters asked him about the possibility of talkies on the horizon. "Novelty is always welcome," he dismissively argued, "but talking pictures are just a passing fad."[4] But after *The Jazz Singer* became a sensation at the box office, such predictions were quickly dropped. Even if we allow Frances Howard some gratuitous hysteria, the astounding impact of sound was undeniable. The success of Vitaphone at Warner Bros. sent all of Hollywood into a temporary panic. The effects were not just psychological but also financial. Aida Hozic notes that retrofitting for sound may have cost approximately $10,000 per theater, in addition to exorbitant millions spent on sound stages and new theaters nationwide.[5] Douglas Gomery suggests that the investments might have ranged from $23 million to $50 million, numbers that appear even more amazing when considering that "the original studios, built over a 15-year period, were valued at only $65 million."[6] However, after the deafening applause received by *The Jazz Singer,* surpassed by Lloyd Bacon's *The Singing Fool* (1928) a year later, conversion came to be seen as sound business practice. As Marilyn Fabe argues, conversion was nearly complete within two years because "so much did the public love the novelty of the sound film that the best-made silent film could not compete at the box office with the worst, most clumsily crafted 'talkie.'"[7] By 1930 or so, silent films had become a relic of the past. With all the hysteria tamed, sound became just another addition to naturalistic filmmaking in Hollywood, and the talkies were standardized within the studio system.

That is the version of the arrival of sound, from chaos to standardization, that Hollywood has created for itself in films about the period of transition. The best known among them, Stanley Donen and Gene Kelly's *Singin' in the Rain* (1952), sets up this narrative. Hollywood is at first shocked and rocked by the popularity of sound. Sound is seen, as the producer tells Don Lockwood (Gene Kelly), as a "sensation." But it is soon integrated into filmmaking, thus revolutionizing the business and making movies better than ever. To be sure, some careers are destroyed, and other stars fade – many due to their own inability to memorize scripts or sound wholesomely middle-American. Overall, however, conversion is represented as a success story. Made at a time when Hollywood was facing a significant threat from a rival medium, *Singin' in the Rain*'s faultless optimism about and faith in the studio system might be understandable. But film historians have naturally been circumspect about such an orderly, classical tale. Donald Crafton calls it the "'revolution' scenario," adopted by the studios because it offers "a usable retelling of the incidents, omitting the complicated parts about capitalization, expansion, competition, and the stylistic maneuvering that had modified cinema practice."[8] So how do we think about the "complicated parts" of the transition from silent cinema to complete synchronization? More importantly, how do we evaluate the sensation caused by sound?

In the last three decades, media scholars and historians have sought mostly to demystify Hollywood's version of the happy transition from turmoil to standardization. Indeed, many have argued against the "chaos" theory, suggesting that sound did not hit Hollywood like a bolt of lightning with the premiere of *The Jazz Singer*. Rather, it was anticipated for many years, and by 1927 it was inevitable. Thus, Scott Eyman's argument that "as 1927 became 1928, the limitless bowl of blue sky that habitually hovered over Los Angeles was about to start falling on explorer and homesteader alike" is usually discounted as being too hyperbolic.[9] Moreover, as Bordwell, Staiger, and Thompson have argued, sound could not have caused such upheaval because silent and sound cinema are not so different after all. "Sound cinema," they contend, "was not a radical alternative to silent filmmaking; sound as sound, as a material and as a set of technical procedures, was inserted into the already-constituted system of the classical Hollywood style."[10] That is to say, sound technology was wholly and relatively smoothly incorporated into the studio aesthetic. If anything, the addition of sound only further streamlined and standardized the assembly-line mode of filmmaking. More recently, Douglas Gomery has insisted that any notion of upheaval during the transition is fully misguided. Focusing entirely on the economic aspects of the transition to sound, Gomery maintains that "there was no chaos, but a consolidation of economic power, the collection of more revenues, and a global colossus known to the world as simply Hollywood."[11] Profits and mergers are Gomery's key words, not confusion or disarray. While Gomery's insistence that the addition of sound was a purely business decision, causing no uproar in the studio backlots, may be an overstatement, film history has generally opted for thinking of Hollywood's conversion to sound more or less in terms of integration into the studio system rather than hysterical pandemonium. But need we consider the moment of conversion in such starkly opposing terms? While sound may not necessarily have been "akin to a cinematic earthquake," the narrative of smooth conversion, as James Lastra suggests, "appears this *tidy* only in retrospect."[12] Is it not more likely that sound, although anticipated and rapidly integrated, also did arrive rather capriciously and sometimes riotously?

Donald Crafton argues that, during the transition era, sound did not behave as Hollywood expected. Disregarding both conventional versions, Crafton suggests that "there was neither a chaotic upheaval nor, at the other extreme, a carefully executed changeover."[13] He does accept that the distinction between silence and sound is not so clear cut and that "the concept of a dividing line between antediluvian silent cinema and the *modern* talkies was coscripted by the industry and the media."[14] Crafton also rebuffs the notion of an insurgency or a revolt. Although the conversion was swift, it was no revolution overthrowing the previous regime, as many studio insiders had feared. Instead, Crafton emphasizes how most of Hollywood's own predictions about sound did not come true. Silent films did not continue to be made alongside the talkies, as expected. The talkies did not attract more sophisticated audiences, as expected. Stars who spoke with European or non-American accents were not instantaneously rejected, as expected. Sound, Crafton suggests, "was more like an experiment that produced unexpected results."[15]

It is this notion of sound as an experiment, almost a kind of gamble, that preoccupies this chapter. Not enough attention has been paid to this aspect of the transition between 1926 and 1929. Everson observes that conversion-era films are "a vast no-man's land of hybrid productions, neither wholly silent nor wholly sound."[16] But he does not fully explore the effects of those films. More recently, Michel Chion has noted "the variety of experimentation going on" during the conversion, but his analysis also does not elaborate the specific forms of such experimentation.[17] If not as expected, how did sound behave? Based on this chapter's opening cinephiliac moment, we might say that Irene Guarry's startled reaction to the silent gunshot in *The Kiss* demonstrates that sound caused a somatic sensation. What draws me to it is that Garbo, long known for her poise, becomes so rattled that she virtually jumps out of her skin. What lingers for me is the feeling that, during this transitional moment, sound is regarded not only as aural or visual but also carnal. Indeed, her stunned response becomes especially intriguing if we see it as an allegory of Hollywood's sensational transition to sound. So, instead of the technological, industrial, and socioeconomic effects of sound, how do we think about that other sense of sensation, as a bodily response, evoked during the conversion era? To put it differently, how do we explore Hollywood's visceral reaction to the aural innovation? And what does the corporeal functioning of sound tell us about the transition era, when filmmakers were still experimenting and gambling with sound and its effects?

BODILY SENSATIONS

Near the end of Aldous Huxley's *Brave New World* (1932), Darwin Bonaparte shoots *The Savage of Surrey*, chronicling John the Savage's retreat to a lighthouse in the countryside, followed by his riotous self-flagellation routine. From his hiding place in the woods, Bonaparte captures his subject's every feral move. This is how Huxley describes the master filmmaker: "He kept his telescopic cameras carefully aimed – glued to their moving objective; . . . switched over, for half a minute, to show motion (an exquisitely comical effect, he promised himself); listened in, meanwhile, to the blows, the groans, the wild and raving words that were being recorded on the sound-track at the edge of his film, tried the effect of a little amplification." The film is released twelve days later. Soon, crowds gather outside the Savage's lighthouse to ogle him; they are so awed by his performance that they whip themselves into a frenzy and devolve into a mass orgy of *soma* and sex. The crowd's hysterical response no doubt parallels the audience's experience at all the feely-palaces, where *The Savage of Surrey* becomes an enormous hit. One morning, when the gawking throngs return to see the Savage, they find his limp body hanging in the lighthouse archway, his feet dangling "very slowly, like two unhurried compass needles" that have lost all sense of direction.[18]

This final cinematic image in Huxley's novel brings the text's critique of mass culture to a close. While Huxley's novel is most often noted for his dystopian imagining of a future where human beings are massproduced and conditioned for lives of conformity and consumption, it also offers a withering account of how popular culture contributes to the mind-numbing zombification of individuals. And cinema bears the brunt of the attack, because in the form of "feelies," it offers titillating pleasures that lull the consciousness and lead to artistic and cultural degeneration. Patrons at the feely-palaces are able to see, hear, and feel the pictures, making them what Mustafa Mond, the grand controller for

Western Europe, regards as "works of art out of practically nothing but pure sensation."[19] In other words, the pictures are no more than fluff, providing a form of mass entertainment similar to hypnosis or intoxication via the *soma* drug.

Earlier in the narrative, a key scene crystallizes this critique of cinema when John the Savage, who has been raised as an outcast on a reservation in New Mexico and is an outsider in the "brave new world," and Lenina Crowne go to the feelies to see *Three Weeks in a Helicopter* – a perfectly inane film about a "negro" falling in love with a "Beta blonde," kidnapping and ravishing her in the skies for three weeks until she is rescued by "three handsome young Alphas." *Three Weeks in a Helicopter* is, as the ad claims in a parody of Harry Beaumont's *The Broadway Melody* (1929), which MGM had advertised as an "all talking, all singing, all dancing" feature, "AN ALL-SUPER-SINGING, SYNTHETIC-TALKING, COLOURED, STEREOSCOPIC FEELY." At the feely-palace, when the audience grabs hold of the metal knobs on the arms of their cinema chairs, they quiver "with almost intolerable galvanic pleasure."[20] Their immersion in the film, however, is purely superficial. There is no distance for intellectual analysis, no desire for digging deep for meaning. Soon "the last stereoscopic kiss [has] faded into darkness, the last electric titillation died on the lips like a dying moth that quivers, quivers, ever more feebly, ever more faintly, and at last is quite, quite still."[21] The audience leaves the feely-palace dutifully, looking for the next thrill in their *soma* ration or games or unrestrained, polygamous copulation. This is why John the Savage criticizes the feelies as horrid. "'But they don't mean anything,'" he later protests to Mond, who argues that in opting for stability, the brave new world has chosen "'between happiness and what people used to call high art.'" Of course *Othello* is better, Mond concedes, but it is the feelies that provide "'a lot of agreeable sensations to the audience.'"[22] Thus, in this dystopian future, high art is sacrificed to transitory pleasures that placate the public and dampen their consciousness. As Laura Frost astutely observes, in his critique of popular culture, "Huxley opposes meaning to sensation and pleasure."[23] This is why it is tragic indeed when John the Savage ultimately becomes a victim of mass entertainment. His dangling, directionless feet are a somber reminder of the fatal effects of sensational distractions.

Taken literally, the feelies, films that one can not only see and hear but also feel, remain a futuristic fabrication. But what is truly noteworthy about Huxley's critique of sensory cinema is how closely it echoes his review of the talkies. Just as John the Savage was creeped out by the feelies, Huxley was appalled by the advent of sound cinema. In "Silence Is Golden," written at the height of the talkie rage, Huxley noted his horror at experiencing Al Jolson sing "My Mammy." "My flesh crept," he lamented, "as the loud-speaker poured out those sodden words, that greasy, sagging melody. I felt ashamed of myself for listening to such things, for even being a member of the species to which such things are addressed."[24] It should be noted that Huxley wasn't primarily offended by Jolson's blackface rendition and its racial implications. Rather, his critical emphasis was on sound as a vulgarizing, sensational addition to cinema. What alarmed him were the bodily sensations offered by the embodied experience of watching the talkies during the transition to sound.

Huxley may have been particularly provoked by sound because he went nearly blind at the age of sixteen, and there is no telling how well he was able to watch movies. But he was not alone in aligning early sound cinema with corporeality at this time. Like him, Ernest Betts claimed that "there is something monstrous about a speaking film." Arguing that "their acceptance marks the most spectacular act of self-destruction that has yet come out of Hollywood," Betts equated the talkies with artistic decay. "The film now returns," he maintained, "to the circus from whence it came, among the freaks and fat ladies."[25] Early sound cinema became associated with base forms of spectacle, the kinds that offer physical stimulation but nothing else. H. A. Potamkin went one step further. Writing in *Close Up*, Potamkin called cinema "no more than a physical attack," suggesting that "the talking film, as it is produced today, has further lowered the level of this physical attack."[26] Such bodily responses suggest that early sound cinema was regarded by cultural critics on both sides of the Atlantic not merely as a novelty but also as a somatic disruption. As Laura Frost notes, these reactions to the new raucous attractions cranking out sensory delights and terrors offer "unexpected insight into a time when cinema's technological innovations were not just observed but were truly felt."[27] Interestingly, they also serve as a reminder of the critical responses to early cinema, when viewers were also terrorized by the strange materiality of the cinematic image. Most importantly, they link the conversion to sound to the nervous stimulations of early cinema – and to the sensory excesses of modernity itself.

Consider an observer's reflections on the new amusements defining America's budding popular culture in the late nineteenth century. "For the insignificant expenditure of five cents," he suggests, they provide "all the sensation of being carried away by a cyclone, without attendant sacrifice of life and limb."[28] These comments focus on the thrill rides of Coney Island, although they might apply to any aspect of modern life. While the railroads had made Coney Island a beach resort after the Civil War, once the Brooklyn Bridge (completed in 1883) connected Brooklyn with Manhattan, it quickly emerged as an amusement destination for the masses. Located on the outer edge of the seat of America's industrial, financial, and cultural capital, Coney Island's amusement rides were the epitome of fun and frolic at the turn of the century. But they also became the site where "the raw embryonic elements of physical sensation and mechanical invention were tested."[29] By turning the potential for physical violence into a source of rousing pleasures, Coney Island epitomized modernity's emphasis on hyperstimulus and its attention to the body.

Modernity revitalized the body, subjecting it to new modes of perception, representation, and commodification. The very notion of what a body means underwent drastic change over the course of the nineteenth century. Whereas it used to be regarded as "the machine in which the self lived," due to a series of advances in medicine, psychology, and socioeconomics, the body "became a more contingent mechanism, incorporating evolutionary survivals, and with a perceptual, neurological, and performative apparatus."[30] In place of a stable entity with well-defined boundaries, the modern body was reconceived as capricious and penetrable. It is this redefined, almost borderless body that Edouard Manet's work focused on. It is also this mutable body that Franz Kafka addressed, particularly in *The Metamorphosis,* but also in "In the Penal Colony" and "A Hunger Artist." And it is this new body that became particularly sensitive to the shocks of modernity – the jolts of rapid industrialization, urbanization, mechanization, and the rise of consumer culture. For these changes not only marked the coming of modernity but also signified an alteration of everyday experience, which was now characterized by a daily assault on old certainties and a barrage of new stimuli – or what Georg Simmel called the "rapid crowding of changing images, the sharp discontinuity in the grasp of a single glance, and the unexpectedness of onrushing impression."[31] The slow and steady pace of daily life was displaced by a more chaotic, disorienting, and frantic experience where life seemed to be in perpetual peril.

Initially, this feeling of being endangered was prompted by the railways, which promised to tear through the natural landscape and create a trail of disaster. In the 1840s, Charles Dickens was already writing about such train terrors. In *Dombey and Son* (1848), the railway is cast as an earthquake: "Traces of its course were visible on every side. Houses were knocked down; streets broken through and stopped; deep pits and trenches dug in the ground; enormous heaps of earth and clay thrown up; buildings that were undermined and shaking, propped by great beams of wood."[32] But the railroad wasn't merely a threat to the old neighborhood or countryside. It also carried the potential for bodily trauma. As Wolfgang Schivelbusch has noted, until it became a "natural" element of the landscape, there was a general sense of peril associated with rail travel. Quoting a traveler from 1845, Schivelbusch suggests that "that anxiety can be explained by the always 'close possibility of an accident, and the inability to exercise any influence on the running of the cars.'"[33] Such anxiety was not entirely unwarranted, since railway collisions were not an infrequent occurrence. Even though steamboat accidents killed many more people, railway crashes became sensational in the nineteenth century because the former were typically considered acts of God whereas the latter became a circumstance of modernity. Controversial new scientific ailments called the "railway spine," thought to be the result of spinal injury caused during rail accidents, and the "railway brain," thought to be the psychological impact of rail accidents, were hotly debated in the latter half of the century.

Such psychological disorders were not limited to victims of railway accidents. A feeling of disorientation and continual danger became a condition of modernity itself. If the railways, Henry Adams observed, "approached the carnage of war," then "automobiles and fire-arms ravaged society."[34] Even walking around the metropolis was not possible without being jolted by a plethora of sensory alarms. Moving through traffic, while being distracted by billboards, advertisements, and other diversions, became treacherous for any individual who felt "nervous impulses flow through him in rapid succession, like the energy from a battery."[35] The masses filling the cities themselves provided unnerving shocks too. All of these elements combined to make it impossible to disengage from the hustle and bustle of modernity. Unlike "the relative isolation, uniformity, and continuity of traditional societies," Ben Singer argues, "modern mobility and circulation entailed the unprecedented diffusion, interpenetration, and hybridization of people and all other social things as they spread out within and across cultures via the media, trade, tourism, migration, and other forms of social contact."[36] Such mobilization of subjects, combined with the speed of technological innovations and the sensationalism of popular entertainments, created an environment where the individual was always at risk of bodily harm – as if he or she were perpetually on one of the Coney Island rides. And this is what is most intriguing about popular amusements in the late nineteenth century. Instead of providing respite from the hyperkinetic shocks of modernity, they replicated those shocks, blending anxiety and exhilaration as well as commodifying and thereby trying to provide a coping mechanism for the visceral jolts of modernity. In fact, the "thrill" became a defining characteristic of modern entertainments, and, as several scholars have pointed out, early cinema became the apogee of such entertainments, where, for a meager nickel, "all the sensation of being carried away by a cyclone" could indeed be experienced.

It has become commonplace to think of early cinema in terms of a series of thrills, or what Tom Gunning has called "an aesthetic of astonishment."[37] Apocryphal tales of spectators shrieking and running for cover at the Grand Café in Paris in December 1895 and after are by now quite familiar. Among the earliest spectators who advanced this account was Maxim Gorky, whose 1896 review of a program of Lumière shorts addressed how terrifying it was to see "the movement of shadows." Many years later, after cinema was no longer feared like the devil, Georges Sadoul was still elaborating this founding legend. "In *L'Arrivée d'un Train*," he argued, "the locomotive, coming from the background of the screen, rushed toward the spectators, who jumped in shock, as they feared getting run over."[38] But while the physical danger posed to or imagined by its initial spectators may have been exaggerated, there is no denying that early cinema's impact was indeed both visual and visceral. As Gunning has maintained, before the birth of the classical spectator, whose investment in cinema was temporal and whose interest was in following the narrative thread of the film, early viewers went to the movies for a different sort of pleasure. Rather than a mythical, credulous audience "submitting passively to an all-dominating apparatus," Gunning distinguishes early spectators for their immersion in a series of sensational instants, as though they were revelers at the thrill rides at Coney Island.[39] It is specifically these bodily thrills of early films that I want to focus on for a moment, in order to connect them to the thrills of early sound cinema.

Consider Edwin S. Porter's *Uncle Josh at the Moving Picture Show* (1902), which encapsulates the varied and contradictory pleasures of early cinema spectatorship. The infamous country rube mistakes the short films flickering onscreen for actual actualités, jumping out of his theater box to interact with, interrupt, or immerse himself into the scenes. At first, Uncle Josh (Charles Manley) tries to mimic and dance with a Parisian dancer; then, terrified of an oncoming train in the next short film, he leaps out of its path and back into his box; finally, apparently agitated, he attempts to thwart the love-making of a country couple but succeeds only in tearing down the movie screen and engaging in a fight with the projectionist hiding behind it. While the spectator of the film is assumed to be more sophisticated than the spectator in the film, *Uncle Josh* nevertheless demonstrates that early film spectatorship, before the institutionalization of narrativity, was characterized by what Miriam Hansen calls "an excess of appeals."[40] It was not only voyeuristic but also kinesthetic. *Uncle Josh's* viewers were seduced and over-stimulated by the heterogeneity of its subject matter. Instead of a linear narrative, the multiple films-within-a-film, which were in fact scenes from earlier Edison films, unfolded like a series of jolts, much like the instantaneous jolts of modernity. That is because early cinema drew inspiration from vaudeville and other variety entertainments that were hugely popular at the turn of the century. In fact, *Uncle Josh's* catalog of earlier films replicates the variety format that was the staple of early cinema. At any given screening, one could see a range of film genres or subgenres, from dance films

to travelogues to comedies to boxing matches to military parades. This
new format changed the way images were experienced. "If the traditional
arts required an extended contemplation of and concentration upon a
singular object or event," Hansen notes, "the variety format promised
a short-term but incessant sensorial stimulation, a mobilization of the
viewer's attention through a discontinuous series of attractions, shocks,
and surprises."[41] That is how early cinema came to be understood and experienced as a visceral medium, offering momentary shocks that caused
bodily sensations.

In addition to the variety format, early films' content often directly
simulated the body blows of modern life, restaging, as Coney Island did,
modernity's perils into visceral pleasures. In Cecil M. Hepworth's *How
It Feels to Be Run Over* (1900), an automobile comes hurtling toward
the camera, as if it might crash into the audience. Biograph's *A Mighty
Tumble* (1901) shows the dramatic demolishment of a building in New
Jersey. In Edwin S. Porter's *Railroad Smashup* (1904), two trains, apparently provided by the Pennsylvania Railroad, crash into each other, a
catastrophe widely feared at this time. Of course, an impending car accident or controlled building explosion or train collision was more than
a visual delight. While these films represented the era's worst fears, they
also offered a kind of respite from those terrors. Drawing on Freud's
work on anxiety as a protective shield against potential trauma, Walter
Benjamin has argued that cinema offered a kind of training for dealing
with the shocks of modernity. "Man's need to expose himself to shock effects," he suggests, "is his adjustment to the dangers threatening him."[42]
So the sensations provided by these films helped viewers adapt to the
shocks of everyday life.

That is perhaps why one of the most popular genres at this time was
the phantom ride film, wherein a camera was secured to the front of a
moving vehicle in order to replicate the kinesthetic sensation of moving
through space. Biograph's *Through the Haverstraw Tunnel* (1897) is the
perfect example of this genre, which placed the viewer at the edge of his
or her seat and seemingly in the path of danger. Hansen cites an early
review of this film that captures its embodied appeal: "The spectator
was not an outsider watching from safety the rush of the cars. He was
a passenger on a phantom train ride that whirled him through space at

nearly a mile a minute." During this ride, the fear is real and palpable, as "the shadows, the rush of invisible force and the uncertainty of the issues made one instinctively hold his breath as when on the edge of a crisis that might become a catastrophe."[43] What might prompt early spectators to want to endure and even enjoy this catastrophic feeling? Robert C. Allen has argued that the phantom ride film was "designed to produce an almost physiological thrill," and Lynne Kirby suggests that "'shock' was the very basis of its appeal."[44] If any early spectators ever shrieked at the arrival of Lumière's train, then within a few years it is clear that they welcomed such shocks.

But this exhibitionist thrill of early cinema, as is well known, gave way to linear causality. Due to a number of interconnected developments in production, distribution, and exhibition, longer, multi-shot films that told stories gained in popularity after 1903. The settling of copyright disputes, intensified competition between the studios, the establishment of nickelodeons, the rising influence of theater and fiction rather than vaudeville, and the increasing use of complex editing techniques all contributed to the shift away from the disruptive effects of early shorts and the emergence of naturalistic narrative principles that controlled (and sometimes repressed) such effects. This does not imply that earlier popular genres disappeared. A portion of Porter's *Railroad Smashup,* for instance, reappeared in another film, *Rounding Up the Yeggmen* (1904), although now it was used to tell the longer tale of a robbery gone awry. The earlier film's sensational energies were thus contained within a larger narrative. Moreover, new genres that drew on the continuity principle emerged, the most popular among them being the chase film, which incorporated the forward momentum of narrativity. For instance, Porter's *Jack the Kisser* (1907), where the protagonist passionately kisses unsuspecting women and is later chased by a group of bystanders, draws on the chase within the context of the romantic comedy. The emphasis in these films clearly shifted from visceral thrills to narrative closure.

By the early 1910s, multi-reel films called "features" became the norm, which further standardized filmmaking and led to the establishment of the vertically integrated studio system. As Lee Grieveson and Peter Krämer suggest, the production of features "depended on the introduction of continuity scripts serving as detailed blueprints to be used

by all production personnel, and the rise of the central producer system, involving greater division of labor between production personnel,
a more layered hierarchy and greater power for company executives."[45]
By the mid to late teens, as Hollywood established itself as the dominant film industry worldwide, the product generated as a result of this
standardization typically followed narrative continuity meticulously,
offered conflict based on character relationships, and adhered strictly to
principles of unity. A film like Maurice Tourneur's *The Poor Little Rich
Girl* (1917) demonstrates how classical narration functioned. Gwendolyn
(Mary Pickford) is ignored by her rich parents, who are only interested
in enhancing their social status; when a nurse's blunder results in her
overdosing on sleeping potion, her parents realize the error of their ways,
and all ends well. In a film such as Tourneur's, the success of the narrative depended on linear causality leading to resolution. There was no
more room for the disruptive jolts of modernity. If cinema had caused
visceral sensations before, they appeared to be successfully buried by
classical narration.

Still, as Gunning has himself noted, the aesthetic of astonishment
did not entirely disappear after the institutionalization of narrative filmmaking. Rather, the thrills that so delighted cinema's earliest audiences
popped up from time to time in otherwise standard narrative films,
"sensed in periodic doses of non-narrative spectacle given to audiences
(musicals and slapstick comedy provide clear examples)."[46] To this list,
we might add moments of action, violence, heightened emotionality or
melodrama, and spectacular sights.[47] These are moments that provide
"an underground current flowing beneath narrative logic and diegetic realism."[48] But the moments that Gunning outlines are arguably intended
for bodily stimulations. After all, instances of spectacular pleasure offered by Rudolph Valentino films, which Gaylyn Studlar addresses, or
moments of couture extravagance in Cecil B. DeMille's films, which
will be discussed in the next chapter, were expectedly thrilling. What is
more intriguing is that early cinema's visceral delights and disturbances,
although suppressed by the establishment of narrative filmmaking, reappeared rather unexpectedly during the transition to sound. At the beginning of "The Evolution of the Language of Cinema," André Bazin charac-
teristically asks "if the technical revolution created by the sound track" in

the late 1920s meant that we had witnessed "the birth of a new cinema."[49] For Bazin, as for most critics since, the answer is no – hence Bazin's case for historical continuity between silent and sound cinema, and Erwin Panofsky's suggestion that "the sound, articulate or not, cannot express any more than is expressed, at the same time, by visible movement."[50] Seen retrospectively, sound becomes just another subordinate element in the classical, realistic narrative tradition, and by logical extension, the conversion to sound appears to have been a sure thing. But during the transition, as Hollywood experimented with aural techniques and tried to incorporate them into the classical narrative, sound was a gamble, which is why the bodily stimulations of early cinema recurred and, for a brief time, rattled viewers and filmmakers alike.

GAMBLING WITH HISTORY

Although all the major studios had eschewed experiments with sound, and his own brother Abe had declared the talkies bunk, Sam Warner decided to take a chance on sound, convincing Warner Bros., which was not too fiscally stable, to invest in Vitaphone – or so the story goes. But, as Gomery shows, the notion that "Warners was broke and thus gambled on talkies" is a myth.[51] In fact, the gamble on talkies can be traced all the way back to the invention of cinema itself. In the beginning, Edison attempted to combine the phonograph with cinema, but nothing came of his experiments. Then, in the first decade of the twentieth century, inventors like Leon Gaumont and E. E. Norton gambled on devices like the Chronophone, the Cameraphone, and the Cinephone. In 1913, Edison's Kinetophone appeared promising, but its synchronization effects were not consistent, and hence it was not widely successful. Even D. W. Griffith wagered on sound for *Dream Street* (1921), which was nothing more than a novelty. The failures of these apparatuses had as much to do with their inherent inefficiencies as with the fact that their outcomes could not be standardized. Each (failed) innovation was merely a bet or a gamble, whose effects could not be replicated.

In a sense, Hollywood's gamble with sound, before and during the transition, resembles Walter Benjamin's sketch of gambling as a series of mostly disconnected yet thrilling events. Benjamin outlines the figure of the gambler in order to trace "the disintegration of coherent experience in modern life."[52] Gambling became an enormously popular cultural practice in the nineteenth century. Initially, it was associated with the excesses of elite, aristocratic society. By the middle of the century, gambling began to take hold among the bourgeoisie and the working classes. But, as Susan Buck-Morss notes, Benjamin is not interested in "the social history of gambling as a pastime among ruling classes" or its effects on the masses.[53] Rather, he is intrigued by the sociohistorical form of gambling and how it represents the fleeting experience of modernity. Gambling enables Benjamin to speculate on the passing of time during the industrial revolution – what he calls the "phantasmagoria of time" – and the gambler becomes a crucial figure for analyzing the bodily sensations of modernity.

The preliminary thrill of gambling, of course, is financial. "Perhaps the next card turned," Benjamin quotes Anatole France, "the ball now rolling, will give the player parks and gardens, fields and forests, castles and manors lifting heavenward their pointed turrets and fretted roofs."[54] But gambling is about much more than money. The real thrill of gambling is the gambler's encounter with shock: "It is the mingling of terror with delight that intoxicates."[55] That is why Benjamin thinks of gambling as a visceral experience. Here is how gambling works: it is not a systematized activity that can depend on logic or rationality. Rather, gambling depends on luck or chance. The gambler cannot use his previous knowledge or skills of observation and analysis to win a bet. He must instead give himself over to the thrill of the game and respond to bodily stimulation, not reason. His bets are placed at the last possible minute, so his behavior is not analytical but reflexive. "The gambler's reaction to chance," Benjamin notes, "is more like that of the knee to the hammer in the patellar reflex."[56] It is almost as if the gambler is constantly at the edge of the precipice. His bets are spontaneous, because what these betting moments offer are fleeting stimuli that resemble the shocks of modernity.

That is why Benjamin compares the gambler to the flâneur and the factory worker. The flâneur wanders aimlessly through the Parisian streets, looking for moments of rapture. His travels have no purpose; he pauses spontaneously to respond to "the magnetism of the next street-

corner, of a distant mass of foliage, of a street name."[57] For the flâneur
as for the gambler, "their reception in distraction, like that of the movie
audience, is not merely visual but tactile, or visceral; it involves their
whole sensorium."[58] Both figures seek out tactile sensations in order to
escape the mind-numbing continuum of history. The case of the factory
worker is slightly different. At first, the hard toil of the factory worker
might seem antithetical to the thrills of gambling. Benjamin, however,
suggests that the two seemingly unrelated activities are connected insofar as they both depend on repetitive, automatic operations. Just as the
gambler repeats himself with each roll of the dice or turn of the cards, the
factory worker replicates his previous actions. But neither figure gains
anything from what has happened a moment before. There is no sense of
logical progression or development in gambling or in factory work. Both
figures only experience a series of shocks in their respective actions.
"The jolt in the movement of a machine," Benjamin argues, "is like the
so-called *coup* in a game of chance."[59] In fact, like the flâneur who thrives
on sporadic sensations, the factory worker and the gambler rely on the
thrill of fragmented experiences.

And that is what makes gambling a productive encounter with modernity. "The wager," Benjamin contends, "is a means of conferring shock
value on events, of loosing them from the contexts of experience."[60] The
bodily sensations of gambling enable the gambler to detach himself from
the long tedium of history. Since each bet is experienced as distinct in a
series of shocks, the gambler is able to experience time as the materialist historian does. In that way, gambling begins to resemble Benjamin's
privileged act of being able to "blast open the continuum of history."[61]
The gambler does not experience time's linear monotony. Rather, he
engages with history through sensational moments.

That is how we might historicize Hollywood's transition to sound
as well. As we know, immediately after the success of *The Jazz Singer*,
studio heads set out to incorporate sound into the classical mode of
production. Their emphasis was on using any means possible to achieve
synchronization quickly and smoothly. If microphones picked up too
much noise on the set, the camera and cameraman were placed in sound-
proof, unventilated booths. If the microphones' range was too short,
they were "concealed in vases, telephones, any object an actor could

address without looking completely balmy."[62] If the variable speeds of cameras and projectors became inconvenient, they were standardized to twenty-four frames per second. Although *Singin' in the Rain* would later playfully mock the process that led to synchronization, the transition was chaotic – and it was far from a sure thing. Viewers who were drawn to early sound films for their novelty also began to notice their strange materiality. With the addition of sound, while the studios strove for enhanced realism, the audience experienced almost the opposite effect for a time. Instead of absorption in the classical narrative, early sound films evoked bodily responses. As Robert Spadoni points out in his astute study of the uncanniness of early sound film and its influence on horror cinema, "the sensations that could result had the power to infiltrate and counteract impressions of the medium's advancement toward greater realism."[63] In that sense, from time to time early sound films inadvertently came to resemble the thrills of early cinema. While audiences may not have shrieked and run out of the way, if they ever did, during the gamble of conversion, they likely responded viscerally.

In the next section, drawing on the methodologies of the gambler-historian, we will locate the thrills of early sound cinema. The gambler is the finest figure for this transitional time because sound in Hollywood was a gamble. In many ways, the studios responded to sound's rising popularity in the way a gambler reacts haptically to bodily sensations. If the gambler relies on erratic sensations of shock, then gambling can be seen as a pretty good metaphor for the practice of filmmaking during the transition to sound. Moreover, the gambler's resemblance to the factory worker, in his incessant insistence on repetition, makes him an ideal historian for a moment when each new sound film appeared to be an experiment that jolted that machinery of the studio system. Instead of standardization, the transition era is characterized by a series of thrills or gambles. However, most traditional film histories trace the transition to sound chronologically from Crosland's *Don Juan* and *The Jazz Singer* to Lloyd Bacon's *The Singing Fool*, as examples of part-talkies that signaled the definitive arrival of sound, and then to Bryan Foy's *Lights of New York* (1928) and Beaumont's *The Broadway Melody*, as examples of pictures that solidified the status of the talkies, charting an irreversible trajectory from silence to realistic sound. These films had the winning formulas.

But for every successful transition film, there were several others at all the studios that were experiments in sound technology. Most of them were more or less failed ventures. In the absence of clear principles for incorporating sound into the narrative, these transitional films tried to imagine what sound could do and ended up allegorizing the sensational impact of the arrival of sound as well as resurrecting the exhibitionist thrill of early cinema. In what follows, drawing on moments of aural cinephilia, we can gamble on their titillating sound effects to uncover a slightly different history of conversion, one that emphasizes the visceral sensations of early sound cinema and analyzes the implications of its many ruptures.

UNSOUND EFFECTS

When Will Hays, president of the Motion Picture Producers and Distributors of America (MPPDA), appeared in front of Don Juan's premiere audience in New York on August 6, 1926, he was ostensibly present to introduce the new Vitaphone technology. But his brief appearance was also meant to showcase the talkies as a clear sign of progress in the history of motion pictures. In the film, Hays suggests that the talkies represent a cinematic evolution. "We have advanced," he argues, "from that few seconds of the shadow of a serpentine dancer thirty years ago when the motion picture was born, to this." Presumably, having broken its ties to early amusements, to the "few seconds of the shadow," cinema can now be considered a mature art. But Hays's introduction, or the short films that follow, or even the part-talkie that is to be the highlight of the evening, are hardly that different from earlier entertainments. Hays's own bow to various sections of the auditorium and direct address to the camera betray early sound cinema's self-consciousness and its temporary return to relying on theatrical techniques. In addition, the program of early shorts that precedes the main feature recalls the variety format of early cinema as well as vaudeville. Most importantly, the novelty of hearing a human being speak onscreen threatens to turn Hays himself into a shadow. Writing about Hays's uncanny direct address, Fitzhugh Green noted that he "seemed to be present, and yet he did not seem to be present."[64] Similarly, of Giovanni Martinelli's booming performance

1.2. *Old San Francisco* (dir. Alan Crosland, 1927).

of "Vesti la Giubba" from *I Pagliacci*, Mordaunt Hall wrote that "the singer's tones appeared to echo in the body of the theatre as they tore from a shadow on the screen."[65] Thus, early sounds were jolting. While Vitaphone bore the promise of synchronization, initially its sounds created aural disruptions.

If the human voice startled audiences, then the varied sound effects used in early sound films caused even more turbulence. Many films during the conversion period were released with some synchronized music and/or sound effects. While these films were meant to ease the transition, both for audiences as well as for theaters not yet wired for sound, they unwittingly exacerbated their aural intrusions. Alan Crosland's *Old San Francisco* (1927), released before *The Jazz Singer*, is one of several Warner Bros. gambles on partial synchronization. The film saves the majority of its sound effects for the climactic 1906 San Francisco earthquake, which may be seen (and heard) as an allegory of the panic generated by

1.3. *Old San Francisco* (dir. Alan Crosland, 1927).

the new technology. Gerald Horne, as mentioned earlier, compares the coming of sound to an earthquake. But even before we get to the film's climactic sequence (Figure 1.3), a single sonic boom exemplifies the disconcerting effects of sound. In the film's prologue, the senior Vasquez (Lawson Butt) hopes to fight off the marauding rebels under Captain Stoner (Tom Santschi) during the gold rush with his family sword. But his traditional weapon and his "Spanish honor" are no match for the captain's gun. With one loud bang, the patriarch is shot dead (Figure 1.2). The film echoes the generational conflict over the technological revolution that is later popularized by *The Jazz Singer*. The sound of the gunshot functions as one of the first shots across the bow signaling the end of silent cinema, and its aural effect may be as jarring as that earlier visual shot fired directly at the audience in *The Great Train Robbery*.

So, when the sounds of people shrieking, buildings collapsing, fires crackling, and police sirens wailing are heard, the narrative recedes so that sound may be foregrounded. As James Lastra suggests, this "gratuitous display of sound" works to "address the audience directly – to hail them – to say, 'Hey! Look and listen! This is important.'"[66] Such hailing harkens back to an earlier era when the technological wonder of cinema was itself the "attraction." Indeed, if the sensational aesthetic of attractions represents the silent narrative cinema's repressed, then that repressed returns during the transition period with a vengeance. For it is precisely such moments of visceral excess, submerged by the force of classical linearity, that now rupture the evolution of narrative cinema. Interestingly, if Warner Bros., Vitaphone, and even Will Hays insisted that sound represented a progressive step forward, then early sound films like *Old San Francisco* suggest that it was also a metaphorical step back – to the days when narrative was not vital to cinema. As Lastra puts it, in early sound films, narrative "clearly takes a backseat to the display of pure technological marvel, and cinematic pleasure momentarily divorces itself from plot."[67] Thus, these earliest moments of aural cinephilia demonstrate that, in the way it actually behaved, sound was unpredictable and not so easily incorporated as a sonic supplement to the classical narrative tradition.

Such is the case with *The First Auto* as well, where sound effects exceed their narrative contexts. Like *Old San Francisco* and *The Jazz Singer*, *The First Auto* presents the arrival of sound in terms of a generational clash between traditional father Hank Armstrong (Russell Simpson), who is a devoted horse racer and stable owner, and his son Bob (Charles Emmett Mack), who becomes charmed by the arrival of the automobile at the turn of the century. As the subtitle points out, the film is "a romance of the last horse and the first horseless carriage." But it is much more than that. More than any other Vitaphone film, *The First Auto* dramatizes the pandemonium caused by the transition.

The film begins nostalgically, with praise for a time when "a horse was a horse" and "a nickel was still respected." Early on, sound effects merely complement the visual track. During Hank's horse race, musical beats provide the effect of galloping horses, while a large crowd cheers "hooray." But soon sound's erratic energies come to the fore. Hank's horse Sloe Eyes has a stroke, perhaps in anticipation of its replacement, the automobile, coming to town. The appropriately named Mr. Hayes (E. H. Calvert) comes to Maple City to introduce the marvelous sensa-

1.4. *The First Auto* (dir. Roy Del Ruth, 1927).

tion, and his lecture aligns the history of cinema with other technological innovations, particularly the automobile. With the help of slides that
Bob volunteers to run through a "magic lantern," Hayes demonstrates
how the horse is destined to become "a curiosity."[68] The arrival of the
"horseless carriage" is proof of modernity; "Everything's speeding up,"
he claims. In an homage to Lumière's *Workers Leaving the Lumière Factory* (1895), Hayes turns to a slide of workers posing for a photograph outside the factory where he manufactures "three cars per month – which
will soon be increased to five!" Until now, the crowd has been mostly
incredulous, and sound has been mostly in the background, but this slide
causes an uproar. The sight of twenty or so men outside a factory is nothing unusual, of course, except for the fact that the slide is momentarily
pictured upside down (Figure 1.4), sending the crowd into a laughing
frenzy (Figure 1.5).

However, their laughter is not fully synchronized. What appeared
to be a silent scene, with intertitles for dialogue, jumps to sound effects

1.5. *The First Auto* (dir. Roy Del Ruth, 1927).

rather disconcertingly. Indeed, it is the asynchronous laughter that is far more jarring than the ominous shadow of a cat walking across the screen, a result of an actual cat walking in front of the projector. This is a highly self-conscious moment of the transition to sound. Even though films using the Vitaphone sound-on-disk technology offered far superior sound than earlier attempts, there were often problems during screenings. Before *Don Juan*, and before Vitaphone's amplifiers, sound features had attracted only boos and heckles. But those catcalls did not disappear with the advent of sound-on-disk, which basically provided recorded sound on a separate disc that was to play in sync with the image track. One can imagine the myriad possibilities for such delicate synchronization to malfunction. The result, as we see and hear in *The First Auto*, was disturbing, and as Donald Crafton suggests, during the conversion, "anything found to be jarring or disconcerting tended to be greeted with jeers or laughter."[69] Roy Del Ruth's film tries to narrativize such instances, but the effect of instantaneous, asynchronous laughter remains grating.

Even more discordant are the numerous jumps between the silent and sound portions of the film. For in place of a sustained musical score and continuous dialogue and sound effects, conversion-era films switch between silent cinema's "background" music and sound cinema's complete synchronization. As John Belton has pointed out, "part-talkie films tend to unravel before the audience's eyes and ears, repeatedly reverting to silence and then back into synchronized sound."[70] Unlike *Old San Francisco,* where the cacophonous sound effects are mostly saved for the end, *The First Auto* gambles with turning sound effects on and off, depending on whether an automobile is onscreen. Maple City's first car is purchased by its wealthiest citizen, Squire Rufus Stebbins (Douglas Gerrard), who wants "to give the town its most breathless sensation." Due to its unpredictability, the car becomes not only a visual marvel but also a spectacle that physically threatens the entire town. Although he doesn't try any "stunts," per the instructions in the owner's manual, Stebbins's new ride does not behave conventionally. As the car zigzags through town, running into the crowd, knocking over yard fences, and trampling horses and poultry, the anarchic sound effects are picked up. While the clanking and jingling are meant to suggest the zany antics of early automobiles, they also sound like gunshots firing intermittently, thrilling yet terrifying. Indeed, each aural shot is accompanied by a visual flash, as seen in Figure 1.6. The automobile, which is now fully associated with nascent sound technology, becomes a different kind of "breathless sensation," sending tiny shockwaves through the audience and replicating the effects of such early automobile films as Hepworth's *How It Feels to Be Run Over* or Alf Collins's *Runaway Match* (1903).

Then, when we get to the car racing sequences, the film tries to reproduce the sensations of the phantom rides by placing the camera right behind or in front of the car itself. Along the lines of the popular Hale's tours, which recreated the physical experience of rail travel, in 1905, Julian Smith notes that "an entrepreneur tried to combine the motoring and movie-going experience via the Tim Hurst Auto Tours, in which an audience sat in a theater designed to look like a huge touring car and watched motion pictures photographed along the main thoroughfares of famous cities."[71] "No jarring, no jolting, no bumping, no discordant noises" were promised by these auto tours.[72] No such promises could

1.6. *The First Auto* (dir. Roy Del Ruth, 1927).

be made by *The First Auto*. Just as the explosion buggy, as Hank calls it, crisscrosses the little town of Maple City and then race tracks in Detroit, jolting and jarring sound effects weave in and out of the diegesis.

Human voices similarly stagger in and out. Mostly monosyllabic words are heard. The father's plea for his son to wake up when Sloe Eyes dies is articulated only with his name "Bob!," while the rest of the dialogue switches to intertitles. The starter of the race between the horse and the automobile exclaims "Go!," although the word is also repeated on the intertitle. Generic cheers of "hooray" are heard from crowds during the races. As Crafton points out, speech is only used "as a 'thrill' to surprise the moviegoer."[73] So, although *The First Auto* ends with a fantasy of standardization, where automobiles have become a permanent and non-threatening fixture of small towns everywhere, and they no longer audibly belch or rattle anymore, such a fate is far from guaranteed for the sound film. In the absence of formulated conventions, early sound films were an admixture of partially synchronized music and sound effects with a few spoken words. Drawing on Rudolf Arnheim, who lamented the loss of the silent film aesthetic, Belton suggests that part-talkies threatened to "transform the medium into a monstrous hybrid."[74] It is no wonder, then, that during the transition period, not all sound films were wholeheartedly embraced by the public. Crafton notes that "*Old San Francisco* grossed only about half as much per seat as *Don Juan; The First Auto* took in about one-third as much and was pulled after a month."[75] Even at the end of 1927, how sound would be absorbed by the principles of classical narration, and what kinds of sounds would be welcomed, remained a gamble.

That is why William Fox decided to hedge his bets by initially subli-censing Vitaphone but also investing in its rival technology, Movietone, a sound-on-film recording system. While Fox offered successful demon-strations of Movietone newsreels – most famously of Charles Lindberg's transatlantic flight to Paris on May 20, 1927, shown with much fanfare that same evening to thousands of patrons at the Roxy theater – the stu-dio did not have as many talkies under production that year. William Fox was more cautious than Sam Warner and seemingly more focused on financial considerations, noting that talkies would be released by Fox "only when and if the Movietone sequences are successful. If not, the Movietone sequences will be scrapped, and further experiments under-taken, before the Movietone picture is presented as a practical commer-cial proposition."[76] That is what makes F. W. Murnau's *Sunrise* (1927), a partial talkie, even more noteworthy. A successful German Expression-ist, Murnau was invited to Hollywood by William Fox at a time when the latter was trying to increase the profile of his studio, a desire that also led him to wade cautiously into sound. Intriguingly, the combination of Murnau and sound in 1927 is anything but cautious. Ironically, while it received praise from the critics, provided Fox with a much-desired prestige film, and helped establish the use of sound-on-film rather than sound-on-disk, *Sunrise* failed at the box office.

Murnau's "song of two humans" is widely regarded as a paean to silent film. Although it was marketed as one of the earliest uses of Movi-etone, it is typically hailed as a *visual* masterpiece. The film's acoustic techniques are generally discussed only in terms of how they visual-ize sound. "Although this is a silent film," Lotte Eisner argues, "sound becomes perceptible everywhere through the power of the images and the eloquence and precision of the acting."[77] More recently, Melinda Szaloky has beautifully analyzed how Murnau expresses aural ideas in a silent narrative with a synchronized music track visually. "Many of Murnau's complex camera movements and shot compositions," she notes, "serve to render . . . crucial sounds audible for the characters and visible (and thus audible) for the spectator."[78] It is true that Murnau utilizes silence, which becomes particularly resonant after the arrival of sound, to convey acoustic signals visually. When the Woman from the City (Margaret Livingston) tries to lure the Man (George O'Brien) away from his Wife (Janet Gaynor) at the beginning of the film, she looks toward the camera, the background music recedes, she purses her lips and whistles; although no sound effects make her whistling audible, it is certainly inferred by the Man turning toward the window. Similarly, before the Man takes his Wife on a boat ride where he hopes to drown her, their dog starts barking violently but to us inaudibly, thus visualizing "a doubly silent voice: that of the (silent) conscience of a guilt-ridden man in a silent cinema."[79] Near the end, when the Wife appears to have drowned, the husband looks for her, calls out to her, but his desperate cries go unheard. In the visual rhythm and grace of these moments, it is easy to see why *Sunrise* is sometimes called the epitome of silent cinema.

But Murnau was not making a silent film. *Sunrise* is yet another partially synchronized sound film with sequences that burst into sound. Sound effects, however, are used very differently in this film. In fact, *Sunrise* does not seem to be interested in realistic synchronization. Rather, it may be the earliest example of the sonic dialectic, where the image and sound tracks blend as well as clash. There are three sequences in particular, all of them located in the city, where sound does more than just complement the visuals. As they lie among the reeds on the moonlit shore in the country, and the Woman of the City tries to seduce the Man to "come to the city," urban images flash in front of them. Alongside images of a dizzying modern city, we hear honking horns, blaring trumpets, and pounding drums. Even when the scene returns to their tranquil countryside reverie, and the sound effects go mute, the Woman keeps jiggling her body frenetically to the city's now silent beats (Figure 1.7). Sound, in other words, lingers moments after it has been heard, ruptur-

1.7. *Sunrise: A Song of Two Humans* (dir. F. W. Murnau, 1927).

ing their stealthy, hushed lovemaking. Sound also interrupts the Man and his Wife, once they get back together in the city. When they get to the city, after the Man fails to drown his Wife, she tries to flee from him, and he follows her, begging for forgiveness. They make their way to a church, where another couple is getting married. As they witness a solemn ceremony, he breaks down, and they reconcile. When they walk down a busy street, the oncoming traffic disappears, dissolving into an idyllic meadow, where they kiss ardently – and that is when the city and its noises interject. The noises of horns hooting, horses braying, and generic voices jeering jolt the couple back to reality. That is, the frenzied city reasserts itself through sound, disallowing the couple to disappear in silence. Finally, before they leave the city, they go to an amusement park, where asynchronous sound effects make their final assault. The amusement park is a place of chaos, where sounds of people cheering clash with ringing bells and clanging whistles and the noise of a squealing pig. The frenzied atmosphere is enhanced by the riotous sound effects that excite and exceed the narrative. Indeed, each time sound effects materialize in *Sunrise,* they are associated with the threatening and deafening city. Therefore, they appear to have a jolting effect.

Molly Haskell has argued that "Murnau's city often seems like a metaphor for the sound film, trying to burst into the peaceful haven of the country, the silent film."[80] If that is the case, then Murnau's notion of what a sound film might be is hardly realistic. The city scenes in *Sunrise* offer a carnivalesque energy, thus linking sound film to the fairgrounds, amusement parks, and, of course, pre-narrative cinema. They are reminiscent of early city films that tried to capture the physical perils and pleasures of urban life, like Edison's *What Happened on Twenty-Third Street* (1901) and Biograph's *Lower Broadway* (1902). The amusement park scene in particular is evocative of films set in Coney Island, like Biograph's *Around the Flip-Flap Railroad* (1902) and Edwin S. Porter's *Rube and Mandy at Coney Island* (1903), which, as Lauren Rabinovitz puts it, were used to "offering the moviegoer not only the voyeuristic privilege of looking at others as among the pleasures of both the amusement park and of the cinema but of the body connected to a device in order to produce moments of physically comical reactions and twists, turns, jolts, and tumbles."[81] The city sequences in Murnau's film recreate these twists and turns with asynchronous sound. Like the Wife, who almost leaps out of her skin at the honking of an automobile that threatens to run her over in the city, the sonic effects expect a corporeal involvement from the audience, unlike the soothing absorption provided by classical narrative cinema. Thus, Murnau seems to imagine an alternate future for sound film, one that does not subordinate the aural to the visual but exploits it to draw out the visceral effects of cinema.

Paul Leni's *The Man Who Laughs* (1928) works in much the same way, bringing the aural carnivalesque to the horror film. Like *Sunrise,* Leni's film is mostly remembered as a silent film – Ian Conrich, for instance, calls it "a horror-spectacular in the twilight of Universal's production of silent movies" – even though it's the sound effects that make it especially terrifying.[82] Like Murnau, Leni had been imported to Hollywood from Germany. After such successful ventures in the Expressionist tradition as *Backstairs* (1921) and *Waxworks* (1924), Carl Laemmle invited him to direct at Universal. Leni's first American film, *The Cat and the Canary* (1927), made in the "old dark house" genre, was a hit, and he was to follow that up with an adaptation of Victor Hugo's macabre novel, *L'Homme qui Rit* (1869). Although the film was completed in 1927, it was held up by Laemmle, who, like William Fox, had signed a contract with Movietone. Like so many other partial sound films from the transition era, *The Man Who Laughs* was released with sound effects and music a year later.

But Leni's film does not use sound in a conventionally terror-inducing manner. As Robert Spadoni suggests, the theatrical precedent for rattling audiences with sound, something the *Motion Picture News* speculated that *The Cat and the Canary* might have benefited from, was "creaking hinges, banging doors, shrieking women, howling cats."[83] His later sound film, *The Last Warning* (1929), seems to have utilized some of these conventional techniques, although not too well, if we are to go by the *New York Times* review by Mordaunt Hall, who was unimpressed with its "too many outbursts of shrieking, merely to prove the effects of the audible screen, to cause any spine chilling."[84] But *The Man Who Laughs* uses virtually none of these devices. Rather, like *Sunrise*, its sound effects are mostly limited to scenes of large crowds, as at the Southwark Fair, where the sideshow clown Gwynplaine (Conrad Veidt) regales patrons with his permanently carved, excruciating grin. The son of an aristocrat who has been sentenced to death by King James II, Gwynplaine is kidnapped and disfigured, so he may "laugh forever at his fool of a father." Along with another abandoned child, the blind Dea (Mary Philbin), he is taken in by Ursus (Cesare Gravina), a mountebank. The three of them form a theater troupe and become a traveling "freak show." Gaylyn Studlar has noted that the "freak show" had been a very popular form of entertainment for over half a century and enjoyed its heyday in the 1920s. Although it came under fire during that decade for being "disgusting and grotesque, as inappropriate and even pornographic," it was absorbed by the movies, where it found a flourishing alternative cultural space.[85] *The Man Who Laughs* is a particularly compelling example in this tradition.

An intertitle suggests that the fair is "a rattle for the masses to make them laugh and forget," and the film seems determined to recreate those rattling effects for its audience as well. The scene begins with "an early replica of a Ferris wheel, carrying a full load of passengers, [which] neatly captures the rotation of the ride and simulates the experience for the viewer, who is spun into the bustle of the fair."[86] Then, like the frenzied carnival atmosphere in *Sunrise*, the Southwark Fair is shown via a montage of fairground shots. Assorted views of the "fire-proof man," the "five-legged cow," and other "strange and weird oddities of nature on earth" are accompanied by raucous and unsynchronized sound effects of catcalls, jeers, and applause. When the scene cuts away to Gwynplaine and Dea contemplating marriage, the sound effects momentarily recede but then erupt just as he leans in to kiss her. Their tender moment is interrupted by the boorish and rowdy catcalls from outside his wagon. Since Dea cannot see the audience, emphasis is placed on how Gwynplaine is horrified by their vocal reactions to him, asking her to "hear how they laugh at [him] – nothing but a clown." Ironically, although they come to hear Gwynplaine, who is the laughing man, all we hear is the wild laughter of his spectators. A little later, on stage, Gwynplaine stands mostly behind the curtain; only his horrific grin is in full view. His voice, even when he laughs along with his patrons, remains inaudible. He does not even grunt or groan, like the monster in James Whale's *Frankenstein* (1931). And it is this silence, in a *sound* film, that becomes ghastly. Add to that the unsynchronized laughter, interlaced with boos, hisses, clanking bells, and tooting horns of the audience, and *The Man Who Laughs* becomes disconcerting, leaving audiences uncertain whether to laugh or scream. Moreover, sound in this transition film is associated with the audience (rather than specific characters). Thomas Doherty reminds us that audiences of early cinema were used to responding audibly to the screen. Having been influenced by "the raucous atmosphere nurtured in the vaudeville hall," he suggests, early audiences believed that films "deserved audible expressions of approval and reproach."[87] This trend continued into the early sound era, but then gradually began to fade, likely because hearing the characters' voices became important for comprehending the narrative. That is to say, once synchronized sound films became the norm, silence became the prerogative of the audience. But Leni projects sound on to the audience in this transition film, thus complicating the term "audience," which etymologically signifies the act of hearing, and echoing the experiential challenges of sound cinema during the conversion era.

Leni's *The Man Who Laughs* might be the perfect example of what Richard Barrios calls "Hollywood at its most vulnerable and sometimes most ludicrous, groping to produce offspring that were, often as not, both trials and errors."[88] Such groping was especially the case at Universal, where Carl Laemmle had not fully committed to sound cinema because he considered it a temporary fad. In his case, hedging of bets makes some sense. The public's affection was indeed waning for part-talkies, not only because their novelty quickly wore off but also, we might argue, because they assaulted their audiences with bodily sensations that they were unaccustomed to. As a reviewer in the *Evening World* reasoned, a part-talkie came to be seen as "a horrible example of the things which might happen if this new toy is not kept within complete control."[89] Since the rewiring of studios and movie theaters around the country was so expensive, "production philosophies began veering away from anything that smelled too strongly of taking chances, or of art."[90] Partial talkies, like the ones we've seen, came to be regarded as too much of a gamble. In this atmosphere, a film like D. W. Griffith's *The Battle of the Sexes* (1928), a part-talkie where musical cues are perfectly synchronized with the action, was far more welcome than the million-dollar gamble that was Leni's film.

That pressure might also explain Foy's *Lights of New York* and Hollywood's eventual move toward complete and realistic synchronization. What started off as a Vitaphone two-reel short, appropriately titled "The Roaring Twenties," became the first full talkie and paved the way for integrating sound smoothly into the classical narrative. *Lights of New York* was a low-budget yarn about two naive barbers whose shop inadvertently ends up as a front for bootleggers. It was widely panned by critics. *Variety* roasted this cinematic milestone, claiming that "this 100 percent talkie is 100 percent crude."[91] But such reproaches could not keep audiences away. Produced on a shoestring $23,000 budget, it made over a million dollars. Critics were shocked that a product this "crude" would be allowed by Warner Bros. to become the first all-talking film. There was nothing sensational about it – and that was its primary appeal. Warner Bros. followed *Lights* with Roy Del Ruth's *The Terror* (1928), another all-talkie, this time without intertitles. Ironically, this staid mystery's tagline claimed that it will "thrill you! Grip you! Set you into tremors of awe!" Like *Lights,* the public cheered while critics rebuked it for offering no such sensory delights. The only tremors it could possibly have sent was among other Hollywood studios, who were eager to cash in on the synchronized sound phenomenon, whether their respective companies or theater chains were ready or not.

In many ways, the least prepared among the major studios was MGM. They had signed the "Five-Cornered Agreement" in 1927 with First National, Famous Players–Lasky, Universal, and Producers Distributing Company. The agreement stressed the benefits of cooperating to find a suitable sound recording process, although it was also meant to counter Warner's early lead in producing talkies. The agreement, of course, did not last long, as terrified studio heads went ahead and sublicensed Vitaphone during the transition phase anyway. Still, throughout 1928 and early 1929, there was some wishful thinking that sound films may not entirely replace silent productions. Publicly at least, studio heavyweights like Carl Laemmle, Adolph Zukor, and Louis B. Mayer claimed that they expected to make silent and sound films. At MGM, under Thalberg's leadership, the plan "was to let the other studios perfect the technology, then enter later to avoid the trial and expense of initial experimentation."[92] And yet, experimentation became unavoidable, so much so that the traits of experimentation were visible and audible throughout the conversion era. As Belton suggests in relation to Alfred Hitchcock's *Blackmail* (1929), it was impossible to avoid "the rupture created by the new technology; from today's perspective, you can see and hear that break in the films themselves."[93] That break reverberates in Feyder's *The Kiss,* which was to be Greta Garbo's and MGM's last non-talkie. It was released at the tail end of 1929, after Beaumont's hit *The Broadway Melody,* which MGM advertised as an "all talking, all singing, all dancing" sensation as a concession that even they could no longer hedge their bets. Conversion to completely synchronized sound finally seemed like an inevitability, and plans were already underway for Clarence Brown's *Anna Christie* (1930), whose draw would be that "Garbo talks." But before she talks, Garbo startles.

The Kiss is among the last of the transitional films. It is generally regarded as a silent film. Upon initial release, a *Variety* review even suggested that "though this is silent it may be stronger that way than with dialog."[94] But while Garbo doesn't speak and the dialogue is conveyed via intertitles, the film does have disc-synchronized music and two disruptive sound effects. Of course, it begins with the sound of Leo the Lion roaring audibly, a practice begun only a year earlier at the premiere of W. S. Van Dyke's *White Shadows in the South Seas* (1928). After the mascot roars, except for William Axt's musical score, everything returns to silence for a while. Unhappily married, Irene Guarry is having a humdrum affair with André Dubail. But, following the "strong convention" of being "a good wife" to a man she doesn't love, she breaks off their relationship. Soon after, she begins a mostly innocent dalliance with Pierre, her husband's business partner's young son. Similar to Clarence Brown's *A Woman of Affairs* (1928) or Sidney Franklin's *Wild Orchids* (1928) or John S. Robertson's *The Single Standard* (1929) in terms of theme and style, the film trundles along predictably. Comparing her with her roles in other films of the late silent era, Lucy Fischer argues that Garbo becomes an Art Deco icon. Deco infuses the sets and costumes of these films, Fischer notes, carrying "great symbolic force, establishing congruity between heroine and decor, marking her as both avant-garde and perilous."[95] It is within this milieu that Garbo as Guarry appears as a hieratic goddess. In fact, her affiliation with the Deco style, coupled with her quiet inapproachability, add to her "air of exhaustion, languor and contemplative stillness."[96] But this typical tranquility is shattered midway through the film, when Irene's husband walks in on her kissing Pierre.

Irene's flirtation with Pierre begins harmlessly enough. He brings fresh energy to her tedious life "of social routine – of striving to forget." Although she is not truly interested in him, and thinks he is "just a boy," Irene encourages his advances and promises to give him a photograph of her as a memento when he leaves for college. Before he goes, Pierre asks a "big favor," a parting goodbye kiss. Irene yields, but Pierre grabs her and begins embracing her. This unrestrained moment is interpreted as a marital transgression by Irene's husband, who returns home unexpectedly.[97] What ensues is an altercation between the two men, with the senior Guarry clearly able to overpower the junior Lassalle. Irene's pleas on behalf of Pierre's innocence go unheard, as the scuffle moves to Guarry's study. As Irene enters the room, the door closes, and the

1.8. *The Kiss* (dir. Jacques Feyder, 1929).

camera tracks out, refusing visual access to the scene of the crime. Then, with the closed door in the center of the frame, the camera freezes as a shot is heard, highlighting, as Scott Eyman points out, "the sound of the gun placing an emphatic period on the gliding sentence of camera movement."[98] This moment crystallizes how the sensational transition to sound affected Hollywood. Like the gunshot that kills the patriarch in *Old San Francisco,* this blast is explosive and has a rattling effect. But unlike that initial gunshot, this one is invisible. Because its source cannot be immediately located and pinned down, it draws attention to the fact that, as Christian Metz has suggested, "spatial anchoring of aural events is much more vague and uncertain than that of visual events."[99] In the early sound era, when sound is unhinged from, and therefore not subor-dinated to, the image, it appears disconcerting. It does not reinforce the narrative but overpowers it, by underscoring that off-screen sound is not really "off." Its absent presence makes it feel like it is everywhere, "'in' the

1.9. *The Kiss* (dir. Jacques Feyder, 1929).

screen, in front, behind, around, and throughout the entire movie theater."[100] The camera literally pauses to absorb its alarming impressions.

A moment later, another sound pierces the narrative, that of a telephone, ringing in the study (Figure 1.8). But this jarring effect does not
last long. Quickly, the sound is united with its image, as Irene leans over
to answer the phone (Figure 1.9). Another swift cut reveals the source of
the ringing – the senior Lassalle calling to check up on Charles Guarry.
Thus, sound switches from being aggravating to being subordinate to
the visual tale and therefore becomes unthreatening. In a sense, this
scene encapsulates the conversion to sound. The novelty of sound, not
yet perfectly synchronized with the image, is initially sensational; but its
thrilling effects rapidly dissipate as it is absorbed by classical narrative
principles. If *The Kiss* is, as Scott Eyman suggests, "a fitting farewell to the
silent film from the studio that made the most glamorous use of it," then
it also bids farewell to the ambivalent transition era.[101] For in Feyder's

film, as in Hitchcock's *Blackmail,* silence is unequivocally linked with guilt. Irene, who ultimately reveals to her lover that it is she who shot her husband and got away with it, does not speak when the phone rings. She also tries to elude the police by claiming not to have heard the gunshot, even though her visceral response to the second shot indicates otherwise. When she finally confesses her crime to André, it does not kill his love for her, as she fears. Rather, speaking, even when it is inaudible to the audience, becomes liberating. The film ends as a comedy, for the gunshot ultimately allows Irene to reunite with her lover and presumably live happily ever after.

By late 1929, Hollywood studios were beginning to hope for such an ending to their own rocky transition to sound by marrying it synchronically to the well-established classical narrative tradition. After that year, sound would no longer remain an auditory spectacle. Filmmakers worked hard to suppress the audience's medium sensitivity and "played down formal expression and novel effects to construct an illusion of unified audiovisual space."[102] They also eliminated what Laura Marcus calls "the multiple auralities of 'the [early] talkies' – music, synch sound/ speech, 'dead' silences."[103] Emphasis shifted from hybrid sequences to linear narrativity. After an initial burst of chaotic energy, sound further streamlined and standardized the classical Hollywood narrative. By privileging the heightened realism afforded by synchronized sound, films tried to eliminate the "feeling of discord within, or a sensation like a tug-of-war" that audiences found disconcerting about early Vitaphone efforts.[104] Indeed, after the transition, sound films became homogeneous and homogeneously harmonious. Jolting sounds surfaced infrequently, if at all. Sometimes they were used intentionally to mock naive audiences. A stray cow in Victor Fleming's *The Virginian* (1929), for instance, is startled by a steam engine's blast and, like Uncle Josh, appears funnily old-fashioned for being unsettled by the sounds of modernity. At other times, startling sounds were absorbed by specific genres like horror, whose spine-tingling terrors were enhanced by sounds that sent the films "rattling into uncanny territory."[105] Otherwise, the heterogeneous vigor and resulting bodily sensations of the part-talkie gave way to the conventional approach of synchronized sound.

"THE ART THAT DIED"

Mere days after the release of *The Kiss,* one afternoon in late November 1929, Sergei Eisenstein met with James Joyce, whom he had praised for bringing a cinematic mode of writing to modernist literature, and whose *Ulysses* (1922) he had extolled as the most significant event in the history of cinema. Taking his cue from Joyce, in the wake of the audio revolution sweeping the globe, Eisenstein was thinking about redefining the dichotomy between silence and sound. Rather than synchronized speech, he argued, by audibly displaying "inner monologue," cinema could realign sound with interiority and with "a feverish inner debate behind the stony mask of the face."[106] This is how montage could, through Joycean stream of consciousness, be allied with sound cinema. When they met in Paris, Eisenstein recalled, they discussed his (silent) films, which he would have liked Joyce to see, particularly for their use of discordant clashes that he admired in and borrowed from Joyce's prose. It was then that he came to realize the extent of Joyce's blindness and how that "external blindness undoubtedly determined that particular penetration of inner vision."[107] This inner vision was once again linked with sound. For after they spoke, Eisenstein listened to Joyce's gramophone recording of a section of "Work in Progress," which would later become *Finnegan's Wake* (1939), a novel deeply interested in the sound of language. Joyce's disembodied, mechanized voice, heard while he was sitting in the same room, must have thrilled Eisenstein for producing the kind of discord between seeing and hearing that other film theorists were then criticizing about the coming of sound. After all, Eisenstein was still hopeful about the radical treatment of sound. In a statement published in *Zhizn Iskusstva* with Vsevolod Pudovkin and Grigori Alexandrov, he had argued for the contrapuntal use of sound, "along the line of its distinct non-synchronization with the visual image," only a year earlier.[108] However, such expectations never came to fruition. Whereas films like Luis Buñuel's *L'Age d'Or* (1930) and Pudovkin's *Deserter* (1933) appeared as clear aural experiments, the majority of films, not only in the United States but around the world, employed synchronized, naturalistic sound. There would not be a real audio revolution.

Still, as we have seen, sound was a gamble even in Hollywood, and it initially behaved erratically. While its arrival was in many ways anticipated, it took the town by surprise. Its rapid standardization was equally astonishing. None of the early predictions came true. Although he had been at the forefront of ushering in sound in Hollywood, Sam Warner did not live to see its glorious success, dying only one day before the premiere of *The Jazz Singer*. Although sound had arrived in Hollywood via Vitaphone, and most major studios had initially signed deals with the company, it was Movietone that ultimately became the standard. By March 1930, even Warner Bros. had opted for sound on film. Although William Fox had pioneered the Movietone recording system, due to a risky financial move in the 1930s, he himself was not triumphant for too long. As Gomery suggests, Fox "took a big risk – the largest in the history of the coming of sound – and uniquely failed."[109] By May 1935, Fox Film had been taken over by Twentieth-Century Pictures. Although sound initially appeared to be an add-on to the silent narrative, it was effortlessly incorporated into the classical style.

But the move from silence to sound was neither as smooth as it now appears nor as chaotic as it was then feared. Many early film theorists deemed the introduction of the acoustic element a fracture, one that would destroy cinema as they knew it. In her memoir, Bryher (pen name of *Close Up* founder Annie Winifred Ellerman) mourned "'the art that died' because sound ruined its development."[110] Instead of seeing it as such a radical break, later film historians have thought of conversion in terms of continuity. Tracing the recent trend of Hollywood's globalization back to the conversion, Douglas Gomery has insisted that the late 1920s evinced "no chaos or confusion, but a speed of transformation which set a record within the mass media of the day."[111] Both versions of the conversion, of course, are accurate. While sound was rapidly integrated into the classical narrative style, sound films did indeed bring an end to the silent era. But both of them miss the sensational effects of the transition, when cinema temporarily rediscovered its corporeality as well as its modernity. Films of that transitory period foregrounded sound rather than submerging it and, as Crafton suggests, "played with the possibilities of surprising, even shocking the spectator with it."[112] For a while, the turmoil of modern technology overpowered the classical aesthetic. Guided by the many moments of aural cinephilia in this chapter, we might think of the transition to sound as a moment of rupture. After all, the acoustic novelty remained a gamble for a time, and it did deliver some unforeseen jolts. These cinephiliac instants from early sound experiments might be seen, heard, and felt as raised seams in the history of classical Hollywood. They suggest that, while we tend to think of the studio era in terms of classical conformity, it was also a time of (modernist) excess. Excess may have been successfully repressed by the return to standardization in late 1929, but disruptive moments never stay buried for too long. As we will see in the next chapter, even when ostensibly settled, classical Hollywood always seemed in a state of virtual transition. During the 1930s, even though sound had been fully subdued, there were other ruptures that created some unsettling effects.

What in the end does it matter to human happiness whether
[Fred Astaire's] trousers do or do not have cuffs?

BRUCE BABINGTON AND PETER WILLIAM EVANS,
Blue Skies and Silver Linings

In my formulation: "The eternal is in any case
far more the ruffle on a dress than some idea."

WALTER BENJAMIN, "B [Fashion]," *A P*

TWO

Show Stoppers

1937 and the Chance Encounter with Chiffons

A FUNNY THING HAPPENS

For a brief moment, a chance encounter between a Wall Street tycoon and an unsuspecting working girl takes on the spectral eeriness of a Surrealist nightmare. Worn down by his profligate wife's spending habits, millionaire banker J. B. Ball (Edward Arnold) decides to teach her a lesson. When their marital spat climaxes on their Fifth Avenue penthouse landing, he flings her most recent purchase, a $58,000 fur coat, off the roof. An overhead shot captures the coat as it slowly descends and assumes the shape of an ominous, bat-like creature (Figure 2.1). Its ghostly glide down seems to envelop a bus that drives in on the street below. When the coat lands on Mary Smith (Jean Arthur) as she rides the double-decker bus to work, the screwball plot gets going again. To the extent that it triggers the coincidental meeting on which the tale depends, this moment is central to the film. But its appearance as a slow, almost dream-like, unmotivated overhead shot is incongruous with the fast-paced screwball action that precedes and follows it. Indeed, it is both excessive and jarring, making it appear virtually extra-diegetic. That uncanny feeling, however, lasts only for a moment. Cut to a medium shot of Jean Arthur as the coat falls on her head, wrecking her hat and scaring her silly, and the comic plot quickly resumes, unfolding through a series of madcap adventures that almost causes the stock market to collapse.

What do we make of this strange moment appearing unexpectedly in a screwball comedy? Of the madcap comedies released during the mid-1930s, Mitchell Leisen's *Easy Living* was hardly the most ingenious.

2.1. *Easy Living* (dir. Mitchell Leisen, 1937).

It was a standard comedy spun out of a chance encounter, neither as fresh as Frank Capra's *It Happened One Night* (1934) nor as lively as Gregory La Cava's *My Man Godfrey* (1936). Preston Sturges wrote the screenplay, turning Vera Caspary's short story into a subtle critique of modern capitalism – all very standard fare during the Great Depression. Although Paramount marketed it as a Sturges comedy, trying to capitalize on the sensation he had created in Hollywood with scripts like *The Power and the Glory* (William K. Howard, 1933) and *Diamond Jim* (A. Edward Sutherland, 1935), the film was not a commercial or critical success. Still, as James Harvey reminds us, everyone remembers the moment when "the fur coat falls on the heroine's head."[1] That is ironic, because Sturges himself did not believe the shot could even be filmed. The script does contain a "very long shot" devoted to the falling fur coat "shooting down," preceded by J. B. Ball and his wife on the penthouse roof and followed by a medium shot of Mary on top of the double-decker bus.[2] Sturges appears to have thought that "the falling will probably not pick up," and the film would advance directly from Figure 2.2 to Figure 2.3.[3]

2.2. *Easy Living* (dir. Mitchell Leisen, 1937).

2.3. *Easy Living* (dir. Mitchell Leisen, 1937).

But the moment did make it to the screen, and what I find most cap-
tivating is that it appears inadvertently in excess. While the falling fur
coat is a crucial plot device, enabling the eventual meeting between Ball
and Mary, it exceeds its narrative function. In addition, it is also visually excessive. Writing about the "material of the film" that surpasses its
motivation, Kristin Thompson has argued that cinematic excess surfaces
when the "narrative function may justify the presence of a device, but
it doesn't always motivate *the specific form that individual element will
take.*"[4] Likewise, the fur coat's surreal appearance exceeds the screwball style. As Sturges had assumed, the film could have easily advanced
from the shot of the roof where the coat is hurled to the shot of the coat
falling on Jean Arthur's head, and the missing "falling" shot would not
have affected our understanding of the scene. In that sense, it functions
like Roland Barthes's description of the moment when the two courtiers are pouring gold over the young czar's head in Sergei Eisenstein's
Ivan the Terrible (1944). There is something in the visual details, Barthes
suggests, that is erratic – something that "exceeds the copy of the refer-
ential motif, [such that] it compels an interrogative reading." There is
something striking about the incongruity between the courtiers' makeup, "thick and insistent for the one, smooth and distinguished for the
other," their facial features, even their hairstyles.[5] For Barthes, this moment becomes intriguing because it hints at the possibility of a "third"
or "obtuse" meaning, one that moves beyond symbolic interpretation.
Barthes is interested in its affective allure, which lies beyond signification. The falling fur coat has a similar cinephiliac appeal. It is likewise
incongruous due to its uncanny excess. And its dreamlike manifestation
appears as if by chance. What gets me every time I watch this scene is
that, unlike the rest of *Easy Living,* for an instant, a familiar object like a
fur coat suddenly appears foreboding, and a screwball comedy seems to
surreptitiously encounter the surreal.

Using a familiar object to evoke the uncanny has been quintessential
to Surrealist discourse. By their own admission, the Surrealists were
interested in everyday objects that could suddenly reveal something
mysterious about the world. In their writing, art, and filmmaking, they
developed ways of interacting with things that could potentially un-
leash the magic contained within them. That is why the Surrealists were

particularly drawn to cinema. As Louis Aragon acknowledged early on, cinema had the ability to alter everyday objects, such that "objects that were a few moments ago sticks of furniture or books of cloakroom tickets are transformed to the point where they take on menacing or enigmatic meanings."[6] But such furtive transformations are more likely in the phantasmic worlds of Louis Feuillade's *Fantômas* (1913) or the dream-like images of Buñuel's *L'Age d'Or*. In a screwball comedy, is such a surreal moment just an odd interruption, to be dismissed as interesting but insignificant, curious but inconsequential?

Visual interruptions have generally appeared to be quite unwelcome in the standardized world of studio filmmaking, particularly after the full integration of sound. As we saw in the last chapter, the transition to sound may have caused real and imagined panic, but the hope was that the industry would soon return to its comfortably classical narrative tradition, which emphasized a seamless flow of action instead of focusing on distinctive details. This does not imply that details did not matter to Hollywood filmmakers. Irving Thalberg would often wonder about seemingly irrelevant details. When he wanted to get to know a character better, Thalberg would ask: "What kind of underwear does he have on? Long or short, light or heavy, clean or dirty?"[7] However, underpants never became the center of attention. In 1923, Erich von Stroheim was fired by Thalberg himself during the shooting of *Merry Go Round* (Rupert Julian, 1923), reportedly for having spent too much time and money getting the guardsmen extras' silk underpants embroidered with the Imperial Guard monogram. The film was turned over to Rupert Julian, who, as Rex Ingram did with *Greed* (1923), had to cut out the excesses. Dazzling details, then, were apparently desirable only so long as they advanced the narrative. Of course, the coming of sound shook up the studio model temporarily, and all kinds of striking interruptions made their way onscreen. By the early 1930s, however, with the onset of the Depression and the easing up of varied experiments with sound, the process of filmmaking was further streamlined. While 1930 was a good year at the box office, for three years afterward, even the so-called Depression-proof industry was in decline. Tino Balio notes that "the major companies could not meet their fixed cost obligations, which simply meant they did not have the cash to pay their mortgage commitments, short-term obligations, and the heavy charges on their funded debts."[8] What they also could not afford was any form of experimentation or excess. A new era of not only economic but also thematic and stylistic austerity set in, which lasted long after the box office stabilized after 1933. In this atmosphere, while the studio system remained a collaborative effort, the script became the essential element of that collaboration. Since "the costs and logistical complexity of sound increased the need for a closely supervised, assembly-line system," Thomas Schatz notes, the shooting script "mapped out all aspects of production – from camera work and dialogue to the shot-by-shot construction of the picture – before the actual filmmaking machinery was set into motion."[9] The screenwriter gained a lot more authority, and anything that did not fit the script was usually left out. In Tay Garnett's *China Seas* (1935), for instance, the details of Jean Harlow's gown – its open back and cut-out sleeves – are hardly seen onscreen. Jane M. Gaines suggests that "the practice of cutting films for narrative coherence and visual continuity" made filmmakers cut some stunning moments out of their films.[10]

Ironically, such details have also been left out of film histories of the period. After all, Fred Astaire's pant cuffs, which Babington and Evans ponder in the epigraph, often matter little if they do not contribute to interpreting, say, the relationship between dance and masculinity during the Great Depression. Such is the case with Leisen's *Easy Living*, too, which has been repeatedly analyzed as a Cinderella story that subverts social hierarchies and redefines femininity in relation to the newly established Production Code, in the mold of Clarence Brown's *Possessed* (1931) or Dorothy Arzner's *The Bride Wore Red* (1937). Bernard F. Dick reads the film as yet another Depression-era fairy tale. Elizabeth Kendall argues that *Easy Living* is a grand vision of social chaos following the Depression. Sarah Berry offers a more comprehensive account of consumer fashion, showing how it "makes fun of class distinctions and presents status as a matter of appearances."[11] While these semiotic readings are valuable in themselves, they fail to account for the cinephiliac allure of the fur coat moment. Its visual effect has been critically missed, likely because its Surrealist look does not fit into the film's symbolic discussion. What can that moment tell us about disruptive cinematic details that appear by chance and distract attention from the linear narrative?

What connections can that instance of Surrealism in a screwball comedy uncover about classical Hollywood that remain cut out of traditional film histories? What would such connections reveal about studio film-making in the 1930s?

"TWO UNLIKELY WORLDS ARE SUDDENLY JOINED"

In early 1937, Salvador Dali traveled to Hollywood to collaborate with the Marx Brothers. Dali was working on *Giraffes on Horseback Salad*, a screenplay about a Spanish aristocrat named Jimmy, who moves to America and falls in love with a mysterious character named the "Surre-alist woman," whose face is never seen throughout the film. With Harpo Marx, Dali co-wrote the initial script and did several sketches for the prospective film. There were other shenanigans too; Dali made some sketches of the brothers, including of Harpo playing the harp and of Groucho being the Shiva of show business, with multiple arms answer-ing phones simultaneously. But their project together never material-ized. As he was wandering through the studios, Dali met an old friend from Paris, composer George Antheil, who was then working on Cecil B. DeMille's *The Plainsman* (1936), starring Jean Arthur as Calamity Jane. When Antheil introduced Dali to DeMille, the Spanish Surrealist prostrated himself in front of the master of mass spectacle, who was quite thrilled by the laudatory gesture. "Ah, Mr. DeMille," Dali reportedly declared, "I have met you at last, you, the greatest Surrealist on earth." Such an encounter is hard to picture. In his Hollywood memoirs, when René Clair takes note of this meeting, he is rightfully skeptical. "If this scene took place as it was reported to me," he adds, "I am sorry that I was *not* an eyewitness."[12] To my knowledge, no photographic evidence of the unlikely encounter exists either. Our skepticism might be fueled by the popular notion that there could be nothing more disparate than the modernist avant-garde and the commercial narrative enterprise. Writing about this encounter, James Morrison suggests that Dali and DeMille seem completely incompatible "because of the vastly different cultural territories each inhabited."[13] They appear to embody "conventional no-tions about the distinction between art and commerce and the related distinctions between 'high' European culture and 'popular' American culture."[14] In other words, they appear to be incarnations of two entirely mismatched registers.

There is a long history of such opposition between high and popular culture, which is traditionally expressed in the arts and philosophy as the distinction between modernism and classicism. Modernism is generally defined as a break from tradition. As Jürgen Habermas has pointed out, the term "modern" has appeared in Europe whenever there has been a sense of the dawning of a new epoch. But what changed after the French Enlightenment is the relationship the modern had with the past or "the ancients." For Habermas, "the belief, inspired by modern science, in the infinite progress of knowledge and in the infinite advance towards social and moral betterment" led to a fundamental rethinking of the power of the past.[15] A new modernism emerged in the nineteenth century "out of this romantic spirit that radicalized consciousness of modernity which freed itself from all specific historical ties."[16] Since then, Habermas argues, modernism has been aligned with that which is new. The value of such newness has traditionally been conferred on works of the avant-garde, not popular culture, whose reliance on formulaic models that can be easily repeated for commercial gain makes it far closely aligned with crass traditionalism. And this broad opposition has been imported to cinema in general and classical Hollywood in particular. Even though the two coincided historically, as Miriam Hansen has adroitly shown, Hollywood cinema has habitually been regarded as being "fundamentally incompatible" with modernism.[17]

Still, in a brief moment, a potential connection between two unlikely registers is revealed. Like most romantic comedies, *Easy Living* is driven by an accidental meeting of two dissimilar worlds. When Mary Smith, a young woman working for a little magazine called *The Boy's Constant Companion*, runs into J. B. Ball, the baron of Wall Street, the economic and social worlds of a working girl and a billionaire suddenly collide in a classic "meet cute" moment. The coat that accidentally falls becomes Mary's, who is then assumed to be Ball's mistress. And everyone, of course, wants to please the mistress of the "bull of Broad Street." She is lavished with gifts, attention, and a free stay at the Hotel Louis. Sturges's script is full of witty dialogue and cleverly contrived situations that unfold through comic misunderstandings resulting from the original rendezvous, as Mary tries to keep up with the fast-paced, screwball world. It ends when she falls in love with a poor but charming young fellow named John (Ray Milland), who turns out to be, in typical fairy-tale tradition, the tycoon's son. It is the initial, incompatible juxtaposition that is the source of the film's comic circumstances. As Andrew Horton reminds us in his practical guide to writing comedic screenplays, incongruities often bring on laughter. Using Woody Allen's line that his parents believed in God and carpeting, he suggests that comedy lies in juxtapositions; in the case of Woody Allen, the combination works between "the cosmic and the daily, the sacred and the profane."[18] Thus, when "two unlikely worlds are suddenly joined" in *Easy Living* by a fur coat, the collision produces a series of comic scenarios.[19]

In the scene that follows their accidental encounter, Ball offers Mary a ride. In the car, the two sit next to each other, but they appear "in the same frame but in different worlds."[20] Ball wants to teach Mary a lesson in computing interest, while she is more interested in finding out if the fur coat is an authentic Kolinsky. The best example of their collision's effect occurs in the automat scene, where a mishap at the coin-operated cafeteria creates a display of zany anarchy. As all the glass lids pop open, customers rush to get their hands on the free food flying in the background, while Mary, still wearing her fur coat, calmly enjoys her pot pie. That juxtaposition, of a sable-clad woman eating pot pie while the masses slip and slide over slippery floors, is hilarious, not the least for "highlighting the extremes of affluence and poverty" and underlining "the Great Depression as a time of fur coats for the fortunate and cloth coats (or no coats) for everyone else."[21] The scene's chaotic energy echoes the frenzy of mechanization gone awry in Charlie Chaplin's *Modern Times* (1936), a derivation of René Clair's *A Nous La Liberté* (1931), released only a year earlier. But nothing will come of this possibility. Unlike Chaplin's film, all ends well in *Easy Living.* Order is restored by the end, as the two unlikely worlds are suddenly and delightfully joined when Ball becomes Mary's father-in-law. The ultimate outcome of their accidental encounter appears to be quite conventional.

But what do we make of that other encounter revealed in the moment of their unplanned meeting? The parties in that encounter too, to use Harvey's terms, are "connected in a way we recognize even if we can't name it."[22] For the image of the coat descending ominously hints at a connection between Surrealism and classical Hollywood, even if we do not have a name for it. It is worth remembering that Antonin Artaud often praised the zany and excessive intensity of the comic disruptions in silent and early sound comedies. He even compared the Marx Brothers' *Animal Crackers* (1930) to the "distinct poetic state of mind that can be called *surrealism*."[23] Man Ray also famously claimed that "there was more Surrealism rampant in Hollywood than all the Surrealists could invent in a lifetime."[24] More recently, Michael Richardson argues that the Surrealists were especially fascinated by Hollywood genre films of the early 1930s, where they found an involuntary Surrealist tendency. However, the relationship between them "has always seemed anomalous, if not contradictory."[25]

It may appear anomalous or implausible, but glimpses of the relationship between Surrealism and the studio system are visible in fleeting moments, like the unlikely meeting between Mary Smith and J. B. Ball or the even more improbable encounter between Dali and DeMille. This connection is usually overlooked, probably because, positioned in opposition to the progressive politics of the avant-garde, the studio system is seen to occupy a vastly different cultural terrain. As Miriam Hansen points out, classical Hollywood is typically regarded "as a mode of representation that masks the process and fact of production, turns discourse into diegesis, history into story and myth."[26] In so doing, it appears to create an illusion of narrative coherence, where disruptive excesses are disallowed. Even when Surrealist elements are noticed in Hollywood films, they are regarded as mere accidents. Jerome Delamater, for instance, detects Surrealist motifs in the fantasy worlds of Busby Berkeley's musicals, but suggests that Berkeley was an "unwitting Surrealist" because he was probably unaware of Surrealism. Similarly, Martin Rubin claims that Berkeley's non-narrative cinema, although different in style from mainstream Hollywood cinema, was extraordinarily popular and therefore less likely to have been influenced by Surrealism and avant-gardism than by the nineteenth-century tradition of spectacle. Robin Wood goes so far as to assert that the studio system and Surrealism are inherently incompatible.[27] He argues that while Expressionist motifs could easily be appropriated by Hollywood because they "proved a fruitful source of subjective effects" that could be linearized, especially in genres like film noir or the horror film of the 1940s, Surrealism was ideologically irreconcilable with the bourgeois narrative tradition.[28] When Surrealism is mentioned in relation to Hollywood cinema, it is generally in reference to Salvador Dali's collaboration with Alfred Hitchcock on *Spellbound* (1945), although Wood hastens to add that, even then, the designs were "modified by the studio and the [Surrealist dream] sequence drastically abridged."[29] This resistance may in part be prompted by Hollywood's self-proclaimed independence. As early as 1934, writing in *Photoplay*, William Gaines declares that the "movie capital is self-reliant as a style center. Designers no longer look to 'shabby' Paris for ideas."[30] The contempt was mutual. For many of his Surrealist colleagues, Dali's work in Hollywood was seen as selling out to mass culture and earned him the nickname "Avida Dollars." The critical consensus, then, seems to be that Surrealism and the studio system are wholly discordant entities. A moment in 1937, however, hints at the potential for an associative link between the explicitly controlled environment of the studio system and the spontaneity-driven avant-garde art.

By chance, just when Mary is suddenly and fortuitously hit over the head by a falling coat, the question of lucky finds also begins to haunt André Breton. Writing in *Mad Love* about an eerie mask that Giacometti had found at a flea market, Breton suggested that the lucky find, *la trouvaille,* is capable of providing the shock of convulsive beauty that Surrealists dreamed of, by breaking the stranglehold of narrative continuity. "Such images," he noted, "are endowed with a persuasive strength rigorously proportional to the violence of the initial shock they produced"[31] Perhaps due to this persuasive shock, the mask appeared to Giacometti as the perfect solution to complete the head of his sculpture. Breton maintained that the solution is an example of the chance object's capacity to embody the subject's desire – to appear as if it were the perfect solution. A lucky find enables the subject to inadvertently uncover repressed desire, or, as Margaret Cohen argues, it is capable of producing a moment "when the habitual veil of repression is rent, allowing a true hidden order of things to surge forth."[32] Ironically, at the moment when Giacometti encounters his lucky find, a mask, *the* mask is torn away, for the order that surges forth is not one of causality – as Breton puts it, a lucky find "could not come to us along ordinary logical paths" – but of irrationality, or, we might say, of chance.[33]

For Breton, chance was not just a singular moment that disrupted the "natural" order of things. Instead, it enabled Surrealists like himself to imagine another order, wherein one gave oneself over to the seemingly arbitrary. Even as early as 1920, Breton asked, "when will one give the arbitrary the place that falls to it in the formation of works and ideas?"[34] Only by giving oneself over to chance can a new order be created, which enables fortuitous juxtapositions. But the Dadaists themselves were much less interested in discovering these juxtapositions. "If the Dadas called spectacular attention to the value of chance," Cohen notes, "they did so in negative fashion, as a force capable of destroying habitual conceptual order."[35] Deeply disturbed by the mass destruction of the Great War, they were a group of young artists and writers who worked spontaneously and collaboratively on pamphlets and publications, paintings and collages, not only to proclaim the rupture between art and logic but also to advertise a kind of destructive anarchism. From Tristan Tzara and Marcel Duchamp to Breton, Phillipe Soupault, and Aragon, they became what Fiona Bradley calls "the randomly christened expression of revolt which exploded into simultaneous life in Zürich, Cologne, and New York."[36] In 1920, Aragon announced, "No more painters, no more writers, no more musicians, no more sculptors, ... NOTHING, NOTHING, NOTHING."[37]

Within a couple of years though, some of them became frustrated with Dada's inflexible negativity. This frustration was voiced by Breton in *Entretiens:* "The *1918 Dada Manifesto* seemed to open wide the doors, but we discovered that they opened onto a corridor which was leading nowhere."[38] Breton and the group of artists who converged around him were more interested in walking down the corridor that would open the door to new ideas, new forms, and to chance. Moreover, Katharine Conley points out that the Surrealists were more drawn to the "door that opens and reopens continuously, like a door pushed by the wind or a swinging door, returning to a singular point of departure yet ever opening new vistas of thought."[39] Early Surrealists were much more intrigued by the logic of circularity and the thrill of the return than the oppression of linearity. Ten years after closing the door on Dadaism, Breton himself produced a work based on that logic. *Nadja,* a text he wanted to leave "ajar, like a door," opens onto a world of endless departures and returns.[40] For *Nadja* is not so much a narrative as a series of unexpected encounters on Parisian streets, woven together through turns and returns that continually disrupt the linear order. Breton's constant, if sometimes inadvertent, visits to sites where the ghosts of past insurrectional activities lie, as well as his unexpected meetings with Nadja, create an eerie atmosphere that Breton concedes gives the appearance of being left "at the mercy of chance."[41] And his repeated fortuitous encounters – as when Paul Eluard turns out to be the same person whom he unknowingly encountered at the first performance of Guillaume Apollinaire's *Couleur du Temps* and coincidentally started corresponding with – produce a world that no longer depends on logical connections. Instead, it becomes, in Breton's words, "an almost forbidden world of sudden parallels, petrifying coincidences."[42] Chance, then, became Surrealism's calling card and its operating methodology.

Remarkably, only a year after Breton wrote *Nadja,* chance became the guiding principle for many at home and abroad. After the speculative boom of the 1920s, a single calamity wiped out bank balances and caused cataclysmic shifts that would last for almost a decade. The stock market crash of October 1929, followed by the Great Depression, seemed to leave everyone at the mercy of chance. Neither tycoon nor laborer was safe from the vicissitudes of a shaky economy. The Dust Bowl further shook confidence, uprooting hundreds of thousands of families and scattering them to the mercy of an uncertain destiny. Simultaneously, the rise of Nazism and fascism, the fall of democratic governments to dictators, and militaristic advances around the globe led to even more insecurity. The decade began with the Nazis winning 107 seats in the Reichstag. Japan invaded Manchuria a year later. The great purges orchestrated by Joseph Stalin, the Abyssinian crisis that weakened the League of Nations, and the Spanish Civil War followed. By the end of the decade, Hitler had invaded Poland, officially triggering another world war. Each crisis sent shockwaves that could virtually be measured on the Richter scale, which was invented in the middle of the decade. Indeed, the 1930s may be seen as a decade in flux, where everything seemed guided by wild shifts of fortune, and everyone's lives seemed marked by disrupted plans and ill-fated reversals. In America, Ina Rae Hark argues, a "head of household could be a plutocrat one day, a pauper the next"; in Europe, "a comfortably bourgeois German Jewish family could suddenly have to flee for its very survival."[43] Life seemed to depend on chance, and luck did not favor too many.

Hollywood was not immune to chance events either. The arrival of the Depression put an end to any residual desire to gamble with film-making. But that did not imply immediate stability. With ticket sales declining in the early part of the decade, most major studios had a lot of debt, and many of them went into bankruptcy or receivership. Some of them also experienced a major reshuffling of the deck. After many years at the top, several founding partners or producers, including Jesse Lasky, Irving Thalberg, and Carl Laemmle, went through a reversal of fortunes. Interestingly, during the 1930s, Hollywood embraced chance as a tactic and appropriated the theme of reversal of fortune. Early in the decade, many theaters, troubled by wary patrons unwilling to spend money on frivolous entertainment, instituted a form of lottery called Bank Night. It was invented by Charles Yaeger, a theater manager in Colorado, as an incentive to draw audiences. The premise was simple enough: on Bank Night, people could put their names in for a lottery of prizes; then, if their name was called, usually during the intermission, they rushed to the stage to claim their winnings. Since no purchases were necessary, Bank Night and other games of chance like Screeno and Prosperity Night were able to skirt bans in many states against gambling. Hollywood hoped patrons would gamble, buying a ticket that might give them "access to a chance, however slight, at actually winning themselves."[44] More importantly, this notion of chance was reinforced by many of the films of the decade. Reversing the real life reversals of fortune, onscreen characters often got lucky. For them, "hard work and perseverance were no longer critical for success within the economic and social system," because they "gained access to affluence largely through dumb luck."[45] In Lloyd Bacon's *42nd Street* (1933), an inexperienced chorus girl (Ruby Keeler) becomes the star of a hit Broadway show. In George Stevens's *Swing Time* (1936), dancer John "Lucky" Garnett (Fred Astaire) succeeds in stopping his sweetheart's wedding at the last minute. And in *Easy Living*, Mary finds love and marriage when a coat falls on her. When the coat first descends on her, it envelops her. Visibly flustered, she turns around, eyes the commuter sitting behind her incredulously, and asks, "Say, what's the big idea anyway?" He happens to be a turbaned Hindu gentleman, who, pointing to the book he is reading, calls the unexpected article "kismet." Looking both amused and annoyed, she shrugs off the fatalistic implications of his response, seeing her mysterious sartorial windfall – recall Jacques Derrida's assertion in "My Chances/*Mes Chances*" that the notion of chance is etymologically linked to the idea of falling – as a lucky find.[46]

In Hollywood, however, chance was mostly used for comic effect. It was incorporated into the classical narrative and fit especially well into genres like musicals and screwball comedies. But the element of chance was not to be integrated into filmmaking itself. In Hollywood, it could not carry the political vigor that the Surrealists deployed to break with tradition and imagine a new way of thinking that lay beyond narrative causality. Consider, for instance, Denise Tual's brief sojourn in Hollywood. Tual, who would soon try to convince Luis Buñuel to direct Lorca's 1936 play, *The House of Bernarda Alba,* was invited by MGM to discuss the possibility of remaking Robert Bresson's *Angels of the Streets* (1943). During lunch one afternoon, John Baxter notes, she mentioned Buñuel to Louis B. Mayer, who claimed never to have heard of him. Tual filled him in, concluding by calling Buñuel a great director. She thought it would be nice if Mayer could arrange for directors like Buñuel, René Clair, and Jean Renoir to "work on new ideas, new ways of making films" in Hollywood. Mayer would have none of it. "If Hollywood needs to change its way of making films," he reportedly retorted, "it'll happen, and quickly. We don't need a laboratory for that!" After that meeting, Baxter notes, "MGM's interest in *Les Anges du Péché* cooled rapidly."[47] Ostensibly at least, any real connection between the studio system and Surrealism appears to be nonexistent. Just as there is no photographic record of the chance meeting between Dali and DeMille, there is no hard evidence of this relationship. What does exist is a displaced picture, a series of cinephiliac glimpses, of that chance encounter. What we need is an alternative way of looking for them.

REFUS[E]ING HISTORY

In Sturges's *Sullivan's Travels* (1941), a Hollywood director, displeased with the studio system of filmmaking, endeavors to make an epic about the essential meaning of poverty. Instead of offering cheap laughs, John "Sully" Sullivan (Joel McCrea) believes that cinema ought to focus more on the grand themes of misery and hardship during the Great Depression. So he sets out dressed in rags, borrowed from the studio's costume department, to write his substantial thesis on poverty, to be titled "O Brother, Where Art Thou?" At first, it is difficult to leave the studio system behind and realize his riches to rags tale. Every time he hitches a ride out of Hollywood, he inadvertently finds his way back. Even his crew follows him in a caravan, filming his adventures. When Sully accidentally encounters two hobos on a freight train who might know a thing or two about living in poverty, he asks them about the labor situation, but they walk away. They are not so keen on discussing his "big idea." When he finally discovers the realities of the Depression, it appears not as a grand narrative about social disorder but in minor details, like a pair of tattered shoes with the front split open and toes exposed. For a short bit, the screwball plot pauses. With his traveling companion (Veronica Lake), Sully ends up eating in soup kitchens and sleeping in homeless shelters, until he becomes a scavenger impaling scraps with a stick in a dumpster.

Sully's attention to rags while he goes on a brief scavenging detour is reminiscent of Walter Benjamin's ragpicker, a figure who rummaged through refuse and detritus while wandering around the nineteenth-century city. The *chiffonier* pursues the rags or *chiffons* that are unattended by traditional history. As Carlo Salzani puts it, for him, "Ruins, fragments and trash are the material for historical reconstruction."[48] The ragpicker rejects nothing, drawing insights even from the most insignificant objects. Benjamin suggests that he "collects and catalogues everything that the great city has cast off, everything it has lost, and discarded, and broken. He goes through the archives of debauchery, and the jumbled array of refuse."[49] And it is in these rags that he finds revolutionary possibilities. For he does not simply hoard his stockpile of leftovers. As Irving Wohlfarth argues, "It is precisely when they no longer circulate, as well-behaved commodities should, that things begin to give signs of a more subversive potential."[50] The *chiffonier* rescues that potential in forgotten objects – a series of *chiffons,* if you will – from the jaws of linear history, to reveal an alternative order of things. That is why he is a fascinating figure, "depicted by some as the *bon sauvage* of the urban wilderness, uncorrupted by the vices of commodity civilization, considered by others a wish-image of *freedom* and *independence.*"[51] As he freely roams the city, he gathers objects whose time has passed. They have fallen in popularity and are therefore discarded as needless trash. But the ragpicker's is not a utilitarian view of objects. Rather, for him, history lies in trash.

The ragpicker's interest in outdated objects echoes Surrealism's affinity for old-fashioned things. Using Breton's *Nadja* as his prime example, Benjamin argues that Surrealism was "the first to perceive the revolutionary energies that appear in the 'outmoded,' in the first iron constructions, the first factory buildings, the earliest photos, the objects that have begun to become extinct, grand pianos, the dresses of five years ago."[52] The Surrealists discovered how to release the radical potential in these antiquated objects and create a world based on uncanny associations between them. Surrealism, for Benjamin, became an alternative mode of writing, and the Surrealists became materialist historians fashioning history out of the outmoded.

Like the Surrealists, Benjamin's ragpicker picks out unattended things, because he is able to "assemble large-scale constructions out of the smallest and most precisely cut components."[53] Moreover, he echoes the Surrealist interest in chance, scaling history, as Benjamin suggests, "rung by rung, according as chance would offer a narrow foothold."[54] The ragpicker's attention to outmoded details, his reliance on chance encounters, and his ability to connect ideas and images through odd associations rather than logical connections yield a method well suited to writing an associative history, drawing on cinematic moments that end up on the cutting room floor of the traditional film historian. For in these moments, we are likely to find the revolutionary potential that the Surrealists discovered in the grand pianos and the old-fashioned dresses of a generation earlier. But how does a ragpicker-historian utilize these scraps? Here is how Benjamin explains the process for ragpicking: "The method of this work: literary montage – I have nothing to say, only to show. I won't purloin anything precious, nor will I appropriate witty turns. But the rags, the remnants: I do not want to inventory them, but let them come into their own in the only possible way: by using them."[55] That is to say, the historical rags are displayed but not appropriated into a singular narrative. The refuse speaks for itself.

Interestingly, Wohlfarth observes that the only place where Benjamin explicitly portrays the ragpicker as an intellectual is in reference to film historian Siegfried Kracauer. Wohlfarth argues that from Benjamin's point of view, "what we see when we visualize [Kracauer] going about his solitary business is a ragpicker at daybreak, impaling verbal rags, scraps of language, with his stick."[56] While impaling these rags, Kracauer refuses to accept history's desire to make order out of chaos. "Whereas academics," Wohlfarth concludes, "vainly arrange the chaos of their 'lumber-room' into neat piles of facts that nonetheless accumulate like so much debris, thereby reflecting the chaos of history without reflecting *upon* it, the ragpicker throws all the litter out *almost* without comment."[57] Following Benjamin, he observes, "He has 'nothing to say,' 'only to show.'"[58] Thus, even the most seemingly insignificant detail, the most undesirable piece of refuse, makes its way into history. In that process, Wohlfarth suggests, the ragpicker comes to embody "the intrinsic connection between refuse and refusal."[59] It is in the refuse that the ragpicker-historian uncovers the past anew by refusing traditional history.

For an era when so many had become virtual ragpickers, depending on scraps for sustenance and perhaps hoping for their own rags to riches story, the ragpicker is a particularly apt figure for historicizing the 1930s. In Hollywood, the rags to riches tale was not only popular onscreen but had been lived by many of its own denizens off-screen. Indeed, one of its founding members began his career as a ragpicker of sorts. Louis B. Mayer, the executive who made MGM the Tiffany of Hollywood, got his start in his father's scrap metal business. From there, the young Mayer started his own junk business in Boston, which helped transform him into a used-clothes dealer, colloquially known as a ragpicker. Like many other early Hollywood moguls, Peter Wollen notes, Mayer emerged from "the lower reaches of the garment industry" and changed the inchoate American film industry into an enormously popular form of mass entertainment.[60] Among Mayer's contemporaries who also came from the clothing industry were Paramount chief Adolph Zukor, a fur coat dealer; producer Sam Goldwyn, a glove salesman; and William Fox, a cloth-sponger. In fact, the film industry became so distinctly associated with the garment business that when Joseph P. Kennedy entered it in the 1920s by acquiring Pathé, Marcus Loew is said to have remarked, "What's Kennedy doing in pictures? He's not a furrier." And this long-standing history with garments was not abandoned when they joined the pictures either. "When they eventually built studios, achieved power and amassed wealth as Hollywood tycoons," Wollen argues, "it was only natural that they should want to associate the cinema with extravagant and spectacular clothes."[61]

Indeed, the idea of the makeover, a literal rags to riches story, fit nicely within the narrative of American self-invention, which many of them, being European émigrés, were eager to embrace. In Hollywood, these young tycoons literally made themselves over completely, and Mayer even expressed his gratitude by adopting the fourth of July as his birthday.[62] It is not surprising that the fashion makeover came to represent the way to the top. As Sarah Berry points out, "fashion was a medium of new beginnings": a working girl, especially in the Depression era, could make herself over "thanks to hard work and a few Adrian outfits."[63] That is certainly the narrative intention of *Easy Living*, where the fortuitous acquisition of a fur coat enables a penniless working girl to cross class lines and end up marrying a billionaire. I will return to that plot in a moment, but what interests me is the way in which, for a fleeting instant, that narrative is ruptured. Insofar as a mundane fashion accessory becomes surreal, it functions as a virtual show stopper, arresting the screwball plot dead in its tracks. So, in this rags to riches tale, let us focus on the rags for now. By unfurling the details of the fur coat that descends uncannily after its wealthy owner discards it like a piece of trash, we might accidentally uncover a different kind of Hollywood tale.

What follows is that tale, told not as a causal narrative but as a series of moments or episodes. It relies on chance encounters between the structured world of the studio system and the unplanned world of the avant-garde. Because even though these two worlds appear to be incompatible, they run into each other often. These encounters are especially guided by the world of couture. Fashion, as Walter Benjamin observes, may be transient, but it offers an alternative view of the past. Benjamin's fashion formulation, about the ruffles on a dress being more significant than some big idea, alludes to Baudelaire's *Tableaux Parisiens*. As Barbara Vinken notes, "The transitory moment versus eternity is the crucial opposition structuring the poem: 'un éclair, puis la nuit'"—a flash of lightning, then the night.[64] Fashion provides this flash of lightning for understanding modernity. It is for Benjamin "the art of the destructive but triumphant moment."[65] In its details, fashion bears traces of *un temps perdu* and therefore enables new discoveries about history. The ragpicker is most interested in these discoveries. As a historian, the ragpicker demonstrates that picking at old articles that were once in vogue but have now become outmoded can yield new ways of seeing the past. Following the ragpicker-historian, the next section digs through articles of fashion, whose ephemeral existence makes it possible to uncover unlikely associations between the mismatched fabrics of classical Hollywood and Surrealism. This is not a history of film couture. Rather, by mining outmoded or cut-out sartorial objects, it asks what *la mode* reveals about *le mode*, what fashion designing unexpectedly reveals about the method of studio filmmaking itself. Along the way, fur coats and chiffon dresses become unanticipated mediators between the studio system and the avant-garde art, and Hollywood looks a lot less like a rational system with a uniform style than a strange network of echoes and coincidences.

EPISODES IN CHIFFON

The element of chance was introduced to *Easy Living* by Preston Sturges. Sturges had moved to Hollywood in the early 1930s from Broadway to fill the demand for talent created by the relatively new phenomenon of the talkies. He saw himself above all as a storyteller and the movies primarily as a medium for telling stories. Arriving during the talkie boom, Sturges believed that the script was the essential component of studio filmmaking. For his first script, *The Power and the Glory*, he negotiated a deal with Fox that was unprecedented for a writer, asking for a percentage of the profits rather than a flat fee. Sturges often championed a kind of reverse auteurism, claiming that "directing is best done through the writing of the script." As he dictated his scripts to his secretary Bianca, his daughter recalls, he "became the characters he was creating as he paced around the office, speaking as they would speak, moving as they would move."[66] In other words, he emphasized the cast of characters and the flow of the narrative. He even moved to Paramount because the studio allowed writers to sit in on conferences with directors. *Easy Living* was his first assignment for Paramount. The screenplay was supposed to be based on Vera Caspary's short story about a poor girl who steals a mink coat. Sturges retained the title, but he remodeled the entire tale. In place of Caspary's dramatic story about the desperate measures a young woman would take during hard times, he created an accidental situation where the coat fortuitously falls on her head. As James Curtis suggests, "the situation carries the action from there. All Sturges had to do then was develop his characters and see how they responded."[67] The script, then, held the *idea* of chance. Indeed, the entire plot turns on the accidental encounter initiated by Sturges's alteration. However, for Sturges, it was solely a plot device – meant to *advance* the linear narrative, not to *disrupt* it, as the Surrealists might have preferred. As we saw earlier, he did not believe chance could be filmed.

But in Hollywood chance was not just a concept. It is true that chance was primarily used as an expedient way to pivot the narrative – after all, "of all the gin joints in all the towns in all the world," Ilsa Laszlo would not have walked into Rick's café had it not been for chance. But studio filmmaking seemed to discredit the value of coincidences. The studio system was ostensibly predicated not on sudden parallels but on predictable standards. Still, chance encounters were not uncommon. Despite its reputation as a rational system, the Hollywood film industry itself began with a classic accidental encounter. The story begins with the inauguration of Woodrow Wilson in 1913 and a young glove salesman's dissatisfaction with the new president and Democratic Congress's lowering of tariffs on imported gloves.[68] That salesman, Samuel Goldfish (later Goldwyn), learned from his lawyer, Arthur Friend, about the potentially lucrative world of motion pictures. A year after a young fur coat dealer named Adolph Zukor formed the Famous Players Film Company and successfully distributed the French silent film *The Loves of Queen Elizabeth* (1912), Goldfish entered into a partnership with Jesse L. Lasky, a vaudeville producer, and Cecil B. DeMille, a Broadway producer and director who hocked the family silver to join them. Together they created the Jesse Lasky Feature Play Company, which merged with Zukor's company in 1916 and later became Paramount Pictures. Not having enough money to set up a studio, the Jesse Lasky company acquired rights to the Western play *The Squaw Man* and decided to shoot on location. DeMille, co-director Oscar C. Apfel, and cameraman Alfred Gandolfi went to Flagstaff, even though the tale was set in Wyoming, assuming that the West was, after all, the West. But they found Flagstaff all wrong and, completely spontaneously, hopped back on the train before it chugged away. Seemingly on a whim, they rode to the end of the line. Last stop, Hollywood.[69]

Soon after DeMille stumbled upon this setting, others followed. By the end of the decade, Hollywood was producing over eight hundred films a year, which accounted for almost 80 percent of movies produced worldwide. Among those who made the journey west was an inspired young designer named James Mitchell Leisen. In 1919, he went to Hollywood to become a movie star. As luck would have it, he was not much of an actor and spent most of his time with family friends, who happened to know Phillips Smalley and his wife, Lois Weber. His entry into Hollywood was as coincidental as the meeting between Paul Eluard and André Breton at the birth of Surrealism, just a year earlier. During a party at the Smalley's, he talked all night with a woman whom he ran into again the next day at the Old Ship Café at Venice pier. Although he did not realize it then, the woman turned out to be Jeanie Macpherson, DeMille's screenwriter. A day later he was hired as a costume designer for Famous Players–Lasky. Leisen, an architectural designer by training, was quite surprised by the offer, but Macpherson reassured him: "You had such interesting hands," she said, "I knew you could do something."[70] As a designer, and later as a director, Leisen did not disappoint. As biographer David Chierichetti notes, "in Leisen's hands [even scripts with little potential] blossomed beyond . . . expectations."[71]

Luckily for Leisen, he entered an industry attracted to spectacle. In the early twenties, Hollywood films were governed by the happy coincidence between two currents: the emphasis on visual image due to the absence of sound, and the postwar craving for "spectacular glamour and display, the signifier of burning passion and intoxicating excess."[72] The spectacle films of the period used couture not only to develop a character or advance the plot but also to create an unapologetic visual extravaganza. As Sumiko Higashi notes in relation to DeMille's films, "As consumption became a pleasurable aspect of modernity, ... compositions were less distinguished by dramatic low-key lighting to articulate ethical dilemmas and more renowned for spectacular sets."[73] Indeed, DeMille was often heard advising his designers to accentuate the visual element, to "get it on the screen," since "the camera has no ears."[74] His suggestion interestingly echoes Walter Benjamin's method of having nothing to say, only to show. And that desire to show sometimes overwhelmed the narrative. Often the camera paused temporarily to absorb couture's visual delights, which were non-narrative. In the silent era, the story could wait. In Joseph Henabery's *Cobra* (1925), one of the earliest films designed by the legendary Gilbert Adrian (with Natacha Rambova), Elsie Van Zile (Nita Naldi) tries to seduce Italian count Rodrigo Torriani (Rudolph Valentino), who comes to America pretending to be a sheik. When the seduction succeeds, the plot literally comes to a halt as Naldi slowly reveals her black gown, whose "only embellishment," Howard Gutner points out, is "a lightning bolt of silver sequins cascading from the right hip to the hem like a shock of desire."[75] In Monta Bell's *The Torrent* (1926), an orange farmer's daughter, Leonora (Greta Garbo), transforms herself into La Brunna, the sensation of Paris. When we are introduced to La Brunna, the narrative pauses on a dazzling medium shot of Garbo in a black and white striped fur collar. There are many such moments that are "heightened," as Lucy Fischer puts it, with "haute Deco couture."[76] Indeed, Feyder's *The Kiss*, which we discussed in the last chapter in relation to sound's jarring effects, is generally remembered for its use of Deco design. Each time, the narrative is delayed in favor of the "glamour shot."[77] Even in DeMille's *Madam Satan* (1930), when Angela Brooks (Kay Johnson) tries to win back her husband by posing as a seductress at a masquerade ball on a moored zeppelin in New York City, she is dressed in a "volcano" gown. Describing the gown as a visual exclamation point onscreen, Jane Gaines argues that it "could only be worn to be photographed and is never properly worn but is rather hung and stuck on the actress who becomes something like a moving mannequin."[78] To put it another way, the dress appears more mobile than the actress; in fact, it seems to be crawling on her. Instead of a seductress, Angela becomes virtually a Surrealist phantom object. In fact, *Madam Satan* was a flop, and Richard Barrios explains its failure by describing the film as the "last baroque gasp of twenties frivolity."[79] What these examples illustrate is that throughout the 1920s, fashion was used not in service of the narrative but for disruptive visual pleasure. Moreover, the effect of "getting it on the screen" could sometimes inadvertently replicate the rupturing tendencies of modernism.

But these spectacular displays, especially in couture, did not survive long after the onset of the Great Depression. Filmmaking in the 1930s reemphasized efficiency, and immoderation of all kinds had to be cut out. This return to middle class values had a direct impact on film couture. While the 1920s had tolerated modernist excesses, the next decade saw increasing restraint. Couture had to be trimmed, as costumes were redesigned to symbolically fit the classical narrative. American culture at large, and women's magazines and films in particular, focused on affirming traditional values for women, who, as unemployment rose, were encouraged to turn away from the labor market and toward their conventional roles as wives and mothers. In this environment, as Lois Banner asserts, the "'lady-like look' once again became the cynosure of the American woman."[80] This "lady-like look" fit nicely into thirties films, from comedies like Frank Capra's *Lady for a Day* (1933) to melodramas like King Vidor's *Stella Dallas* (1937), particularly after the wholehearted enforcement of the Production Code.

Coincidentally, just when Hollywood was turning toward sobriety, the Surrealists began borrowing from haute couture in order to rupture the logical order. The first generation of Surrealists, still under the sway of Dadaism, was invested in language, exploring its social and psychological functions. But within a few years they turned to the fine arts. At that point, as Richard Martin suggests, "fashion and its instruments were at the heart of the Surrealist metaphor, touching on the imagery of woman and the correlation between the world of real objects and the life of objects in the mind."[81] For the Surrealists, the mannequin became a familiar phantom object, allowing them to illustrate the relationship between the real and the simulacrum. In Jean Cocteau's *Blood of a Poet* (1930), a calcified Lee Miller is at first a surrogate for a living figure, brought to life when the poet wipes off his disembodied mouth from a self-portrait on to the Hellenistic model.[82] Also that year, in "Self-Portrait," Herbert Bayer established the relationship between the living and the phantom object with an image of the photographer himself as a mannequin whose arm is being disassembled. By the mid-1930s, at the *Exposition Internationale du Surréalisme* in Paris, mannequins were displayed as dream-like sculptures at city thoroughfares. As Richard Martin puts it, in that spectacle, "Pygmalion was meeting Freud in a dramatic encounter."[83]

But the appropriation of mannequins was part of a much wider exchange between Surrealism and haute couture. The Surrealists were not only interested in accentuating the artificial but also in creating moments where the unreal would lead to a new order of things. Rummaging like a *chiffonier* through older texts at the National Library in Paris, Breton had discovered the nineteenth-century poet Comte de Lautréamont, pseudonym of Isidore Lucien Ducasse. Lautrémont's *Les Chants de Maldoror* provided what would become the paradigmatic Surrealist metaphor, the chance encounter of an umbrella and a sewing machine on a dissecting table, which shows that couture offered the ideal imagery for expressing Surrealist interest in displacement and illogic. In couture, the Surrealists found an ideal dissecting table where the bizarre in the banal, the marvelous in the everyday, could be revealed. They were fascinated by couture because it seemed to possess inherently an air of surrealism. In *Une Vague de Rêves,* Louis Aragon drew attention to sartorial details that could be transformed in an instant: "There is a surrealist light," he argued, that "lingers till late on the avenue de l'Opéra at Barclay's, when the ties transform themselves into phantoms."[84] And, like Walter Benjamin, the Surrealists sought to investigate history through these fragmentary sartorial glimpses, which were capable of evoking "the erotic and mysterious."[85] The most audacious example of this evocation is René Magritte's "Homage to Mack Sennett." The painting shows a dress in human form, hanging in a wardrobe, but the human body no longer inhabits it. What is left is an undeniable trace or memory of that body in the arresting visual detail of female breasts exposed underneath the surface of the dress. In its absence, the body becomes strikingly excessive. The hanging nightgown enables another unlikely juxtaposition of incompatible things, summed up perfectly in Herbert Blau's phrase: "the ominous slapstick."[86]

Ironically, while Magritte was painting his homage to comedy's chaotic impulses via couture, both Mack Sennett and fashion's spectacular ability of instantaneously disrupting the linear narrative were fading in popularity in Hollywood. Along with the Great Depression, it was the standardization of the talkies that made slapstick comedies like Mack Sennett's, whose films had markedly negligible script outlines, almost obsolete. They were succeeded by dialogue-based comedies, especially of the screwball variety, and the continuity script became sovereign. Although moments of anarchic energy did not entirely disappear, such as the diner scene from *Easy Living,* they were accommodated into the linear narrative. Couture too, which tends to emphasize the thrill of the moment, was tailored to fit the requirements of the narrative, and striking visual elements that could not be contained were usually jettisoned. As Jane Gaines suggests, costumes had "the potential to distract the viewer from the narrative, which could result in breaking the illusion and the spell of realism."[87] Therefore, in the sound era, Gaines adds, the linear narrative demanded "subordinating an especially evocative aesthetic to narrative designs."[88] The most striking example of this occurs in George Cukor's *The Women* (1939). Hedda Hopper, playing the prying columnist Dolly DePeyster, appears in one scene wearing a sequined butterfly with a matching hat with antennae, to suggest that she is picking up gossip signals from the Casino roof. Gaines quotes Cukor himself as saying that the ideal costume was one that enabled narrative coherence: "If the costume 'knocked your eye out,' he goes on, it was not good for the scene or for the entire film."[89] In fact, even the fashion show itself, inserted as an extended color sequence in Cukor's black-and-white film, becomes part of the narrative.

Still, the anarchic ruffles of fashion have a way of knocking your eye out, stopping the show, and inadvertently juxtaposing the standard and the strange. In Gus Meins's *Nobody's Baby* (1937), two nurses stranded outside New York City take a breather on a convertible's running board. When the automobile takes off, they hang on for dear life. They are only discovered when Detective Emory Littleworth (Lynne Overman) notices the tops of their hats fluttering in the wind. For a split second, as the

2.4. *Shall We Dance* (dir. Mark Sandrich, 1937).

feathers flutter in the oncoming breeze, their hats appear to be floating, disembodied and surreal. In Mark Sandrich's *Shall We Dance* (1937), an American ballet dancer, Pete P. Peters (Fred Astaire), falls in love with a showgirl, Linda Keene (Ginger Rogers), while faking a marriage with her for publicity. In the film's finale, Pete looks for Linda among a bevy of chorines, who are all dressed exactly alike and are all wearing Ginger Rogers masks. Just as Pete is obsessed with combining classical ballet with modern jazz dancing throughout the film, in this number, Sandrich combines modern dance moves with the nineteenth-century ballet convention where "the hero walks onstage, finds a large number of women who look alike and are dressed alike (the corps de ballet), and seeks among them for the one woman who is his."[90] Their multiplicity is meant to satirize the assembly line. But their identical black dresses and veils, blond wigs, and Ginger Rogers masks held in place with matching gloved hands represent a collective sartorial excess that is uncanny (Figure 2.4). Hansen has suggested that, given "its contemporaneity with twentieth-century modernisms and modern culture," it would be impossible for classical Hollywood to not have encountered Surrealism.[91] Even though the studio system claimed to have eschewed excess in the 1930s, these sartorial moments possess an air of cinephilia because they appear suddenly and incredibly surreal.

That is partly because fashion designing, even in the rigidly controlled studio system, was far closer to the ragpicker's method than to the assembly line worker's. Caroline Evans compares the roles of the ragpicker and the fashion designer, arguing that "the historian/designer's method is akin to that of the ragpicker who moves through the city gathering scraps for recycling."[92] She makes this analogy, however, only in relation to postmodern designers who deliberately rummage through fashion history in order to quote it. I find the inadvertent scavenging within Hollywood's vertically integrated system much more compelling. In *Talking Pictures,* an insider's account of classical Hollywood written in 1937, Barrett C. Kiesling observed that the design departments at major studios were quite impressive, often set up "in an enormous twelve-story building, [where] some thirty thousand different costumes of every known historical period are stored."[93] Similarly, Jane Powell thought of the MGM costume department as a museum, with "a glorious collection of real and unreal [clothes], of every period, every style you could imagine."[94] That kind of eclectic raw material enabled designers to stroll up and down the vertical promenade of fashions, reviving forgotten styles and creating startling juxtapositions of sartorial articles, as if by chance.

The designer who most adroitly executed such juxtapositions was Gilbert Adrian. Before Mitchell Leisen ran into him in New York and brought him out to Hollywood, Adrian had gained experience working with chiffon (and plenty of other fabrics) mainly through *chiffons,* validating Elizabeth Nielsen's contention that costume designing depended more on the designer's resourcefulness than creativity, on "a kind of spontaneous adaptability found in individuals who because of necessity have to do something with very limited resources."[95] As a struggling designer, Adrian had learned to assemble designs out of the scraps left on the cutting room floor. While he was studying at the Parsons School of Fine and Applied Arts in Paris, he decided to participate in the *Bal du Grand Prix*, where designers like Paul Poiret met each year to create extravagant costumes. This was to be his "sacred rite of initiation into the Parisian world of art and design."[96] But without much time or money for an original design, Adrian put together a costume by rummaging through "the workrooms at Parsons looking for whatever [he] might take that wouldn't be missed."[97] The result of his scouring was a brightly colored design that, luckily, caught the attention of Irving Berlin, who happened to be in Paris looking for a designer for his Broadway revue. When he finally moved to Hollywood and took over as designer at MGM, Adrian brought his scouring talents with him. Despite Mayer's apparent refusal to allow the studio to be turned into a laboratory, this talent for experimenting with old scraps proved especially useful during the austere, cost-cutting thirties.

All of these threads, combining couture, economics, and the avant-garde, come together in what is considered the most cited dress in Hollywood fashion history: from Clarence Brown's *Letty Lynton* (1932). Indeed, since the film itself has not survived, this may also be the most outmoded of sartorial objects from the era.[98] Joan Crawford had been a fashion icon since her flapper days. In the 1930s, that image was toned down, so she could play a rags to riches working girl or an unlucky in love socialite, helped out by a few Adrian outfits. But the *Letty Lynton* dress has outlived those narratives. Indeed, the white chiffon organdy dress with built-up shoulders and puffed sleeves has persisted like a still from Gilbert Adair's album of "flickers."[99] It became popular immediately upon the film's release, so much so that Macy's claimed they had sold 500,000 copies of it, and an article in *Vogue* reported that "the country was flooded with little Joan Crawfords."[100] What kind of dress would create such a fashion furor across the country? Instead of following the realistic trend in costume designing of the early 1930s, Adrian borrowed a detail from the gay 1890s by reviving the puffed sleeves, which were ruffled at the shoulder and tight from the elbow down. Incidentally, rather than a fashion statement, the puffed sleeves were simply meant to cover Joan Crawford's unusually broad shoulders. By chance, fashion historian Jane Mulvagh notes, the 1931 *Exposition Coloniale* in Paris had reintroduced the wide shoulders, showing "Japanese and Balinese costumes and Bangkok temple dancers with winged shoulders and tiny waists."[101] The *Letty Lynton* puffed sleeves – also called mutton sleeves, appropriately echoing Surrealism's penchant for the bizarre – arose out of the juxtaposition of neo-Victorian femininity and Oriental chic. To the outmoded but now revived sleeves, Adrian added other heterogeneous elements, such as "the Buster Brown collar, the hip treatment and the flared bottom of the skirt, both ruffled and tucked," confessing to the *Ladies' Home Journal* that the *Letty Lynton* dress "may have seemed to have several ideas."[102] The dress, which became synonymous with 1930s Hollywood fashion and defined Adrian's reputation as the quintessential Hollywood designer, was in fact put together almost inadvertently as a collage, out of bits and pieces from different eras. Moreover, David Wallace notes that the dress was not produced by a lone artist, Adrian, but by "a small army of up to 250 cutters, tailors, beaders, embroiders, jewel craftsmen, feather workers, and seamstresses."[103] Kiesling had correctly identified this collaborative environment as the key to understanding studio filmmaking: "Picture making is not like the manufacture of gloves, or of overcoats, or of shoes," he argued, for it is not the repetition of a standardized product.[104] The result of all this collaboration was that *Letty Lynton's* starched chiffon dress signified in excess of its look of innocence and vulnerability demanded by the narrative. Although Joan Crawford is supposed to look "demure and submissive in the frothy fantasy dress," if we look at the ruffles closely, the dress does not appear to follow those script requirements.[105] In a striking cinephiliac moment, as Elizabeth Wilson points out, "when Joan Crawford stood framed in a doorway the sleeves stood out like twin powder puffs or embryo wings."[106] The visual details of Adrian's collage, then, made the dress unmistakably surreal. The design suggests that, like the accidental meeting between Dali and DeMille, incompatible juxtapositions were inevitable in classical Hollywood. Indeed, fashion designing encouraged such juxtapositions, thereby allowing the irrational to coexist with the otherwise rational method of studio filmmaking.

Coincidentally, Elsa Schiaparelli, the doyenne of Parisian high fashion, had introduced the exaggerated puffed sleeves a year earlier. In the early 1930s, haute couture responded to the somber mood following the collapse of the stock market by eschewing both opulence and triviality. Therefore, in the designs of Parisian fashion houses, conservatism prevailed. To break this cycle, Surrealism happened to gain currency in fashion's graphic designs. First, Coco Chanel decided to revise Paul Poiret's restrictive outfits by freeing women of the corset. William Wiser notes that Dali became one of her friends, because he "could offer a surrealist touch to the Chanel line, and contributed his flair and capricious whimsy to the more staid designs."[107] In 1936, Elsa Schiaparelli adapted Dali's "The Study of Drawers" for her famous desk suit, with pockets simulating a chest of drawers. The Surrealist returned the favor. At a lecture in London, Dali arrived wearing a diving suit to show "that he was plumbing the depths of the human mind."[108] Two years later, he collaborated with Schiaparelli on the Mutton Chop Hat, which oddly echoes the *Letty Lynton* sleeves. This hat was part of a series of sartorial articles that Dali and Schiaparelli co-produced through a surrealist juxtaposition of dissimilar objects. Around the time of the release of *Easy Living,* Dali and Schiaparelli joined forces to create the Mad Cap, a pixie-like hat that could be manipulated into a series of bizarre shapes. Paraphrasing Richard Martin, we can say that fashion and Surrealism were meeting in a dramatic, often comic (might we say madcap?) encounter.

In 1937, that encounter included one other member: classical Hollywood. Although Hollywood stars like Norma Shearer and Joan Crawford had been interested in Parisian haute couture since earlier in the decade, in 1937 Schiaparelli invited Mae West to adapt her bosomy curves for a perfume bottle. When West arrived in Paris, Martin points out, "she was stretched out on the operating table of [her] workroom, and measured and probed with curiosity."[109] Based on West's silhouette, Surrealist artist Leonor Fini created an hourglass-shaped flacon. In that singular moment, with Mae West as a kind of moving mannequin, Schiaparelli's "operating table" became the charmed dissecting table where Surrealism met Hollywood through fashion, as if by chance.

BY CHANCE

That encounter made an impression on Hollywood too. Long before Hitchcock worked with Dali on *Spellbound,* Surrealism was briefly invited to the studio system. Both Chanel and Schiaparelli were asked to design costumes, at MGM and Paramount respectively. Schiaparelli did

Mae West's costumes for Edward Sutherland's *Every Day's a Holiday* (1937), and Chanel was invited to collaborate with Leisen and Adrian. That association did not last long, because these Parisian couturiers seemed too eccentric for the fast-paced studio system.[110] What Hollywood wanted was to incorporate Surrealist-inspired designs symbolically into their scripts, mostly for laughs. In Leisen's *Midnight* (1939), for instance, an American gold-digger goes from being Eve Peabody of the Bronx (Claudette Colbert) to the Duchess Czerny of Hungary with the help of some Parisian couture. In a scene at Simone Chapeaux, the owner, Simone (Elaine Barrie), emerges wearing a centipede brooch and asks for a decidedly surreal hat, "with the stuff on it that looks like spinach." That movie has none of the visual intensity of Surrealism. The Brackett and Wilder script does not linger on Surrealist details; it moves swiftly along to the next joke. And we might conclude that the enthusiasm for Surrealism in Hollywood faded just as quickly. What remained, however, were occasional glimpses where the worlds of Surrealism and the studio system accidentally collided. For even in the rigidly controlled 1930s, moments of sartorial excess had a way of inadvertently breaching the classical style. Like the overhead shot of the fur coat that falls on Jean Arthur's head.

At the end of *Easy Living*, another unsuspecting girl gets hit by a fur coat. After the confusion is finally cleared up, J. B. Ball finds his wife in possession of a disruptive fur coat once more. Yet again, he throws it off the roof, and it falls on a young girl who happens to be standing nearby. She lets out a slight scream. John and Mary recognize her puzzlement. Mary grabs his arm and walks away, saying "Johnny, this is where we came in," leaving open the possibility that chance will offer another opportunity for all sorts of comic misunderstandings. Ed Sikov argues that *Easy Living* issues from "Sturges's and Leisen's glorifying appreciation of kismet."[111] Although Sturges's script contains this sense of predetermination, in Leisen's hands, the film becomes a little less predictable, so that the script is momentarily disregarded in favor of unplanned moments that reflect an appreciation not of kismet but of chance. Like the other sartorial excesses discussed in the previous section, the unmotivated overhead shot momentarily suspends the narrative order. In fact, we might say that it takes on the qualities of what René Crevel called "a

single minute's lyricism," which is "capable of making us forget all sorts
of wretched [or funny] stories."[112] The enigmatic fur coat is certainly
capable of making us forget the screwball script – but just for a moment,
because Leisen cuts back to Jean Arthur, and the plot resumes. This
moment shows the negotiation that is at the heart of 1930s studio filmmaking: on the one hand, the film tries to move from one plot point to
the next; on the other hand, it becomes the script's "screwball." Ed Sikov
notes that the term screwball came from baseball: it was coined in the
1930s to suggest an erratic, counterintuitive pitch meant to confuse the
batter. It became especially popular when, at the All-Star Game of 1934,
New York Giant Carl Hubbell surprisingly "struck out five future Hall-
of-Famers in a row – Babe Ruth, Lou Gehrig, Jimmie Foxx, Al Simmons
and Joe Cronin – all with screwballs."[113] The excessive sartorial moment
that turns suddenly surreal similarly strikes out the traditional narrative
in and about classical Hollywood. Even if only for an instant, it reveals
the contradictions and combinations that lie just beneath the surface
and between the folds.

The mysterious fur coat or the starched chiffon dress, then, become
perfectly fitting instances of the fortuitous juxtaposition of classical Hollywood and Surrealism, experienced not in the planned collaborations
between the European émigrés and the Hollywood natives but in the
unplanned moments that happened by chance during the 1930s. Writing
about the decade's dislocations, Ina Rae Hark argues that at no other
time "did the Hollywood film industry and its product look so different
at its conclusion as compared to its beginning."[114] This is because while
the previous decade's turmoil had been primarily caused by a singular
event, the transition to sound outlined in the last chapter, the thirties
saw numerous cultural, economic, and moral transformations. Even as
the studios tried to consolidate power, mature into an oligopoly, and
standardize filmmaking, the world seemed more and more to be ruled by
chance – which inadvertently made its way into some of the studio's most
standard stories, sometimes thematically and at other times in momentary juxtapositions that appeared surreal. Indeed, one way to think about
thirties cinema, Hark notes, is in terms of hybridity. With "an equal measure of transgressive desire and normative pressure," the decade's films
strive to balance competing ideas, such that "sepia-toned Kansas [ex-

ists] in a parallel universe with Technicolor Oz."[115] In a similar fashion, thirties filmmaking appears to balance the tension between systematicity and disorder. As is clear in the cinephiliac moments traced above, chance does appear onscreen. While we tend to think of the studio era in terms of predictability, it was also a time of accidental encounters. These encounters were particularly likely during a time when the world was making the transition from one chaotic disaster, the Great Depression, to another, World War II. In the next chapter, we will see what happens after the war ends, when Hollywood responds to the terrifying unpredictability of a different kind: the rise of proto-McCarthyism.

Goethe? Shakespeare? Everything they put their name to is supposed to be good, and people rack their brains to find beauty in the silliest little thing they bungled. All great talents, like Goethe, Shakespeare, Beethoven, Michelangelo, created not only beautiful works, but things that were less than mediocre, quite simply awful.

LEO TOLSTOY, *Diary 1895–99*

Yet something, many things, blocked satisfying development [of *Mr. Arkadin*]. The failure was not in talent, certainly, but in control over the circumstances in which the talent had to work.

ROBERT GARIS, *The Films of Orson Welles*

THREE

Signature Crimes

1946 and the Strange Case of the Lost Scene
(as Well as the Stranger Case of the Missing Auteur)

WHODUNIT?

Strike One

The scene that exposes the former Nazi's identity is rather unremarkable. Standing in a phone booth at a local drug store, Charles Rankin (Orson Welles) draws his signature, almost inadvertently, on a notepad hanging on the wall. There is no mistaking this symbol. What he signs is not his personal name but the moniker of Nazism itself. A standard over-the-shoulder shot captures Rankin sketching a swastika on the notepad, while he faintly whistles "Deutschland über Alles" (Figure 3.1). Then, just before his wife Mary (Loretta Young) appears at the other end of the line via a cutaway, he begins to cancel the signature with brief diagonal strokes that distort the swastika's symmetrical design, ending with an X across the page (Figure 3.2).

While intriguing in itself, this revelatory moment from Orson Welles's *The Stranger* is unexceptional. It is not visually stunning. And yet, it carries a peculiar cinephiliac appeal. It has none of the poignancy of the close-up of quivering lips slowly whispering "Rosebud" in *Citizen Kane* (1941) or the solemnity of the long shot of a fading artist walking off into an apocalyptic evening in *F for Fake* (1973). Nor does it have the flamboyant, innovative flair of the hall of mirrors sequence in *The Lady from Shanghai* (1948). Quite simply, the "signature" shot in *The Stranger* is highly unlike a classic Wellesian moment. It appears almost banal and does not support neatly our understanding of the Wellesian aesthetic. For me, this is precisely its appeal.

3.1. *The Stranger* (dir. Orson Welles, 1946).

The entire scene comprises standard medium shots of Charles Rankin waiting in a phone booth, doodling his signature as he urges his wife
Mary to meet him at the church tower, where the film's denouement will
unfold. The notepad is in the lower right corner of the frame; therefore,
it never appears to be the focus of the shot. It competes with another,
slightly larger sign in the background, evidently also in Welles's handwriting. That sign matter-of-factly advises callers not to "deface walls" and
instructs them to "use pad," a suggestion Rankin clearly complies with.
But nothing will come of this scene. Nobody will discover the swastika
as evidence of Rankin's guilt. Nowhere will this Nazi symbol reappear.
As the phone conversation ends, Rankin tears the signature sheet off the
notepad, and the camera tracks him in profile out of the phone booth.

The erased signature is a rather heavy-handed illustration of Rankin's identity. By this point in *The Stranger,* it is obvious that Charles
Rankin, a history professor at a boys' prep school in Harper, Connecticut, is in fact the escaped Nazi mastermind, Franz Kindler. Although

3.2. *The Stranger* (dir. Orson Welles, 1946).

the townspeople consider him "above suspicion," his actions leading up
to this scene – especially his strangling of fellow Nazi fugitive Konrad
Meinike (Constantin Shane) as well as his fierce insistence that Marx
was not a German because he was a Jew – have left no doubt about his
character. So, the delayed revelatory signature shot does not seem to
reveal much at all.

But the signature moment was to occur right at the beginning of
this film.

Strike Two

A few quick strokes would have revealed that the former high-ranking
s s officer and architect of the Final Solution, Franz Kindler (also Orson Welles), had indeed transformed himself into Charles Rankin. The
moment was to occur during the opening Latin American sequence,
which begins right after the Allied War Crimes Commission releases

Konrad Meinike, a Nazi bureaucrat, with the hope that he might lead them to the fugitive Nazi mastermind. While elements of this expressionist sequence remain in the released version of the film, some details have been lost. In search of Franz Kindler, a schizophrenic Meinike was to travel to Argentina.[1] In a moment that would have eerily anticipated the acclaimed entrance of Harry Lime (Orson Welles) in Carol Reed's *The Third Man* (1949), Meinike was to appear shuffling anxiously down a cobblestone path, wanting to deliver a message "from the All Highest." He was to come in contact with the "Nazis of 1932 . . . plotting for 1952," who would assume that he had been sent by the Führer and therefore guide him to a morgue attendant specializing in fake passports.[2] Besides issuing counterfeit travel documents, the attendant was to "take a paper from [Meinike] with Franz Kindler's name on it and draw a series of diagonal lines through the letters F, Z, D, L, E, R until it spells Rankin."[3] The strikes across Kindler's name would have immediately established his Möbius strip-like connection to Charles Rankin.

But in the released version of *The Stranger,* only snippets of this expository episode have survived. After being allowed to escape, and unaware of being followed by a female agent who is presumably working for the Allied War Crimes Commission, we see Meinike sneaking into a morgue in a vaguely Latin American country. Although the expressionist mood still prevails – heightened by low-angle photography during the chiaroscuro exchange between Meinike and the photographer – the sequence is abridged to report only the most essential dramatic details that will lead to the escaped convict's journey to the United States in search of the transformed Nazi war criminal. Besides, this sequence appears superficially shadowy, lacking the Gothic depth of a noir thriller or a Wellesian film. While being photographed for his fake passport, Meinike demands to know the whereabouts of Franz Kindler. After some hesitation, the morgue attendant hands him a postcard of Harper, Connecticut. There is no mention of Rankin's name, since Meinike claims he already knows Kindler's current identity. The scene cuts to a picture postcard of a bucolic old town with a Gothic clock tower at its center, but this two-dimensional image once again betrays the absence of depth at the heart of this mystery. Then, a fade-out suggests the change in location, and the town of Harper, an all-American setting with ostensibly no troubles at all, springs to life.

The long Latin American segment, which the director saw as an opportunity to explore "a whole series of very wild, dreamlike events," was apparently edited by producer Sam Spiegel in collaboration with editor Ernest Nims.[4] Up to thirty minutes of footage was reportedly deleted from the introduction, never to be restored, thus cutting out almost entirely what Welles considered the signature sequence of the film. For the studio, "a dreamlike sequence around South America did not necessarily smell like box office – especially in the mid-1940s."[5] Welles may have been inspired by a State Department White Paper, written by Cordell Hull, who served as secretary of state from 1933 to 1944 and was a strong supporter of the Good Neighbor policy in Latin America.[6] The document suggested that Juan Péron harbored Nazi sympathies and intended to establish a fascist state in Argentina. That would have made Latin America an ideal location for the wild opening segment of *The Stranger*. A year earlier, it had served as the location in Edward Dmytryk's *Cornered* (1945), where ex-POW Laurence Gerard (Dick Powell), in search of his bride's murderer, tracks a Vichy collaborator to Buenos Aires. That film was enormously controversial, and it couldn't have given any confidence to the studios about locating renascent fascism in Latin America. Moreover, as Jennifer E. Langdon points out, even after World War II came to an end, "the Hollywood studios, still fearful of jeopardizing their foreign markets, tried mightily to avoid antagonizing those South American nations that were neutral or even sympathetic to the Nazis."[7] Welles himself often spoke of the clashes with the studio over the opening sequence in *The Stranger*. While admitting that the majority of the deleted segment was not central to the plot, he told Barbara Leaming that Nims was "the great supercutter, who believed that nothing should be in a movie that did not advance the story."[8] Since the identity of the Nazi mastermind is revealed more overtly later on, these striking wild and dreamlike images could not have done anything to develop the plot. Hence, they were cut out.

But the opening sequence may have been lost before it was even filmed.

Strike Three

According to the shooting schedule, there were days assigned for all the scenes in the shooting script of *The Stranger*. But then, some scenes were cancelled. As Clinton Heylin points out, the schedule "has a series of lines drawn through the scenes deleted from the film, perhaps suggesting their elimination at the outset."[9] In other words, *The Stranger* may have been pre-edited. Welles would insist that the opening scenes were shot and deleted later, even claiming "a deep wound" in his leg that occurred when he "stepped on a baby's coffin" while shooting in Latin America, a wound that "always reminds [him] of what was lost from the movie."[10] But whether the sequence was altered during pre- or post-production is not the most magnificent piece of this puzzle. Unlike the recently recovered film *It's All True* (1942; unfinished), another Latin American project that Welles worked on just before *The Stranger,* this original sequence, if it ever existed, has been lost. What we have in its place is a generic Hollywood opening with a few superficial embellishments. Indeed, the entire film looks that way, because, as James Naremore puts it, *The Stranger* "barely deviates from industry habits."[11] The final authority seems to have ended up in the hands of Nims, the great supercutter.

Welles had in fact signed an extremely restrictive contract for this film. It gave Ernest Nims the license to edit any part of the film "in the interest of telling its tale as simply and swiftly as possible."[12] The memories of Welles's much-publicized struggle with RKO over *The Magnificent Ambersons* (1942) were still fresh. As is widely known, that film was shortened considerably by editor Robert Wise, and its elegiac ending was replaced by a resolution that was happier in tone, after Welles submitted his final cut to the studios. Those edits were undertaken following unfavorable reviews from preview audiences, while Welles was in Brazil shooting *It's All True.* During that scuffle with RKO, he not only lost control over his film but also developed the reputation for being unbankable. Following that disaster, Welles found it difficult to get rehired as a studio director. He worked some in radio, guest-starred on variety shows, and appeared as an actor in other directors' films. On September 20, 1945, he signed what would have seemed to be quite an unpleasant deal with International Pictures to direct a film that was then titled "Date with Destiny," based on Victor Trivas's story called "The Trap." Heylin regards the contract as "Hollywood's ultimate revenge on the Boy Wonder of 1939."[13] The terms of the agreement required Welles to surrender control over the finished product. "Just four days after inscribing his moniker on the dotted line," Heylin tells us, "he delivered a 164-page final shooting script which bore telltale thumbprints on every page."[14] But it appears that, as the shooting proceeded, a number of these thumbprints began getting erased. The final product reflects all the elements of a classical Hollywood film: a linear plot, continuity editing, and a neat and predictable resolution of conflict at the end. In fact, cuts to the opening sequences were apparently only the first in a series of edits that transformed the film into what is unanimously regarded as a standard studio product.[15] The studio system seems to have won over Orson Welles, "depriving him of many little strokes he'd planned to apply to his thematic canvas."[16]

So, in the case of *The Stranger*, the auteur appears to have struck out.

IN THE NAME OF THE AUTHOR

On November 21, 1864, believing that she had lost all five of her sons in the Civil War, Abraham Lincoln wrote a letter to Mrs. Lydia Bixby of Boston. The brief missive was meant to offer condolences, but it also acknowledged "how weak and fruitless must be any words of mine which should attempt to beguile you from the grief of a loss so overwhelming." Along with the Gettysburg address and the second inaugural speech, the Bixby letter is regarded by many Lincoln biographers as a masterpiece and is often cited as evidence of his literary genius.[17] Intriguingly, the letter is treated by just as many historians with skepticism, not for the quality of its prose but for doubts about its authenticity. As it turns out, the letter is historically inaccurate, since Mrs. Bixby only lost two sons in the war. Of the remaining three boys, one deserted the army, the other was honorably discharged, and the third may have either deserted or died as a prisoner of war. Besides, Mrs. Bixby was said to have been a supporter of the Confederacy and therefore may have destroyed the letter after receiving it. There remains in circulation what might be a lithographic facsimile of it. Other copies have materialized too from time to time. These facts have led some historians to suggest that the

extant letter may be a fake or speculate that John Hay, Lincoln's secretary of state, may have composed the letter, imitating the president's
voice and perhaps even forging his signature. Noteworthy in this debate
is the use of the word "beguile," which evidently appears repeatedly in
Hay's correspondence but never in Lincoln's. On the other hand, noted
biographer Roy Basler has argued that the letter is comparable "to the
best of Lincoln's lyrical passages" from the Gettysburg address and the
farewell address. Basler is convinced that "the internal evidence of style
seems to mark the letter as Lincoln's."[18] But since the "original" letter has
been lost, and multiple copies appear in circulation, uncertainty over its
authorship persists.

The debate over the Bixby letter, especially since the death of its pur-
ported author, has been similar in form to that engaged by connoisseurs
when trying to validate the originality of works of art. The dispute over
this letter highlights the issues surrounding the vexed idea of authorship, including its relation to uniqueness, authenticity, and authority. It
also reminds us, as Michael North rightly suggests, that "authorship has
never been an unassailable concept, and modern doubts about it, radical
though they may seem, recast in new form an uneasiness that has always
haunted literary creation."[19] While authorship has always been fraught
with anxiety, however, that concern is compounded with the invention
of mechanical means of reproduction. The anxiety over the Bixby letter,
intensified by the existence of multiple copies with seemingly no clear
original, in effect parallels the problems of authorship highlighted by
the rise of photography, also in the latter half of the nineteenth century.
As Roland Barthes argues in *Camera Lucida,* photography – and later
cinema – caused a "*disturbance* (to civilization)."[20] Therefore, debates
over authorship have been particularly contentious in film studies. Of
course, no other director has been more troublingly synonymous with
auteurism than Orson Welles, whom I will return to in a moment. But let
me first trace a brief history of the birth, death, and continued survival
of the author.

The notions of authorship as a site of creative autonomy and of the
author as a romantic genius are relatively recent ideas. At least until the
early modern era, literary authority rested in the classical past, and the
auctor was a craftsman whose work consisted of "sifting, recasting, or

engagingly imitating ideas that had been common property as long as ideas had been written down."[21] Writing in the thirteenth century, for instance, St. Bonaventure suggested that a book may be produced by a scribe, compiler, or commentator, all of whom would have worked collaboratively.[22] Until the Renaissance – the word *author* first appears as a variant of *auctor* around 1550 – authorship was typically understood as a transcription of ideas handed down by tradition. "From the Middle Ages right down through the Renaissance," Martha Woodmansee argues, "new writing derived its value and authority from its affiliation with the texts that preceded it, its derivation rather than its deviation from prior texts."[23] But this attitude began to change in the early modern period. As Jacqueline Miller suggests, authorship became an act of imitation that, like Petrarch's definition of imitation as "the resemblance of a son to his father," implied the addition of a "mysterious something" to the original.[24] However, while the "author" was thus born, he did not fully come to life until later.

Even after authorship wrested itself from the pull of antiquity, it continued being seen as a collaborative activity. As Woodmansee notes, even Dr. Samuel Johnson's *Lives of the Poets,* which helped create the notion of individual authorship, was itself a collective and collaborative composition "between Johnson, the poets he immortalized, the London booksellers – and countless others."[25] While Johnson is associated with the birth of authorship, his own work was far more of the *auctor* variety. Indeed, Johnson himself may have become the modern author due to the efforts of biographer James Boswell, whose *Life of Johnson* posthumously conferred a romantic aura on him. Still, Johnson's *Lives* went a long way in "establishing a pantheon of great authors whose 'works' differ qualitatively from the sea of mere writing" – a gesture, as we will see momentarily, that was very similar to early auteurism practiced at *Cahiers du Cinéma* – and helped foster the myth of the solitary genius.[26] Also contributing to the transformation of authorship were the rise of print culture and the subsequent development of copyright laws. Print regulated the relation between author and text, thereby bringing into sharp focus the role of the individual writer and his proprietary right over his literary work. The work was no longer merely rhetorical: it was an object that had to have a creator. And it is precisely this reconceptualization of writing as intellectual property that led to the Romantic revolution, when the modern author came alive.

If the emergence of a mass market for printed texts and the consequent formulations of copyright lent materiality to those texts, they also recast the idea of authorship. By the mid-eighteenth century, after print had transformed writing into a commercial act, knowledge came to be regarded in terms of individual property. Mark Rose suggests that this discourse of authorship as a proprietary right grew out of a Lockean assertion of possessive individualism. Since an individual's "person" was now seen as his own property, his writing could be construed as his property as well.[27] In that context, authorship became radically reconceptualized. No longer was a writer a mere scribbler of handed-down, communal truths. Genuine authorship, especially since it now merited legal protection, could no longer be found in adaptation, imitation, or reproduction. Instead, the notion of originality became the basis for establishing authorship and authority. In 1759, Edward Young argued in *Conjectures on Original Composition* for a new way of thinking about writing, suggesting that "an *Original* . . . rises spontaneously from the vital root of Genius; it *grows,* it is not *made: Imitations* are often a sort of *manufacture* wrought up by those *mechanics, art,* and *labor,* out of pre-existing materials not their own."[28] Young's thesis about literary independence was enormously influential on an emerging profession of writers, especially in Germany, where it contributed to the development of Romanticism. "In a country where youthful writers were chafing at the long subjection of the native literary tradition to foreign models and rules," M. H. Abrams has argued, "Young's suggestions that a great work of literature grows out of the impenetrable depths of the mind of genius" found a receptive audience.[29] Nearly two centuries before another generation of young writers would denounce the "tradition of quality" in favor of the individual artist, German theorists from Herder to Goethe to Kant formulated a new literary tradition in which the author was reborn as a romantic genius. This notion of authorship, redefined as individual expression, became ubiquitous by the turn of the nineteenth century. In England, William Wordsworth declared that genuine authorship was not the imitation of life but "the introduction of a new element into the intellectual universe: or, if that be not allowed, it is the application of powers to objects on which they had not before been exercised, or the employment of them in such a manner as to produce effects hitherto unknown." The true author was thus transformed into a genius, who could do "what was never done before."[30] In America, Ralph Waldo Emerson appropriated this reconceptualization to declare literary independence, proclaiming "imitation is suicide." Thus, by the mid-nineteenth century, the author was severed from tradition and steadfastly aligned with originality.

It was this author that the critics at *Cahiers du Cinéma* invoked almost a century later, when they contended that even a Hollywood director might be considered an auteur. Interestingly, etymologically an auteur had been around long before an author was born, but in cinema, he (almost always a "he" at this stage) gained particular authority after World War II. As the title of Irving Pichel's article in the November 1946 issue of *Revue du Cinéma* declared, "Creation must be the work of one person." This provocative contention assigned the attributes of romantic authorship to directors who expressed their personal vision through thematic and stylistic consistencies, in spite of the constraints of the studio system. True authorship in cinema was no longer collaborative production but individual self-expression. As Helen Stoddart suggests, an auteur became the name for a director who "was distinguished by the presence in each film, above and beyond generic variations, of a distinctive personality, expressed as a world-view or vision, which would thereby constitute a trace or 'personal stamp' of the director's presence in the film and therefore within their *oeuvre*."[31] The emphasis on tracing that personal stamp implied that an auteurist critic could discover, across a diverse body of films, a single, innovative thread that tied those films together.

But the auteur theory was more than just a question of style. Using such studio directors as Howard Hawks and Nicholas Ray as their test cases, auteurist critics worked "to discover the director within the given framework, to find the traces of the submerged personality."[32] In this sense, auteurists closely resembled the Romantics, who came to dominate aesthetic and literary criticism throughout the nineteenth century. M. H. Abrams has characterized their discourse in terms of detection; if artistic genius was an expression of individual personality, then the literary critic would dig deep to unearth evidence of it. "Furnished with the proper key," he argued, "the romantic extremist was confident he could decipher the hieroglyph, penetrate to the reality behind the appearance, and so come to know an author more intimately than his own friends and family; more intimately, even, than the author, lacking this key, could possibly have known himself."[33] At *Cahiers du Cinéma*, where the *politique des auteurs* was formulated, the auteurist critic was similarly a detective uncovering the deep, dark mystery of cinematic auteurs. In his essay "The Genius of Howard Hawks," for instance, Jacques Rivette argued that "Hawks is a director of intelligence and precision, but he is also a bundle of dark forces and strange fascinations; his is a Teutonic spirit, attracted by bouts of ordered madness which give birth to an infinite chain of consequences."[34] What Rivette accomplishes here goes beyond an analysis of *Monkey Business* (1952), which is ostensibly the subject of his piece. Instead, his essay demonstrates what William Routt likely means when he argues that auteurism is more "a point of view or a critical *regard*."[35] Rivette's critique shows that auteurism was not so much a theory as a polemical way of looking in order to find evidence of an auteur's genius.

In his seminal piece translating the *politique des auteurs* for American film criticism, Andrew Sarris made a similar observation, contending that the most significant identifying feature of auteurism was at the crucial third level, which was concerned with "interior meaning, the ultimate glory of the cinema as an art. . . . It was not quite the vision of the world a director projects, not quite his attitude toward life." While it was connected to these, the interior meaning was not expressed in terms of technical competence (first level) or even consistency of visual style (second level). The interior meaning was produced by that creative tension between the auteur and the apparatus. In fact, interior meaning was indefinable; it was that "intangible difference between one personality and another, all other things being equal." From Sarris's perspective, auteurism appeared to be a quasi-mystical unearthing of that which was "imbedded in the stuff of cinema and [could] not be rendered in non-cinematic terms."[36] Ultimately, it was this notion of interior meaning that transformed a *metteur-en-scène* into an auteur. Therefore, the auteur theory, as practiced by the *Cahiers* critics and translated by Sarris, enabled the reevaluation of popular cinema in aesthetic terms and, at least for a time, conferred considerable authority on even commercial film-makers by reexamining them in terms of romantic authorship.

Interestingly, although the characterization of the author in terms of originality and genius became widely accepted in the nineteenth century, anxiety over authorship did not dissipate. Invented during the (late) romantic era, photography destabilized the relationship between authorship and ownership, between intention and authority – causing, in Barthes's words, a disturbance to civilization. First, it collapsed the difference between the original and the copy. Imitative images weakened the notion of uniqueness, which, as we have seen, was so important to the Romantics. As Liz Wells points out, with the advent of photography, "what is called into question is the originality of authorship, the uniqueness of the art object and the nature of self-expression."[37] Second, it deconstructed the notion of depth and its relation to genius. Writing as early as 1859, Oliver Wendell Holmes feared the shallowness of photography. In an intriguing passage, he argued that even though there is only one Coliseum or Parthenon, we would no longer be interested in what is within them. Instead, we would "hunt all curious, beautiful grand objects, as they hunt the cattle in South America, for their *skins,* and leave the carcasses as of little worth."[38] Because photography, for Holmes, represented a move away from depth. Finally, photography also caused a disturbance in civilization in a more direct fashion, by undermining the very foundation upon which modern authorship was erected. Michael North argues that "arriving just as Wordsworth phrases in its most uncompromising form the Romantic claim of individual authorship, photography establishes a counterregime, one in which authority and authorship are set at odds."[39] A photograph, in other words, could be produced without human intervention. When he invented the daguerrotype, Louis Daguerre argued that the camera could not be protected by the laws of copyright. Due to what the Surrealists later called its "automatism," photography, rather than revealing the depth of individual genius, appeared to limit, if not entirely erase, the role of the human intermediary. A photograph was not as dependent on its artist as, say, a painting.

A similar argument was initially also made by André Bazin, who became the first to attack the *politique des auteurs.* For Bazin, the process of producing a photographic image was so completely different from the other arts that it complicated the notion of personal expression. In "The Ontology of the Photographic Image," Bazin argued that since a photograph is produced "automatically," the personality of the photographer enters into the proceedings only insofar as he selects the actual "object to be photographed and by way of the purpose he has in mind. Although the final result may reflect something of his personality, this does not play the same role as is played by that of the painter [or the writer]. All the arts are based on the presence of man, only photography derives an advantage from his absence."[40] This position overturns the assumptions of the auteur theory. Rather than focus on the creativity of an individual director, Bazin emphasized "the impassive lens" of the camera, capable of representing reality "in all its virginal purity to [his] attention and consequently to [his] love."[41] Even though the photographer chooses the object to be photographed, it is the mechanical process of photography that triumphs. For Bazin, then, the automatism of the cinematic apparatus and the collaborative pieces of the studio system were far more important than the genius of this or that auteur.

This is not to say that Bazin did not value individual directors, especially those working within the constraints of the studios. After all, he inaugurated the *Cahiers* critics' enthusiasm for popular cinema through the work of Hollywood directors, an enthusiasm that led directly to the articulation of the *politique des auteurs*. As Colin MacCabe has argued, "If Bazin presented them with Welles and Rossellini, then the young critics would present their master with Hitchcock, Wyler and Hawks."[42] But these directors, Welles especially, energized Bazin to return to an appreciation of the studio system. "For all film-lovers who had reached the age of cinematic reason by 1946," Bazin remarked, "the name of Orson Welles is identified with the enthusiasm of rediscovering the American cinema."[43] For Bazin, American cinema seemed to have gone through a renaissance during the war years, and Welles "epitomized the conviction, shared by every young critic at the time, of being present at a rebirth and a revolution in the art of Hollywood."[44] For Bazin, the rebirth of that cinema, which ultimately led to the development of his theory about the genius of the system, was far more significant than the genius of Orson Welles himself.

What Bazin decried was the *Cahiers* critics' blind faith in individual expression. His argument was against François Truffaut's famous remark, "There are no works, there are only auteurs," an aphorism the latter had appropriated from novelist Hippolyte Jean Giraudoux. In his most vigorous critique of the auteur theory in "On the *politique des auteurs*," Bazin challenged the younger *Cahiers* critics for exclusively focusing on "the personal factor in artistic creation as a standard of reference."[45] Unlike the later poststructuralist attack on the very notion of authorship, arising out of the dismantling of (romantic) subjectivity, Bazin was not opposed to celebrating auteurs. His chief objection to the *politique des auteurs* was that according to this theory, "any old splash of paint can be valued according to its measurements and the celebrity of the signature."[46] His essay began with Tolstoy's concern, cited in the first epigraph, with seeing every work of an author as having artistic merit just because that author signed it. Bazin wanted to value cinema using less personal criteria. What he disapproved of was the obsession with the author at the expense of the cinematic text. The exclusive practice of auteurism, he believed, led to the danger of "the negation of the film to the benefit of praise of its *auteur*."[47] The trouble with auteurism was that a film was judged a success or failure based solely on how closely it resembled the critic's conception of that particular auteur – or how nearly it represented what the auteurist considered what Andrew Sarris later termed the "élan of the soul."[48] Bazin feared that the *politique des auteurs* was more likely to ignore "good" films from non-auteurs or *metteurs-en-scène*, like John Huston, because it reserved authorship for a select few directors. Following Tolstoy, he insisted that even "mediocre *auteurs* can, by accident, make admirable films, and . . . a genius can fall victim to an equally accidental sterility," a proposition that has serious implications for our understanding of *The Stranger*.[49]

Of course, the auteur is no longer as provocative a figure in film criticism. Successive critical positions have discredited or at least weakened the *Cahiers* approach to auteur theory. Since Roland Barthes pronounced the author dead by declaring that "it is language which speaks, not the author," arguments about creative authority have been associated with a naive intentionality and have been appropriately dismissed.[50] By the late 1960s, the author appears to have died. But although the author may be dead, the auteur has survived. He has now been transformed into an industrial auteur. While there is no longer the baggage of Romantic expressionism, the "commerce of auteurism," as Timothy Corrigan puts it, promises "a relationship between audience and movie in which an intentional and authorial agency governs, as a kind of brand-name vision that precedes and succeeds the film."[51] Grounded in cultural and reception histories, this new auteurism raises valuable questions about the auteur's role in an industrial and economic context, questions that had been largely ignored by the earlier generation of auteurists. The new auteur, we might say, has become an extratextual authorial agency, whose body of work still gains meaning by the virtue of his signature. As Thomas M. Leitch puts it in his analysis of contemporary Hitchcock criticism, "poststructuralists, who ought to have no truck with Hitchcock the auteur, have found not only his films but 'Hitchcock' the director as a paradigmatic figure, equally useful."[52] In other words, while we are no longer talking about the élan of an auteur's soul, we continue to emphasize a coherent authorial figure whose films can be pulled together under the name of the author.

But what about individual films that do not conform to that author's signature? How can we evaluate films that exceed the auteur's appellation? It was exactly these questions that bothered Bazin, who ended his rebuttal of the *politique des auteurs* by arguing for a reevaluation of the notion of auteurism itself. Rather than focusing on this or that director, he wanted to reassess auteurism as a critical discourse. "This does not mean one has to deny the role of the *auteur*," Bazin posited, "but simply give him back the preposition without which the noun auteur remains but a halting concept. *Auteur,* yes, but what *of*?"[53]

This question becomes especially difficult to answer in the case of *The Stranger.* Orson Welles is a good test case for Bazin's rebuttal of the *politique des auteurs.* He is widely regarded as an auteur, even *the* auteur. That is, Welles is usually considered, as Richard Macksey suggests, the "presiding model of Romantic genius, the myth of the explosive, comprehensive talent challenging corporate power and ultimately becoming the victim of his own genius."[54] However, his oeuvre does not cohere as neatly as Alfred Hitchcock's or Howard Hawks's. In other words, not all of his films can be praised in the name of the author. In fact, *The*

Stranger poses exactly this problem. The Welles film that led to a renewed enthusiasm for Hollywood after the war was not the one released that year (in 1946), *The Stranger,* but the original Welles film, one that his later films would be measured against and found deficient in relation to, *Citizen Kane.* Ironically, while auteurism was just being formulated, Welles himself was making the most generic film of his career. But *The Stranger* is also generic in another way: no matter how it was conceived, its released version is a standard genre film. So, how do we think about this un-auteurist film? What might it tell us about being an auteur and working within the studio system?

On the surface, *The Stranger* is a mediocre film, a generic thriller with some noirish accents. It is easily explained in terms of this familiar tale: a lone artist, consistently working against the system, is finally trapped by it. His authority is undermined, his signature style overturned. The auteur does not prevail. In a sense, there is no mystery here. *The Stranger* seems to be a straightforward case of the triumph of the vertically integrated studio system. The film came in under budget and on time, and it was the only Welles venture that was successful at the box office upon first release. But it is widely considered a Wellesian failure, the kind of film Tolstoy might call "quite simply awful."

Following Bazin, who declared the film a "parody" of a Welles film, critics have paid scant attention to it, almost unanimously dismissing it as the worst work in the director's oeuvre. Peter Cowie, for instance, notes that "the film is as uncomfortable an experience to watch as it must have been for Welles to make." Writing about its conventional linear structure, Barbara Leaming argues that this was Welles's "least personal film," because "missing was the disjunctive cinematic style that Orson had made his signature in *Kane.*" And while Joseph McBride allows that it may not be as bad a film as it seems upon first viewing, he still finds *The Stranger* "a disappointing piece of work." Even James Naremore, who investigates the Welles canon more deeply than any other historian, concludes that the artist has been so completely suppressed here that it "could have been directed by anybody."[55] In fact, the film has been of little interest to Welles scholars. Aside from lamenting the censorship of artistic vision, especially in the "lost" scenes, critics have found little that is even worthy of discussion. This attitude toward the film is best summed up by Robert Garis's recent pronouncement that "*The Stranger* has been generally condescended to, mostly because it deserves to be."[56] The film, he argues, "isn't very interesting and doesn't matter very much, particularly to people who value Welles's work highly."[57] Thus, *The Stranger* is not an important film, ostensibly because it is the farthest from Welles's authorial signature and presumably his intent.

To a certain extent, Welles is himself responsible for this sort of reception. In an interview with André Bazin, Charles Bitsch, and Jean Domarchi, he proclaimed: "There is nothing of me in that film." Stressing that he had little control over the script or the editing, he argued: "It's the one of my films of which I am least the author."[58] Welles's desire to disassociate himself from the film seems to anticipate the Allen Smithee phenomenon. Allen Smithee, as is well known, is the pseudonym used by directors who wish to disown films when they feel that creative control has been wrested from them by the Hollywood machine. This practice didn't begin until two decades after Welles had signed his name to an enormously restrictive contract for *The Stranger*. Considering the production struggles over his first Hollywood venture since the public showdown with RKO over the mid-shooting cancellation of *It's All True*, one can imagine that Welles might have disowned the film and asked that his name be struck from the credits, if that convention were available. But we might ask, as Peter Conrad does in a recent reassessment of the stories the self-proclaimed genius told about his life, "how could Welles – who as usual directed it, acted in it, and wrote a good deal of the script – leave himself out"?[59]

Here's another way to think about Welles's supposed absence. Welles would often claim that he stayed on this picture to show that he could work within the studio system, that he could "say 'action' and 'cut' just like all the other fellas."[60] Welles sometimes asserted as well that with *The Stranger* he had intended to make a picture worthy of the institutional mode of filmmaking, almost to debunk the myth of the romantic genius and show that he "didn't glow in the dark."[61] While I hesitate to privilege one strand of directorial commentary over another, especially when talking about someone as mercurial and self-contradictory as Orson Welles, I highlight this point because it is often left unaddressed in any assessment of the film. *The Stranger* is considered the least Wellesian of his films, characteristic of the oppressive studio system's triumph over art. This is a convenient explanation, and it is why the film has not mattered much in the debate over Welles's authorship. Yet, *The Stranger* is deeply concerned with questions of authorship and authority. Even though Welles-playing-Kindler-playing-Rankin strikes off the swastika, his/their authority is not obliterated. Indeed, that is what is most striking about the otherwise conventional moment that opens this chapter. So, while the most Wellesian scenes may be lost and the genius may be missing, an ostensibly un-Wellesian film has significant implications for the role of the auteur in the studio system during the immediate postwar era. What we need in this case is a different way of thinking about auteurism and the name of the author.

DETECTING HISTORY

Here is a story about another missing letter. This is a simple mystery, for the criminal is known to all. He uses a stolen letter to blackmail its author, who is a person of prominence. This should be a fairly straightforward case to solve: if the police retrieve the letter, the extortion ends. So they launch a series of systematic investigations, but to no avail. Despite their best efforts, the police are unable to unearth that letter. The crime remains unsolved, the letter unfound – perhaps because of the simplicity of the thing itself. While the police frantically dig away for clues that might lead them to the original dispatch, the criminal and the letter are in fact hiding in plain sight. Having seemingly exhausted all possibilities, they approach a private detective. A month later, that private detective recovers the letter by stealing it back from the original thief. He claims that the police could not find it because it was hidden in the most obvious place. The letter is then returned to its original author, and the blackmail, we assume, promptly ends.

The detective I am referring to is, of course, C. Auguste Dupin, who solves the mystery of that infamous purloined letter. Along with "The Murders in the Rue Morgue" (1841) and "The Mystery of Marie Rogêt" (1842), Edgar Allan Poe's "The Purloined Letter" (1844) is usually seen as inaugurating the detective genre. Poe is credited with authorizing the modern detective, an intuitive intellectual who examines evidence and resolves mysteries using a process that is quite different from the standard practice employed by the police. In that sense, Poe's detective story is a reflection on method. Consider, for instance, *how* Dupin recovers the purloined letter. The tale begins with Monsieur G –, the prefect of the Parisian police, visiting Dupin with a problem that has him "a good deal puzzled because the affair *is* so simple."[62] The prefect's problem is that a letter of utmost importance has been stolen from the queen's quarters, in her presence, by Minister D –, who has now acquired undue political power and is using it to blackmail the queen. During the course of his investigation, the prefect claims to have searched "'every nook and corner of the premises in which it is possible that the paper can be concealed.'" He then proceeds to describe the systematic, almost mathematical, fashion in which his agents have explored the interior of Minister D –'s apartment, rummaging through every potential hiding space, believing that "'to a properly trained police-agent, such a thing as a *"secret"* drawer is impossible.'"[63] Still, the letter remains missing. Thus stumped, the prefect now approaches Dupin, who is not so interested in the search. Instead, he asks for a detailed description of the stolen object itself. He is intrigued not only by the letter's internal content but especially by its external appearance. According to Dupin, the prefect has conducted a less than thorough search by assuming that "*all* men proceed to conceal a letter, not exactly in a gimlet-hole bored in a chair-leg, but, at least, in *some* out-of-the-way hole or corner."[64] In other words, the prefect assumes, incorrectly, that every criminal would try to hide a stolen object by burying it in the deepest recess. However, as Dupin discovers, Minister D – is hiding the letter in plain sight.

Rather than scouring Minister D –'s apartment for hidden clues, Dupin inverts the prefect's expectations by looking for the letter in the most obviously unlikely place. And he finds it there: inserted carelessly into a card-rack made of pasteboard. At first glance, it looks soiled, crumpled, and rather common, not something that would involve a royal personage. Minister D – has concealed it so far by hiding the letter in plain view of every visitor and by having "'turned [it], as a glove, inside out, re-directed and re-sealed.'"[65] Dupin recovers it by stealthily replacing it with a facsimile of the purloined letter, appropriately turned inside out. He succeeds where the Parisian police have failed precisely by not making their fatal error of equating truth with depth and eschewing all that seems superficial. As James V. Werner correctly notes, "If, as Dupin points out, truth is not always found 'in a well,' but is frequently discovered on the 'surface' of a situation, then the ability only to plumb the 'profound' and 'deep' detail of an event's intricate 'recesses' amounts to blindness, no matter how adept the viewer is at this type of scrutiny."[66] Thus, Dupin's method of investigation entails inverting the clues – or turning them inside out. The three Dupin stories demonstrate Poe's most complete realization not only of how the detective functions in modernity but also of his ability to remain outside of modernity in order to investigate it. Detection amounts to a method of reading clues that destabilizes the bourgeois boundaries between interiority and exteriority, depth and surface, inside and out. The detective, in other words, functions on the threshold.

It is precisely this liminality – the ability to be "neither in nor out," as suggested by the subtitle of an earlier Poe story – that attracted Walter Benjamin to the detective. For Benjamin, the dialectical relationship between the interior and exterior becomes vital for analyzing the shifts precipitated by modernity. Benjamin observes that, starting in the late eighteenth century, and coinciding with the birth of the (romantic) author, the "private individual makes his entrance on the stage of history."[67] This individual is defined primarily in terms of separation between his private home and his public place of work. Since the city begins to be seen as a place of terror out there, the individual tries to feel secure by believing that the interior is absolutely segregated from the exterior space. However, such orderly distinctions are only a fantasy. For crime cannot be kept outside the bourgeois home or confined to the city. That is what Poe's detective fiction demonstrates: terror lies as much within as it does without. And that is what Benjamin admires most about Poe, whose detective stories transform the bourgeois interior from a place of rest and relaxation to a claustrophobic space, filled with dull and lifeless commodities, as horrifying as any crime scene. Moreover, in this new interior, "where doors and walls are made of mirrors, there is no telling outside from in."[68] It is this alluring interweaving of interior-exterior that the Benjaminian detective investigates. Even the arcade presents itself as an external space configured as interiority. In an interesting exploration of the arcade's spatial dialectic, especially as observed by the flâneur, who, we will see, gets transformed into the detective, Benjamin suggests: "It opens up to him as a landscape, even as it closes around him as a room."[69] Like the domestic dwelling, the arcade provides a space for interpenetration of exteriority and interiority, which undermines the traditional division between public and private, upon which bourgeois society is founded. As Tom Gunning points out in an essay on the arcades, "the opposition between street and intérieur does not form a simple dichotomy; the significance of the arcade lies partly in its simultaneous embodiment of both aspects of this apparent contradiction."[70] Gunning argues that Benjamin locates the significance of the detective story in precisely its ability to stage this interpenetration. While he accepts Carlo Ginsburg's contention that the detective story originates with the scrutiny of the indelible trace as a clue, Gunning suggests that the key to the detective's method for Benjamin is "the optical exchange between interior and exterior."[71] Because if the outside can seep in, then the inside can be turned inside out.

The detective is often considered the rightful heir of the flâneur, whose idling around the arcades often led to unforeseen discoveries. The flâneur enjoyed his Parisian glory days in the 1830s, and just as he was beginning to fade away, Poe began authoring his detective tales. In fact, there is one particular short story that traces the transformation of the metropolitan stroller into the modern detective. "The Man of the Crowd" is that story, which exists at the threshold between these two figures and clarifies the method of the detective. Interestingly, in his analysis of the transition from flânerie to detection, Benjamin ties the story to the rising impact of photography, calling it "an x-ray picture of a detective story."[72] It begins with idle flânerie and shows how the flâneur's sketches develop into an investigation. In the opening scenes of "The Man of the Crowd," Poe offers a remarkable portrait of the flâneur, who observes London life from behind a coffeehouse window. He waits there, detachedly surveying the crowd, confident that he can read, "even in that brief interval of a glance, the history of long years." The flâneur believes the city and its crowd to be legible, until he notices a man in that crowd who cannot be analyzed or figured out. He is, he says, "singularly aroused, startled, fascinated" by the stranger, who appears, for the first time, to be a threatening mystery.[73] He is so intrigued by the stranger that he decides to give up his invisibility, pursuing the odd individual as he traverses the city, which suddenly becomes, like a strange city in a film noir, indecipherable. In fact, the stranger's real crime is illegibility. For he does not fit into any preexisting categories or *physiologies* and therefore frustrates the narrator/detective's attempts at identifying or interpreting him. The flâneur concludes that his mode of interpretation is inadequate in relation to the man of the crowd, whom he now considers "'the type and the genius of deep crime.'"[74] After this stage, Benjamin believes, "No matter what trail the *flâneur* may follow, every one of them will lead him to a crime."[75] Thus, we might say that the detective comes into being in order to investigate the strange genius of deep crime.

But his method for scrutiny involves scanning the surface, rather than digging deep, for clues. This is partly because the detective does not possess a panoptical view of the scene of the crime. As Gunning puts it, the detective activates "the complex dialectical optics of modernity," so that he "not only observes and investigates but also – at least potentially – investigates his or her point of view."[76] Instead of observing from a detached, exterior perspective, the Benjaminian detective's gaze is always caught up in the optical exchange between exteriority and interiority. Therefore, instead of the visual mastery afforded by surveillance, detection involves picking up evidence that may be missed by conventional methods. Many scholars have noted that it is not coincidental that the detective story appears on the scene at the same time as photography. As James Lastra points out, like photography, the stranger in Poe's story is "simultaneously compelling and threatening, signaling the fragility of our familiar ways of knowing, while trumpeting the arrival of new and disconcerting epistemologies."[77] More importantly, like photography, the detective's method involves investigating traces that may be lying on the surface. Indeed, the most effective way for a detective to figure out "inner" secrets is to look for clues that may be hiding in plain sight. The detective thus problematizes the traditional opposition between inner and outer, private and public space.

The detective would be particularly suitable for investigating the strange case of Orson Welles in the Hollywood studio system. In place of the traditional auteurist approach, the detective's method will enable us to focus on the surface, thereby circumventing the urge to dig deep for interior meaning. Film historians regard the name "Orson Welles" either as a mark of genius or as a sign of failure. Both camps employ tactics similar to those used by "the investigative reporter Thompson's staff editor in *Citizen Kane*," who is "bent on finding a single formula for explaining a man's life."[78] But no such single formula exists. That is where the detective comes in. As a historian, Benjamin's detective could help us investigate the varied ways in which Welles, especially in a film such as *The Stranger,* navigates the tensions between the auteur and the studio apparatus as well as the relationship between autography and authority. The wildly romantic discourse of the *Cahiers* critics, James Naremore notes, "formed canons and fixed the names of people we should study."[79] Orson Welles's name is certainly fixed at the top of that canon. But what if we un-fix these names? What if, instead of considering the directorial signature as a source of interior meaning, we turn his name inside out?

Like the purloined letter, the name of the author is actually hidden on the surface of the text. As Dudley Andrew puts it, "Always a problematic and very special sign, the signature of the author is a mark on the surface of the text signaling its source."[80] It is this problematic sign that the detective-historian can explore by inspecting the significance of the name as well as its meanings, associations, and variations. If the signature is used as a clue, the investigation becomes similar to the way Jacques Derrida examines literary texts through the name of the author. In *Signsponge,* Derrida proposes a way out of the Romantic form of literary criticism by demonstrating how unstable the name, the proper noun, can be. The signature experiment involves inverting the name into a common noun. By doing so, Derrida argues, you "lose the identity, the title of ownership over the text; you let it become a monument or part of the text, as a thing or a common noun."[81] The loss of identity also results in a loss of a set of values or characteristics taken for granted by the auteurist critic. In the case of Welles, what is lost is the assumed "Wellesian" signature. But what is gained from that loss is the multiplicity of meanings generated by the common noun, which can be employed for an investigation of the text and the auteur. Rather than an individual who stands outside the text and confers meaning on it, which is the auteurist assumption, the name of the author becomes an integral part of the text. Such a move enables the interpenetration of interiority and exteriority that the detective himself first introduced. For the signature is an articulation on the threshold. It exists outside the text but its resonances can be found within it. It is "the mark of an articulation at the border of life and letters, body and language"; moreover, it pulls in both directions, "appropriating the text under the sign of the name, expropriating the name into the play of the text."[82] For the Benjaminian detective-historian, the signature can work to rethink auteurism. Rather than a way to uncover the auteur's submerged personality, the signature can be used as a "superficial" entrance into the text – particularly a text like Welles's *The Stranger,* which does not appear to be as deep as most films attributed to the name of that author.

There is yet another reason to investigate names and naming at this time. In classical Hollywood, names – not only of directors but of actors and characters too – were always strictly regulated. That is why a plain-Jane name like Constance Ockleman was transformed into Veronica Lake or an ethnically accented name like Margarita Carmen Cansino was changed to Rita Hayworth. This kind of policing became even more crucial in the immediate postwar era, where naming names would soon result in dangerous consequences. The Waldorf Statement, a declaration issued by Eric Johnston, president of the Motion Picture Association of America, in December 1947, outlined the industry's policy of not knowingly employing any Communist. The statement was signed by forty-eight studio executives, and their signatures effectively authorized the blacklist, which initially contained the names of ten screenwriters and directors who had refused to testify before the House Un-American Activities Committee (HUAC) and were therefore cited for contempt. The names on the list would multiply throughout the immediate postwar period. And these postwar shifts would result in enforced anonymity for several prominent writers and directors, who would not be able to sign their own names to their projects for many years to come. Some careers would be ruined. Others would work sporadically and pseudonymously. Welles appears to have anticipated these cultural changes by making the most standard film of his career, an average genre film that does not appear to bear his Wellesian strokes. In this context, following the detective, I would like to investigate the signatures in and of *The Stranger*. Gilbert Adair has argued that Orson Welles "was the sole American filmmaker to have created, as director and actor, a set of characters whose *names*, as well as faces, we continue to remember."[83] The next section will remember the name of Orson Welles in his most forgotten film, but we will also forget its auteurist implications in order to rediscover it as something else. If, as Poe suggests, "'Truth is not always in a well,'" then the detective-historian can look at the film's surface for clues and uncover an alternative understanding of authorship within the studio system.[84]

NAMING NAMES

The Stranger is a model detective tale. It chronicles the pursuit of a Nazi war criminal, Franz Kindler, by detective Wilson (Edward G. Robinson), an officer with the Allied War Crimes Commission. During the war, unlike Goebbels or Himmler, Kindler apparently "had a passion for anonymity." Before leaving Germany, he has "destroyed every evidence, down to the last fingerprint." Therefore, tracing him will not be an easy task. Wilson's only clue is that the notorious Franz Kindler has a "hobby that amounts to a mania": an avid interest in antique clocks. His trail leads Wilson from Germany to a quiet New England town called Harper, which has a highly conspicuous, eighteenth-century Gothic clock tower at its center. When Wilson arrives there, he expects to investigate an ex-Nazi who has gone underground in this sleepy American town. He decides to proceed systematically, by scrutinizing every stranger who has relocated there in the last few months. By a literal process of elimination – striking off the names of new arrivals in Harper in the past year, ~~Black, Maynard, Young, Shepard, Sudder~~ – he is left with the one name that oddly echoes Kindler's: Rankin. To his surprise, what he discovers is that this stranger is the beloved new history professor at a boys' prep school, and he is about to marry Mary Longstreet, the daughter of a state supreme court justice (Philip Merivale), the most respected man in town. Several clues begin to point to Rankin, but the most obvious one is his fixation on clocks. He is obsessed with fixing the church clock. Mary even wonders about what would happen to Harper if the clock worked again, because "the clock's hands have never moved." For the townsfolk,

Rankin is merely an odd enthusiast, his hobby as quirky as the old clock itself. Only Wilson finds Rankin suspicious, seeing something amiss when the clock rotates counter-clockwise as Rankin is trying to fix it. Interestingly, the former Nazi mastermind has not chosen to conceal himself at all. Except for a slight name change, he is hiding in plain sight. Through his tenacious detective work, Wilson finally convinces Mary and the rest of the town of Rankin's horrific past. During the thrilling finale, the stranger is discovered hiding in the clock tower. As he tries to escape, he is impaled by the sword-carrying figure in the tower and falls to his death. Wilson reasserts control over the town, proclaiming it "V-Day in Harper." Thus concludes this generic thriller. Ostensibly, the mystery is resolved; all's well that ends well(es). There is nothing remarkably auteurist about the film.

However, anxiety over authority becomes clear in *The Stranger* right in its opening credits. Over the backdrop of a Gothic clock tower, where the film's gripping conclusion will unfold, the title sequence displays the names of people involved in the making of the film on both sides of the camera. Our first clue may be the directorial credit, which appears at the very end, after the producer, and is rather unusual. While the production credit is listed as "Produced by S. P. Eagle," for the director, the title only reads, "Direction Orson Welles." Curiously, the preposition by, which would confer directorial authority, is not available to him in the credits. One might say that the signature is not very firmly attached to the film. It clearly functions differently from the way it does in *Citizen Kane,* which offers the title "A Mercury Production by Orson Welles" even before the name of the film is announced. Authorial voice is also asserted more directly in *The Magnificent Ambersons,* where Welles announces the closing credits, concluding with "My name is Orson Welles." Not so with *The Stranger,* which is made in a very different context. Having succeeded at failing expectations with his first two authorial efforts, and with a third film incomplete, Welles did not have much free rein on the next project. As outlined earlier, this film is a generic noir thriller, where his signature is not very firmly moored. Thus unfixed, we can use the name of the author to disperse its effects in the text. Fortunately, the name Welles connotes multiplicity. Unlike other auteurs, such as Ray or Ford or Hitchcock, whose names allude to the singular, Welles indicates plurality. Therefore, we can assume that it will be difficult to demarcate Welles. To put it differently, while there is a brand called "Welles," when we convert it into a common noun, the brand name will not be so singularly dependable. So what is this thing called welles?

To begin with, Welles's name signifies depth. We can ignore the second e for now, since Welles is just "his own fancier, more quaintly olde English spelling" of Wells, which was his family name in previous generations.[85] Of course, there is also another connection here, to H. G. Wells, whose *War of the Worlds* Welles adapted for the radio in 1938. That unauthorized adaptation was a notorious broadcasting disaster. It was the Halloween episode of *The Mercury Theater on the Air*, presented as a series of news bulletins to suggest an actual Martian invasion, and it reportedly sent many listeners into panic, some fleeing the area, others claiming to see flashes of lightning in the distance. Welles later wondered how his listeners did not recognize the voice that always opened with "Ladies and Gentlemen, this is Orson Welles." Even if his listeners did not, Hollywood took notice, for it was that fake broadcasting disaster that brought Welles's name to the attention of RKO chief, George Schaefer, who signed in 1940 an unprecedented deal giving the inexperienced director complete creative control.[86] It was the deal that made Welles an auteur *avant la lettre*. Interestingly, that same year Wells met Welles, whom he called his "little namesake"; Wells "challenged Orson to drop the supernumerary, affected 'e' in his surname, and said he could see no reason for it."[87] Orson didn't, except for a brief instant when signing his name on a painting in *F for Fake*. What if we take up Wells's challenge? If we think of this signature in terms of an enclosed, deep space that extends vertically, such as a well or an abyss, then we find that the name corresponds with the traditional understanding of Welles as a profound genius. Further, his genius is primarily defined in terms of his use of deep focus cinematography. So, the "well" may be taken as our clue to the classic auteurist signature.

We need only recall the oft-cited scene from *Citizen Kane* where Susan Alexander (Dorothy Comingore) attempts to commit suicide, in order to think about how the use of depth of field exemplifies the Wellesian signature. After suffering a humiliating opera debut, Susan tries to commit suicide, but Charles Foster Kane (Orson Welles) and another man break into her bedroom to save her. There are several planes of depth (Figure 3.3). In the foreground, we see an enormous glass with a spoon in it as well as a medicine bottle, which together occupy at least a quarter of the screen. The bed where Susan is assumed to be lying is located in the middle ground, but it is barely visible, overshadowed by the objects in the foreground. However, we are made aware of this plane due to the sound of her weak breathing. Except for all kinds of distracting objects, where the viewer's eye may democratically wander, the large bedroom is, from a narrative point of view, empty. We hear knocking first, and then Kane bursts into the room. The entire scene takes place in deep focus, revealing all three planes at the same time. Combined with the long take, this sequence demonstrates Welles's distinctive use of deep cinematic space. But depth of focus here is not merely a stylistic device imposed on an otherwise regular *mise en scène*. As Bazin has suggested, "the decoupage in depth becomes a technique which constitutes the meaning of the story. It isn't merely a way of placing the camera, sets and actors."[88] In a very real sense, depth becomes the fundamental distinction between Welles and other filmmakers. Some of this use of deep focus cinematography must, of course, be attributed to Gregg Toland, who worked as Welles's cinematographer on the film. As Bordwell, Staiger, and Thompson point out, influenced by an increased desire for realism during the war, Toland had been working with deep focus, combined with low-key lighting and continual frontality, on earlier films like William Wyler's *Wuthering Heights* (1939) and John Ford's *The Long Voyage Home* (1940). In *Citizen Kane,* Toland consolidated his previous efforts, such that, even though the unusually deep focus "came under considerable criticism within the industry," it made "Toland the only Hollywood cameraman whose name was known to the general public."[89] While Toland may have helped inaugurate this style, it was Welles who became most closely associated with it. Indeed, we might say that depth became the auteur's signature. But there is more to this signature than just depth of cinematic space. The notion of depth was used over and over again by the Romantics as a true test of genius. Edward Young urged the poet to dive deep within himself in order to find "the stranger within" and to "let thy genius rise (if a genius thou hast) as the sun from chaos."[90] From a traditional auteurist perspective, then, Welles's signature conforms to

3.3. *Citizen Kane* (dir. Orson Welles, 1941).

his association with depth, of focus and of vision, which translates into a profound sense of him as a romantic artist.

This particular signature, however, is missing in the case of *The Stranger*. In this film, Charles Rankin enters his wife Mary's bedroom while she is lying in bed, apparently dreaming. The camera follows Rankin as he slowly walks into the room and stands next to Mary's bed (Figure 3.4). He casts a large shadow, which towers over her as she begins to stir. In fact, through most of the scene, all we see of Charles is his shadow on the wall. Unlike *Citizen Kane,* where deep focus cinematography enables Welles to explore different spatial and temporal planes in a single shot, here the focus remains on the linear narrative. Mary begins telling Charles about her dream, in which she sees Meinike, Charles's most recent victim, "walking all by himself across a deserted city square, where every move he threw a shadow." The shadow in her dream is a manifestation of the shadow her husband casts on her and on the narrative, thus connecting her nightmares to him. While there is some spatial depth,

3.4. *The Stranger* (dir. Orson Welles, 1946)

all the action takes place on a single plane. Nothing in the foreground conflicts with anything in the background, therefore allowing the linear narrative to retain momentum. Indeed, it is a fairly standard shot – quite common in films noirs by this time and used often to suggest that deep, dark anxieties were visible right there on the surface.

Writing about how the use of deep focus cinematography evolved in classical Hollywood from the innovative late 1930s to its full-blown use after the war, Bordwell, Staiger, and Thompson argue that while Welles's cinematographic advances in *Citizen Kane* and *The Magnificent Ambersons* were flamboyant and controversial, the studios quickly found a way to appropriate those innovations in the service of storytelling. After 1942, "Hollywood cinematography adopted a less picturesque deep-focus style better suited to the demands of classical narrative and decoupage."[91] In other words, the seemingly radical shifts in *mise en scène* are standardized by the studio system, such that a shot that is "so rare in 1937" becomes "quite ordinary a decade later."[92] Two instances can illustrate this point:

the moment where two hoodlums plan to kidnap a rich man's son in the foreground while a woman pushes a baby carriage in the background in William Wyler's proto-noir *Dead End* (1937) is certainly more exceptional than the moment in George Cukor's *A Double Life* (1947) when theatrical producer Max Lasker (Philip Loeb) offers the part of Othello to troubled Broadway star Anthony John (Ronald Colman) while a secretary brings in coffee from the background. A decade later, the background is used only for the purpose of blocking. Bordwell, Staiger, and Thompson argue that the reason deep focus cinematography became standardized has a lot to do with the paradoxical role of the American Society of Cinematographers (ASC) in the studio system. As a technical agency, the ASC reflected the tension between standardization and innovation: "On the one hand, the ASC asked the cinematographer to be a craftsman, cleanly obeying the rules. At the same time, he was expected to originate techniques," echoing the tension between the roles of auctor and author.[93] In *Citizen Kane*, Toland was clearly interested in the latter role. But over time, classical Hollywood was really adept at appropriating those innovations and pushing in the opposite direction; by the mid-1940s, deep focus shooting itself became incorporated into the studio style. *The Stranger* belongs to that tradition in its "ordinary" use of deep focus. Fittingly, in place of Gregg Toland, who saw himself as an artist, *The Stranger*'s cinematographer is Russell Metty, whose name fortuitously alludes to that standard craftsman of the studio system that Welles himself appears to become, the *metteur-en-scène*.

So if the Wellesian signature is missing, let us turn to the other signatory on the credits, S. P. Eagle. S. P. Eagle was in fact the name briefly assumed by independent producer Sam Spiegel until 1954. Like so many other Jewish European émigrés, Spiegel came to Hollywood as a stranger. A fugitive from Germany in 1933, Spiegel stopped over in Mexico before coming to the United States. Once in Hollywood, biographer Andrew Sinclair explains, "he lived under an assumed name on the charity of other refugee filmmakers from central Europe."[94] Then, Spiegel reinvented himself in the American tradition, telling varied stories about his past to different people. He even renamed himself S. P. Eagle, apparently "struck by a burst of patriotism."[95] But the name change wasn't as innocuous as that. As a producer, Spiegel himself operated like an eagle, much like other authoritarian producers before him, such as Irving Thalberg, Darryl Zanuck, and David O. Selznick. Indeed, Spiegel's name became synonymous in Hollywood with forceful persuasion, so that "to be 'spiegeled' meant to be soothed, cajoled, or conned."[96] Under Spiegel's watchful eye, Welles had to surrender artistic control, having been forced to sign a very restrictive contract. In other words, under Spiegel's supervision, Welles's own vision had to be suppressed. What Spiegel preferred was a lean and uncomplicated tale, "with none of the ambiguities that usually made Welles's films so rich and rare."[97] In opposition to Welles's deep desire for innovation, Spiegel insisted on following convention. His films reflected what RKO had printed on their stationery after Welles's spectacular financial failures there in the 1940s: "Showmanship instead of Genius." In that sense, Spiegel seems to stay true to his original signature. It is noteworthy that in German, "spiegel" is a common noun meaning looking-glass, mirror, or reflecting surface. Spiegel's authority, we might say, derives from a pre-Romantic conception of authorship. Recall M. H. Abrams's basic distinction between two types of authorship, the mirror and the lamp. According to the mirror conception of aesthetics, literary critics valued imitation over innovation. What was praised was an author's ability to mirror already established standards. As Abrams suggests, in this model, the poet was regarded primarily as "the maker of a work of art according to universal standards of excellence."[98] The task of a critic was to uncover how well those established standards had been followed. Spiegel similarly advocated close adherence to, or mirroring of, the established rules of genre filmmaking in classical Hollywood. A director was to be like an auctor, a craftsman who could successfully reflect the conventions of that system, assuredly regarded as the "universal standards of excellence." By those standards, things had gone well with *The Stranger*. It was an average thriller that cashed in over three million dollars, almost three times its cost, upon initial release, enabling Spiegel to reflect his name, even if Welles could not stay true to his own.

Perhaps things had gone too well – and this might be our next clue. By some accounts, Welles had signed up for *The Stranger* in order to make a conventional film. After struggling to make ambitious projects like *War and Peace* and *Crime and Punishment*, Otto Friedrich tells us, he wanted to convince "a suspicious Hollywood that he could make a perfectly orthodox film."[99] This new project would be completed on time and under budget, thus disproving accusations that he was undependable. To a certain extent, these were false accusations, since "he was never 'inclined to joke with other people's money.'"[100] *Citizen Kane* was actually made on a relatively low budget of $749,000. Yet, during the 1940s, Welles developed the reputation of being an unaffordable director. Therefore, *The Stranger* would be different. The film would still carry his name, but the name would not mean the same thing it had before. Rather than the "director's cut," what we end up with is a highly efficient narrative, proving that Welles could indeed "say 'action' and 'cut' just like all the other fellas." To put it another way, it is Welles the auteur who becomes the ultimate stranger in the picture. Like a dutiful auctor, Welles estranges himself from his signature in order to make a film that is all too familiar. If that is the case, then we might do well to look not at depth but perhaps its inverse, the surface. In so doing, we would be following that other O. W., Oscar Wilde, who appears to be channeling the Benjaminian detective in *The Picture of Dorian Gray* when he argues, through Lord Henry Wotton, that "it is only shallow people who do not judge by appearances. The mystery of the world is in the visible, not the invisible."[101]

To investigate the visible or to judge by appearances is to point out that *The Stranger* is an imitation of Alfred Hitchcock's *Shadow of a Doubt* (1943), which, Welles claimed, was the only American film directed by Hitchcock that he admired. In the Hitchcock version, Charles Oackley (Joseph Cotten), a strangler of wealthy East Coast widows, hides in the idyllic Northern California town of Santa Rosa. There, his sister Emma (Patricia Collinge) and her daughter, his namesake Charlie (Teresa Wright), are thrilled to welcome him into their home and community, because they believe he can "save them from their suffocating ordinariness."[102] But what Uncle Charlie introduces to the small town is an outside world of crime and deception. *Shadow of a Doubt* presents an ironic portrait of wartime America. As Palmer notes, "the Capracorniness of the film's Santa Rosa makes room not only for a full gallery of oddball grotesques, but implies (as Emma and young Charlie both testify) sexual immaturity and failure."[103] That is, the film explodes the illusion that crime exists out there, disrupting the boundaries between the underworld of crime and the moral world of upstanding small-town America.

Hitchcock, whose fascination for Poe has been well documented, ruptures the binary opposition between interiority and exteriority, turning the small world of Santa Rosa upside down – or, we might say, inside out. Hitchcock's Charles becomes the kind of criminal Poe's Dupin would find intriguing.

Welles's Charles, on the other hand, seems not to be such a character. As Naremore suggests, *The Stranger* has only "a superficially Hitchcockian sense of the absurd."[104] Otherwise, as an imitation, it is a shallow copy. François Truffaut once said that Wellesian characters were always exceptional; they were "geniuses or monsters, monstrous geniuses."[105] Charles Rankin exhibits no such depth. Welles plays him fairly unambiguously. That Rankin is in fact the Nazi fugitive Franz Kindler is never in much doubt. One of his first acts in the film is the murder of old comrade Meinike, who claims he has been sent by the All Highest. This scene with Meinike becomes the key, albeit a very obvious one, to figuring out Rankin's identity. While the boys at his prep school are out trailing a paper chase, Rankin drags Meinike into the woods and murders him with his bare hands. In a rare long take, Welles shows Rankin quickly burying the dead body in a shallow grave. That is all it takes. In fact, it turns out that the film is not about our detection of Rankin's guilt but of his wife Mary's eventual discovery of his genocidal crimes. That is why Rankin is not a conflicted figure. Unlike the Charles in *Shadow of a Doubt,* Charles Rankin is unmistakably guilty. Nor is he a very complex character. Unlike other "monstrous geniuses" in the Welles oeuvre, "the 'otherness' of the unheimlich Kindler is not identified with either relentless power or hypnotic sexuality."[106] Although the names Kindler and Rankin echo other Wellesian monstrous geniuses, like Charles Foster Kane, Gregory Arkadin, and Hank Quinlan, in this film nothing comes of those alliterative associations. Nor still is he the ambivalent noir hero. Borde and Chaumeton have argued that one of the central features of postwar noir is its moral ambivalence: "In it, 'vice' is seductive; it is nevertheless experienced as 'vicious,' and the lawbreaker seems obsessed by a sense of anguish and a feeling of guilt."[107] Charles Rankin, however, is simply vicious. There are no signs of an interior struggle.

In fact, Rankin is fairly one-dimensional. Although he plays the role of Rankin, Franz Kindler never remains buried. Wilson's task is not to "lure the guessed-at presence out into the open where it will show it-self."[108] The monster is always right there on the surface. During a dinner at Judge Longstreet's, where he comes face to face with Wilson for the first time, Rankin does not try too hard to keep Kindler hidden. When the conversation turns to the German "problem," Rankin becomes an authority on Nazi philosophy, claiming up front that he has "a way of making enemies when [he's] on that subject." He says he believes that equality or democracy could never take root in Germany. "Mankind is waiting for the messiah," he asserts, "but for the German, the messiah is not the prince of peace – he's another Barbarossa, another Hitler." When Noah cites Marx as a possibility that perhaps Germans might embrace equality, Rankin immediately rebuffs the notion: "Marx wasn't a Ger-man, he was a Jew." The others remain skeptical. Eventually, the judge wonders whether conceding Rankin's argument implies that "there is no solution," to which Rankin responds, "annihilation." Yet, even these overt references to the Final Solution do not raise any suspicions around the table. Rankin's words are dismissed as the odd notions or ramblings of a delightful pedagogue. And the dinner scene is not the only one where Rankin's obvious guilt goes undetected by the local community. During his wedding reception, Rankin disappears to bury the body of Meinike a little more deeply. The body refuses to stay buried, and it is dug up by the dog, Red, whom Rankin kicks and later kills. Still, nobody finds him devious. He is also prepared to kill Mary. "Murder can be a chain," he argues, with "one link leading to another until it circles your neck." These circles end up with Rankin/Kindler waiting in the phone booth doodling a swastika that unmistakably, if heavy-handedly, binds the two together.

What, then, can we investigate about such a superficial character? Links in the associative chain between Kindler and Rankin exist in the names themselves. Indeed, one clue that Wilson intuitively notices while striking off the names of other strangers in Harper is the kinship between Rankin and Kindler. But they have more than a few letters in common. David Thomson hints at these commonalities in passing when he observes, "The unruly bundle of Kindler and Rankin (containing the name Kane as well as the dreamy threat of a Kain for kinder – the puzzle fiend cannot quite *not* notice these things)."[109] Although Thomson does not, let us try to unravel this unruly bundle of names. Kindler is the one whose name obviously signifies the most authority, since to kindle means to excite or arouse or set going. As the presumed architect of the Final Solution, the name fits. Similarly, Rankin, which is an old English name meaning little shield, provides a fitting nominal shield for Kindler. In German, the names are appropriately inverted. Kindler, with its agent derivative in "kind" for children, is sometimes used as the occupational name of a schoolteacher, which he will later become in his incarnation as Rankin, whose German roots in "ränke" implies plotting or scheming, which suits the Nazi mastermind well. Once again, as at the narrative level, the mystery is resolved simply.

Perhaps the mystery appears to be too simple. There is another nominal connection, also lying on the surface, that may become our next clue. Well before Welles and Edward G. Robinson were named among the 151 presumed Communists working in broadcasting in *Red Channels,* or Joseph McCarthy gained renown by waving a piece of paper supposedly containing the names of 205 known Reds working in the Truman State Department during a speech in Wheeling, West Virginia, or unfriendly witnesses were renamed the Hollywood Ten, a congressman from Mississippi had made a name for himself as a tough anti-Communist. A ranking member of HUAC, which was renamed and made permanent from the Special Committee on Un-American Activities in 1938 on his suggestion, this congressman was known for his racist and anti-Semitic tirades. "Six months before the attack on Pearl Harbor," David Everitt notes, he "declared on the floor of the House of Representatives that 'Wall Street and a little group of international Jewish brethren' were trying to drag the country to war."[110] During World War II, he negotiated the amount paid for the deadly munitions disaster at Port Chicago down to $2,000 when he learned that the victims were mostly black. In the immediate postwar era, he rejoiced "every time a witness [for HUAC] refused to name names," because that was seen as "proof of disloyalty to the Stars and Stripes."[111] When HUAC began investigating Hollywood, he took to the House floor to "reveal" the Jewish origins of mainstream stars – "There is one who calls himself Edward Robinson. His real name is Emanuel Goldenberg. There is another one who calls himself Melvyn Douglas, whose real name is Melvyn Hesselberg," and so on – in order to discredit them and link them to Communism.[112] This anti-Communist crusader was Congressman Rankin, whose proto-McCarthyism succeeded in linking any expressions of liberalism to Communism and then to anti-Americanism. He was thereby "able to wrest a full-blown domestic Red Scare out of international tensions."[113]

In reverse, in *The Stranger*, Rankin comes to embody an internal threat while ostensibly representing an external threat. In his daily editorial column for the *New York Post*, taking stock of a post-Roosevelt era in 1945, Orson Welles began arguing that "the phony fear of Communism is smoke-screening the real menace of renascent Fascism."[114] So how does an auteur represent the perils of impending fascism, which would soon be renamed McCarthyism, after Wisconsin's junior senator, whom Welles himself considered running against in 1946? And how to accomplish that representation politically without being labeled a Communist and being blacklisted from Hollywood? During the war, political filmmaking was encouraged. "The Popular Front, an antifascist alliance of radicals and liberals," Langdon argues, was able to "integrate their artistic vision with their antifascist, antiracist politics, significantly shaping wartime constructions of Americanism."[115] Since Americanism was then being defined explicitly against the white supremacist propaganda of Nazism – with America being the "free world" in stark contrast to the "slave world" of fascism, to use Frank Capra's terminology from *Why We Fight* (1942–1945) – the ostensible liberalism of films like John Ford's *Tobacco Road* (1941) and Michael Curtiz's *Mission to Moscow* (1943) was permissible. However, following the war, such content would be condemned for being Communist. Led by Congressman Rankin, the campaign against the Red Menace in Hollywood implied that filmmakers had to either edit their work or be kicked out. Langdon has astutely covered the uproar over Edward Dmytryk's *Cornered* and *Crossfire* (1947), both politically charged films where the "message was not incidental and would not be lost in either the narrative conventions of the investigative thriller or the visual conventions of noir."[116] Orson Welles's *The Stranger* works in the exact opposite direction. It fulfills the narrative conventions of the investigative thriller by uncovering the mystery straightforwardly and follows the standardized conventions of noir. But is it simply a conventional, un-auteurist film?

In 1969, only a year after the author was officially declared dead, *Cahiers du Cinéma* published an influential piece aiming to redefine the object of film criticism. In this manifesto, titled "Cinema/Ideology/ Criticism," Jean-Louis Comolli and Jean Narboni call for a reclassification of narrative cinema. In place of a naive intentionality that characterized so much early *Cahiers* criticism and defined the auteurist approach, Comolli and Narboni propose seven categories, from (a) to (g), for rethinking individual films and their relationship to ideology. While most of these categories are fairly predictable, from films that abide by mainstream politics to those that deliberately break with it, the most intriguing of these alphabetized listings is category (e), which describes those films that disintegrate from within, in spite of the intentions of its director. In these films, they argue, "an internal criticism is taking place." These are distinct from auteurist films, where the intention to disturb the dominant ideology, be it of the studio system or of American culture at large, is clearly or implicitly stated. Instead, films belonging to category (e) are very conventional. "This is the case in many Hollywood films," Comolli and Narboni suggest, "which while being completely integrated in the system and the ideology end up by partially dismantling the system from within." What can we do with such films? In their initial manifesto, their recommendation is "to show the process in action."[117] This form of criticism acknowledges those spaces where an otherwise conventional film begins to crack at the seams. To put it differently, category (e) enables a form of film analysis that lies beyond strict auteurist interpretation. For category (e) helps us see how a generic film turns itself inside out.

I would argue that *The Stranger* is that kind of film. It is indeed a model genre film, a formulaic tale told in a familiar fashion. There is no deep, multi-layered text to be unraveled. The viewer knows too much. The mystery is simple, and it is simply revealed. That is why it has been regarded as an auteurist failure. But perhaps it appears to be too simple. After all, even though Rankin's guilt is never in doubt, his criminality is established to the point of absurdity. In narrative terms, he remains a superficial villain, who plainly represents the banality of evil as well as the (not too deeply) hidden dangers of fascism. In stylistic terms, the film faithfully follows the standardized look of noir. Given that in the postwar era, Welles's "films became more radically stylized than ever, as if the limitations in subject matter and budget had to be overcome by an utter strangeness of *mise-en-scène*," *The Stranger* appears ridiculous.[118] Writing about another troubled film, Alfred Hitchcock's *The Trouble with Harry* (1955), François Truffaut focuses on its absurdity, arguing that "as the film goes forward, it destroys itself."[119] For Truffaut, the Hitchcock film becomes a trick. Could *The Stranger* be seen that way too? After all, as Michael Anderegg suggests, "Welles wants to play Kindler, while Kindler wants to play Rankin. In this contest, Welles wins throughout."[120] Welles ends up making a generic film, one whose critique is not buried thematically or stylistically in a deep well, but it is right there on the surface.

There is another way to connect category (e) with *The Stranger*. A hint of what Welles accomplishes here may be found in the German meaning of his name, with the letter e carefully reinserted. In German, a *welle* is a wave or a ripple. If we think about this undulating ripple as a small agitation or disturbance to the surface, we can see how paradoxical the Wellesian signature can be. Rather than the deep, brooding auteur, Welles becomes someone who causes small waves, like a trickster or a prankster. This would not be the first time that Welles has engaged in trickery. There is a long history of this other side of Orson Welles. Writing about his childhood, Thomson notes Welles's early interest in magic. He had very large hands, which were "his first gesture of conjuring before he had thought of tricks, black velvet rabbits in his deep pockets."[121] This early pursuit of trickery was not abandoned even when Welles joined show business. Indeed, his penchant for farce predates the *War of the Worlds* fiasco. His first venture as a filmmaker was in fact not *Citizen Kane* but a short silent film called *The Hearts of Age* (1934), which Welles himself regarded as a spoof of an avant-garde film like Luis Buñuel's *Un Chien Andalou* (1929) or Jean Cocteau's *Blood of a Poet*. But even in its ostensible simplicity, it is more than that. In this Surrealist fake, Welles plays a dandy playing a grinning fool playing Death. Under deep layers of makeup, he is still recognizable. Besides his preference for trickery, what this first film also reveals is Welles's complicated relationship with the notion of authorship. As McBride points out, "The credit cards list only the title and the actors, but they are all in Welles's handwriting."[122]

Thus, right from the beginning, it shows the simultaneous appearance and disappearance of the auteur.

Later in his career, of course, there is also Welles's most comprehensive meditation on trickery, *F for Fake*. About the notorious art forger Elmer de Hory, the film is filled with hoaxes: not only de Hory's but also Clifford Irving's and Orson Welles's. In fact, Welles admits deception up front, calling it "a film about trickery." It begins as a film about Elmyr de Hory's art forgeries, then turns to his biographer's forged biography of Howard Hughes, then to Welles's own history of trickery, and to Picasso's dalliance with forgery. At each turn, rather than setting them up as polar opposites, *F for Fake* becomes a consideration of the relationship between fakery and authorship. Andreas Huyssen suggests that there is "a certain family resemblance" between an artist and a faker, a notion that Picasso confirms when, confronted with some of his own paintings, he rejects them by saying "I can paint fake Picassos as well as anybody!"[123] Thus, the film investigates whether our traditional conception of authorship itself must be redefined. Near the end, while contemplating the medieval cathedral of Chartres, Welles returns to another crucial question: how to untangle the connection between the self-promoting auteur and the self-effacing auctor. Welles admires the Chartres, whose unknown creators from centuries past make it a work "without signature." Joseph McBride ruefully notes that "the man who often boasted 'My name is Orson Welles' is the least anonymous of filmmakers. Not for him the self-effacing craftsmanship of the builders of Chartres."[124] It is true that Welles's name preceded him even before he went to Hollywood, in large measure due to his *War of the Worlds* prank, and his name/fame would never allow him to be the anonymous craftsman of the Chartres. However, the unavailability of anonymity of craftsmanship does not imply that Welles is entirely attached to his name either. Just when we think we have identified his signature, he turns it inside out. Time and again, Welles tries to unmoor himself from his name by making fakery another way of thinking about the auteur. François Truffaut was convinced that Welles had made *F for Fake* as a critical response to Pauline Kael's claim that he had stolen much of the credit for *Citizen Kane* that rightly belonged to Herman Mankiewicz. In the film, Welles declares himself a charlatan, but even that ostensible admission is an act of fakery, as he later claims that he was "faking even then. Everything was a lie. There wasn't anything that wasn't."[125]

This contradictory position has particular relevance for our understanding of the case of *The Stranger*. For the detours offered by its varied signatures show how, by copying the conventions of the studio system closely, the film turns those conventions into a joke, which is especially ironic in 1946 – the best year for box-office receipts. Thomas Schatz describes it as the "heyday" of the studios in general and the genre film in particular.[126] In an atmosphere of blacklists and paranoia, the studio system began its slow decline after that year. Welles appears to anticipate trouble on the horizon and ends up making the most standard film of his career, in order to estrange himself from his own signature. Let us return, then, to the signature moment in the film, with Orson Welles playing Franz Kindler playing Charles Rankin, standing in a phone booth and doodling a swastika. If we observe the swastika carefully, we see yet another inversion. The swastika that the presumed author of the Final Solution sketches turns in the wrong direction. Just like the Wellesian signature, the very moniker of Nazism itself is playfully reversed.

The swastika was adopted as a symbol of the Nazi party and Aryan supremacy in 1920. When it first appeared, Hitler took credit for its design. In *Mein Kampf* he speaks at length about the laborious but inspired process of creating the swastika, even though it is believed that he only copied it from Dr. Friedrich Krohn, a dentist from Starnberg. "Since Hitler was a wannabe architect, painter, and dabbler in commercial art," Steven Heller argues, "as leader of his movement he chose to be its art director and image manipulator."[127] Of course, like the Bixby letter, the story of the swastika's origins is less than reliable. Versions of the swastika were in existence long before Hitler decided to claim authority for it. It was originally meant as a symbol of good luck, especially in Hinduism, Jainism, and Buddhism. Its name itself derives from a Sanskrit word meaning the thing associated with auspiciousness. In appropriating this image as the artist/author of Nazism, Hitler also manipulated the long tradition of regarding the swastika as a signifier of well-being. Malcolm Quinn, on the other hand, argues that the swastika should be included within another tradition, drawing on its associations with the discourse of awakening or coming to consciousness. "In the writings of Goethe and Schelling, of Coleridge and Novalis," he points out, "the symbol is defined not so much as a representation as an event, a sudden revelation which restores the alienated subject to a richer, fuller existence."[128] In other words, per Quinn, the swastika might also be seen as a sign of Romantic vision.

But in the revelatory moment in *The Stranger,* this Romantic revelation is undone. Here, the swastika rotates in the counter-clockwise direction, like the clock Rankin is trying to fix initially. Its arms lean leftward, thus reversing the original symbol. Interestingly, it resembles a satirical Saul Steinberg cartoon, showing a frustrated Hitler drawing swastikas on the wall. Most of the swastikas have been sketched inaccurately, and then there are strikes across them to cancel them out. The cartoon is untitled; it is usually called "Hitler Drawing Faulty Swastikas." It was created in 1946, the same year *The Stranger* was released. In the cartoon as well as in the film, the swastika ultimately turns out to be a fake. Rather than thinking of the film as an artistic failure, then, can we not see it as a productive parody and use it to complicate the boundaries between authorship and fakery? Because signatures can be less stable than traditional auteurist critics would have us believe. As Welles puts it in *F for Fake,* "maybe a man's name doesn't matter all that much."

"THIS IS ORSON WELLES"

In another cinephiliac moment that turns on the complexities of naming, we have a powerful financier (Orson Welles) hiring a small-time American smuggler as a detective (Robert Arden) to investigate himself. Here is the narrative Arkadin knows: in the winter of 1927, he finds himself walking down a deserted street in Zurich with nothing but the suit he is wearing and two thousand Swiss francs in his pocket. He uses the money to build an empire. He is now a ruthless billionaire, with no memory of how he started off that winter night in Zurich in 1927. He wants detective Guy van Stratten to explore the rest of the story, starting with this clue: the subject's name is Gregory Arkadin. This deal is offered in Welles's *Mr. Arkadin* (1955), another one of his "failed" ventures. This film was left incomplete due to disagreements with Welles's chief financial backer, Louis Dolivet. We do not know exactly what the final

version, the "director's cut," would have looked like, because the notorious pattern of Welles's inability to finish the film under budget and on
time led Dolivet to remove it from the auteur's hands. Garis reports that
although Welles had planned a nonlinear structure for the film, it was
edited under Dolivet's supervision to follow "a straightforward linear
structure, supposedly to make it more easily understood."[129] There are in
fact multiple versions of the film, including the British version originally
released under the title *Confidential Report*. That title reflects the truth
behind the odd offer, which is fake because before asking the American
crook to serve as a private detective and investigate his life, Arkadin has
already compiled a "confidential report" on van Stratten. That report
has uncovered van Stratten's secret: that his aristocratic name is in fact a
cover for his original, more ethnic name, Guy Straitheimer. Perhaps preoccupied by his own name change, Guy diagnoses Arkadin's problem of
having no memory before 1927 as amnesia and then poses this intriguing
question: "So what makes you so sure your name is Arkadin?" He adds,
"Well, maybe it's Arkadine, or Arkadini, or Arkapopoulos – or Smithee."
He is quickly chided by Arkadin: "Don't be a fool. I know my own name."

Like Arkadin, auteurist critics usually put too much faith in the stability of names. But, as Guy van Stratten's seemingly random question
suggests – random because the other associative versions of Arkadin
make sense in terms of different ethnic possibilities in Europe, but why
Smithee? – names themselves are slippery and can form associations that
go beyond the intentions of this or that director.[130] More importantly, it
demonstrates that there are fewer than six degrees of separation between
Orson Welles, whose name invokes auteurism itself, and Allen Smithee,
whose name was invented to stand in place of those directorial names
that had to be willfully erased. It is fitting, then, that Bazin's primary
example in his critique of the *politique des auteurs* was in fact Welles's
highly un-Wellesian *Mr. Arkadin*. But if we want to be "foolish," to use
Arkadin's terms, and start from the premise that names are unreliable
as well as unstable, what do we learn? Following the Benjaminian detective's emphasis on the interpenetration of exteriority and interiority, we
can discover that the signature does not need to lie safely outside the
text, governing its interpretation; its nominal effects can also be scat-
tered within it.

Rather than exploring the auteur's stylistic competence, thematic unity, or personal vision, the signateurist detective can improvise, finding that, while being the consummate auteur, Welles's name can also be placed within a long tradition of twentieth-century artists who pose a serious challenge to the regime of authorship. For Welles's nominal connection to Smithee reminds us of another playful artist, Marcel Duchamp. Duchamp is generally remembered for his work on readymades, which were also deeply engaged with undermining the signature, in that a readymade is a nominal piece of art. It is nominated by Duchamp, following what he called pictorial nominalism, to become what the proper noun designates as art – even though the actual object is merely a product otherwise called by a common noun. Comparing Duchamp's work to Allen Smithee's, Jonathan E. Eburne suggests, "With the readymade, Duchamp, like Smithee, did not 'invent' or 'create' so much as devised ways of exhibiting or reproducing other objects, even other works of art, under aliases designed to complicate the all-too-automatic process of using art 'as a proper name.'"[131] Like an ordinary auctor's product, the readymades present a way out of assigning authority to the author. That is why Duchamp may be seen as the first in a long line of thinkers who used the snapshot effect to undercut authorship. In a 1961 lecture on readymades, Duchamp said that "the choice of these 'readymades' was never dictated by aesthetic delectation," emphasizing a "total absence of good or bad taste."[132] Intriguingly, while disowning *The Stranger* in an interview with Bazin, Bitsch, and Domarchi, Welles appears to echo Duchamp, claiming he didn't know "if [the film] is good or bad."[133]

With that connection, we might return to the question Bazin posed at the end of his critique of auteurism – *Auteur*, yes, but what *of*? In the case of *The Stranger*, Welles is the "auteur" of what can be seen as a virtual readymade. Indeed, there is more than one way to interpret Welles's verbal signature that opened up all his radio shows, "This is Orson Welles." Welles is the name of deep, original genius, but it may also connote its opposite, a trickster or a duplicate. Thus, we might turn the Wellesian signature inside out. In relation to the readymade, it is also not entirely coincidental to think of *The Stranger* as a copy made in 1946, at the height of studio Hollywood's powers, as that is also the year that xerography is invented. That year, 1946, was the year that inaugurated "the world as simulacrum, or copy," because "costly Photostats were eliminated and it became a matter of relative ease to duplicate all manner of documents, be they legal, economic, or creative."[134] *The Stranger* is that kind of copy, a generic thriller that is perhaps too perfect an imitation. Rather than an auteurist failure, it can be seen as a sort of joke. It shows that, even in the rigidly standardized studio system, a standard film can unexpectedly offer a counterregime to authorship and therefore subvert the rules of genre filmmaking right there on the surface. Such "superficial" moments of subversion make sense in the immediate postwar era, when the threat of declining audiences and prestige loomed for Hollywood. As we will see in the next chapter, anxieties about the studio system's very existence manifested even more overtly in the next decade in disruptive moments that appeared to sado-masochistically relish the end of cinema as we know it.

The public will no longer buy tickets at the theater, except to see the very highest form of entertainment, far superior to what they can see on television free. For this type of entertainment they will pay an admission price. For anything less they will not.

Y. FRANK FREEMAN, Select Committee
on Small Business, U.S. Senate

There is something contagious and morbid about all this shrinking.

BOSLEY CROWTHER, *"The Incredible Shrinking Man"*

FOUR

Apocalyptic Antennae

1954 and the End of Storytelling

A TEST OF THE EMERGENCY BROADCAST SYSTEM

By direction of the President of the United States, all broadcasting is interrupted for a few moments to declare the city of Los Angeles under martial law. Inside the briefing room, amid now-quieted news reporters, civilian and military leaders gather to inform the public about "the most serious crisis this city has ever faced." A tight medium shot of General Robert O'Brien (Onslow Stevens), looking straight into the camera and addressing the public directly, follows. His grim visage spells doom as he declares that curfew begins at 1800 hours, at which time any person seen lingering outdoors might be arrested by the military police. Then he begins to explain the reasons for such drastic measures, and the scene cuts to a series of shots of men and women gathering around television sets and radios. When the apocalyptic threat of gigantic mutant ants – originally discovered in the New Mexico desert but now nesting "somewhere in the storm drains beneath the streets of Los Angeles" – is televised, viewers stand aghast, gazing feebly at the small screen in bars, diners, and department store windows (Figure 4.1). In the background, military trucks rumble through the city streets, although their presence seems to provide no comfort to the assembling crowds, who only watch the televisual transmission in terror.

This alarming moment from Gordon Douglas's *Them!*, where an existential threat from an unfamiliar and seemingly invincible enemy is finally and fully acknowledged, is quite typical of science fiction films of the 1950s, when the political and cultural climate of the Cold War

4.1. *Them!* (dir. Gordon Douglas, 1954).

made America appear to be in a perpetual state of emergency. And yet, there is something inexplicably terrifying about it. For me this terror has little to do with the threat of the gigantic ants themselves. Rather, it is the fact that, at this catastrophic moment, television offers little hope or comfort. What I find most intriguing is that General O'Brien's outsized face appears ominous on the tiny television frame, which magnifies the sense of impending catastrophe. What is supposed to be a reassuring site for communal gathering during times of social crisis itself turns into a source of scopic dread.

Like the ferocious prehistoric monster that crushes everything in its way in Eugène Lourié's *The Beast from 20,000 Fathoms* (1953) or the extraterrestrial parasites that colonize people's bodies and intend to re-place the entire human race in Don Siegel's *Invasion of the Body Snatchers* (1956), the discovery of gigantic ants about to destroy Los Angeles in Douglas's film plays up fears generated by the Cold War. Film histori-ans have generally maintained that the wave of sci-fi films in the 1950s was a direct result of Cold War paranoia. Until then confined mostly to serials like *Buck Rogers* (1939), *The Crimson Ghost* (1946), and *Bruce Gentry* (1949), science fiction developed and multiplied rapidly to address all sorts of existential anxieties, especially after the Soviet Union successfully tested an atomic bomb in 1949. While other subgenres of sci-fi were not uncommon, following the release of Howard Hawks's *The Thing from Another World* (1951), the epidemic of fifties sci-fi films portrayed a pervasive fear of imminent invasion. Indeed, 1951 is the moment Mark Jancovich identifies as "the year the aliens arrived," and over the course of the decade, mutants, monsters, and Martians all became displaced figures for the national fear of the Other.[1] It is not surprising that during the Cold War, "'invasion' became a key metaphor, central to understanding larger social processes in postwar America."[2] Indeed, the notion of invasion encompassed numerous (and sometimes contradictory) threats, perceived and real – most immediately from Communism, nuclear warfare, McCarthyist witch-hunts, rising crime and juvenile delinquency, and "mad" science, but also more subtly from the "feminization" of civilization, secularism, rock 'n' roll, racial tensions, conformity, and repressed desire. And what other genre could better represent this cultural panic than science fiction? What other genre could portray what Peter Biskind calls "the hysteria behind the picture window" of the fifties?[3] After all, as Sean Redmond argues, "Above any comparable genre, science fiction seems to be able to represent and reproduce the individual and collective fears, paranoias and cultural and political transformations that exist in society."[4] That might be particularly true for this decade, which became increasingly skeptical of science itself as a conduit for reason and progress.[5] Science fiction of this era focused primarily on the potential of humanity plunging into a Dark Age and remained "haunted by dystopian sentiments and apocalyptic scenarios."[6] Therefore, it became the most effective vehicle for portraying invasions on the horizon.

Along those lines, we might say that *Them!* conflates multiple fears. As David Seed suggests, the film "picks up the double metaphor of ants-as-monsters and ants-as-people to dramatise the unpredictability of the Bomb and fears of Communist attack."[7] The ants are shown to be unfeeling aliens seeking to destroy the city of Los Angeles and beyond. But they are not just cinematic apparitions of the Red Menace or nuclear

warfare. *Them!* links "nature, ants, women, and Russians, [and] imagines
Reds as monsters from the id."[8] Moreover, the mutant ants represent the
worst fear of the era, articulated by one of the journalists before the official press announcement: "Has the Cold War gotten hot?" That is to say,
the ants' arrival in Los Angeles is seen in terms of an imminent threat of
extinction. Finally, because the ants' mutation is initiated by bomb testing, they serve as a reminder that human beings are capable of their own
destruction, embodying what Cyndy Hendershot calls "fears of the human race's evolutionary eclipse."[9] In that sense, *Them!* fits nicely within
the narrative of sci-fi's emergence during the Cold War, allegorizing the
threat of a superior power seeking territorial domination, which results
in collective paranoia and a state of crisis.

But there is another kind of fear, one that has gone curiously unnoticed in discussions of Hollywood's turn to science fiction at this time
and that elucidates the cinephiliac moment outlined at the beginning of
this chapter: fifties sci-fi films seem to conflate the nation's fear of invasion by a superior power with "primitive" cinema's anxieties about extinction in the face of "advanced" television. The fifties was a tumultuous
time for Hollywood studios. They started the decade fearing that their
best years were behind them. The war years had been good for box office
receipts, and the industry reached unprecedented heights in 1946, before
its rapid descent in the latter half of that decade. It is estimated that the
national rate of movie-going fell approximately 10 percent each year for
ten years after 1947. During that period, "annual box office receipts declined from $1.692 billion to $1.298 billion, or about 23 percent."[10] Many
factors – suburbanization, loss of overseas markets, legal setbacks that
severed the studios from their theater chains, panic over the blacklist,
among others – were responsible for the sharp decline in movie atten-
dance. However, the studios settled on television as their chief existential
threat and primary scapegoat. Jack Warner even went so far as to declare
that a T V set would never appear in the studio's films. Indeed, in Warner
Bros.' *The Beast from 20,000 Fathoms*, released the year that *T V Guide* de-
buted, emergency alerts are communicated only through radio bulletins.
Similarly, in William A. Wellman's *The Next Voice You Hear* (1950), even
God's sermons can only be tuned in on the radio, although the use of T V
sets both in and outside of homes was becoming quite prevalent at this

time.[11] In fact, although it had appeared as a scientific curiosity when it was introduced by RCA at the 1939 New York World's Fair, Lynn Spigel notes that "between 1948 and 1955, television was installed in nearly two-thirds of the nation's homes."[12] That kind of predominance proved hard to ignore, even for the hard-nosed Jack Warner. So his stipulation about not showing television on the big screen is disregarded in an unusual way by the middle of the decade. In *Them!*, also released by Warner Bros., the warning about gigantic mutant ants on the loose in Los Angeles, a city virtually synonymous with Hollywood, is broadcast over television. However, at that moment, the image of television itself appears threatening, as the traditionally dispassionate and reassuring figure of the news reporter looms large and menacing. Instead of consoling scopic anxieties, the undersized, claustrophobic screen heightens the impression of doom. Moreover, a different kind of peril is echoed in the emergency broadcast. The voice announcing the invasion urges its viewers to stay in their homes, presumably with their eyes glued to their TV sets. And it is this retreat of viewers to their homes, likely in the suburbs, that Hollywood considered the most dangerous menace to itself during the fifties.

A striking feature of 1950s Hollywood is the cinema's profound underlying anxiety about its own demise. Under threat from its newest media rival, the industry's fears of extinction reverberate across fifties films, appearing in films noirs like Billy Wilder's *Sunset Boulevard* (1950), epic spectacles like Cecil B. DeMille's *The Ten Commandments* (1956), even comedies like Wilder's *The Seven Year Itch* (1955) and dramas like Elia Kazan's *A Face in the Crowd* (1957). But the most evocative and deeply ambivalent expressions of the studio system's looming downfall appear in the decade's sci-fi films, which are saturated with tales of collective annihilation at the hands of a superior technology emanating from the Beyond: the future, an alien planet, or a foreign adversary. And television fits that bill perfectly. It is regarded, sometimes rather hysterically, as a monstrous technological force, capable of invading and soon surpassing America's principal culture industry.[13]

In fact, starting in the late 1940s, with the postwar boom fully underway, television is often marketed in sci-fi terms. It is promoted as a superior entertainment technology that functions as a harbinger of futuristic lifestyles while guarding against the ills of the city as well as the troubles of the world. An ad for DuMont, for instance, affirms television as "a force of unparalleled power." In the ad, a family watching TV in their living room is directly beamed into outer space. "The world," the copy claims, "stands on the threshold of an astonishing age," but this advanced era is also kept at a safe distance, as television becomes an ultramodern device that provides a window on the world from the comfort and security of one's own home. Another ad, for General Electric, proclaims "Tomorrow is Here!" to sell its redesigned Space Age TV units. And in 1955, Zenith introduces Flash-Matic, the first wireless remote control, marketed as "a flash of magic light from across the room." Thus, as TV's popularity grows, so does its capacity to market itself as the medium of the future, thus attempting to redefine the spatial terrain of American popular culture. It is no wonder then that Hollywood construes the advance of the cool medium in the age of the Cold War as an alien attack. As Thomas Doherty points out, the metaphor of invasion seems apt, at a time when "aerial antennae sprout like noxious weeds from apartment rooftops and suburban homes while video-born catchphrases spread like viruses through the vocabulary of children."[14] Drawing on cinephiliac moments from standard sci-fi films, in this chapter I investigate how Hollywood responds to this invasion and represents its own eschatological anxieties during the 1950s. How does it engage in technophobia onscreen while at the same time working with television networks behind the scenes to create a new entertainment order? How does it tell and retell tales about itself, at a time when its gradual collapse is already underway? How does a seemingly rational industry represent its irrationally excessive antagonism toward its media rival?

THE INCREDIBLE SHRINKING SCREEN

Imagine a world that is ostensibly bursting with optimism and belief in technological progress but is in fact ambivalent about its highly mechanized way of life. Where unfettered capitalism rules, and commercial advertising dominates the landscape. Where cities and suburbs are connected by airplanes and helicopters that transport people from one place to another at lightning speed. Where the mastery of electric energy has led to the potential for building new continents and controlling the weather. This is a world too that has discovered new diseases, biological warfare, and atomic bombs. Where one can learn about wars and massacres around the world, watch something playing at the theater, or indulge in home-shopping through a televisual device that connects the family to the outside world from the comfort of one's living room.

This is the fantastical world of Albert Robida's mid-twentieth century. Set in the 1950s, his illustrated sci-fi fantasy trilogy, written in the 1880s, paints a panorama of daily life in Paris with remarkable accuracy.[15] Especially interesting is his projection of technology's role in overhauling transportation and (tele)communication. A contemporary of Jules Verne, Robida could not entirely escape nineteenth-century sci-fi's technological fetishism. However, his work's primary focus is on "the social impact of coming technologies, not simply the wonders of the hardware."[16] Of particular note is his illustration of the ubiquity of a "distant vision" device in homes and its effect on families in the 1950s. Robida calls this gadget a *téléphonoscope*, which "consists of a simple crystal screen, flush with the wall or set up as a mirror above a fireplace."[17] His sketches illustrate the device's capacity not only to entertain but also to inform, educate, facilitate shopping, and enable people to metaphorically reach out and touch each other. In the late nineteenth century, even before the invention of cinema, televisual fantasies were not uncommon, and Robida accurately forecasts that a *téléphonoscope*, or television, would become widely available in the 1950s.

But where Robida misses the projection is in the size of the TV screen and what that implies about its rivalry with cinema. His sketches consistently suggest a very large screen, functioning like a home theater and thereby virtually annulling the cinematic medium altogether. Ironically, it resembles the screen we see in Norma Desmond's home in *Sunset Boulevard,* although that large screen has the opposite objective. Norma's Gothic abode lionizes the silver screen and trivializes the television screen – as Paul Young argues, "It's hardly coincidental that Norma's home screen circa 1950 is not a TV but a movie screen" – even as it nostalgizes a bygone era.[18] As several commentators have suggested, her wide screen has more than a hint of paranoia about the invasion of television. But while Norma herself tries to hold on to the old glory days and resist change, claiming "I am big. It's the pictures that got small,"

Hollywood was quite aware that they would have to deal with television, which may have been small in size but was becoming a monstrous crisis. Indeed, one can imagine how television in the 1950s came to resemble, at least in the darkest imaginations of studio bosses, gigantic mutant ants, prehistoric monsters, and colossal fifty-foot women (more on the gendered dynamics of this fear later).

How did television grow into such an outsized, outrageous dilemma for the studios? After all, the miniature T V set, limited programming, as well as early broadcasting's sometimes erratic reception, lack of color, and typically poor audio quality, could barely compete with cinema's technological wizardry in the 1950s: anamorphic widescreen, 3-D, and stereo sound. Besides, the two entertainment media were not always destined to be foes. Hollywood studios had assumed that they would be involved in molding the fledgling "visual broadcasting" industry from its beginnings. When it was merely a theoretical possibility, the Motion Picture Producers and Distributors of America (MPPDA) prepared studies of television for the studios in the 1920s and 1930s. In 1939, when NBC began offering limited, experimental broadcasts to a few thousand households in the New York area – the first among these was the opening ceremonies of the New York World's Fair, where RCA introduced the T V set – they turned to Hollywood to provide legitimacy. In December 1939, NBC broadcast the most important event in American popular culture, the Atlanta premiere of *Gone with the Wind*. The budding television industry received a much-needed boost, primarily "by paying homage to the country's preeminent form of popular culture," the movies.[19] And although the T V business was mostly dormant during the war, "in late 1943 the studios began applying for station licenses and developing plans for production," in keen anticipation of commercial television becoming a viable, vibrant entertainment sibling during the postwar boom.[20]

But that early optimism came crashing down with the 1948 Paramount decree, which found the studios in violation of antitrust laws and required them to divest themselves of theater holdings. In many ways, the more lasting consequence of this ruling was that the studios could not expand into television. In 1948, the Federal Communications Commission (FCC) issued a six-month freeze on all applications for new T V stations to investigate whether the studios' entry into television might further abuse the antitrust decree. Paralleling a general public unease about the studios in the wake of the Paramount decision, the FCC freeze lasted for four years, effectively crippling the studios' ability to control and shape the new medium. As Douglas Gomery argues, the FCC freeze "guaranteed that the majors would not take a significant place in the ownership of U.S. television networks and stations" but the radio industry would.[21] Thus, the major studios had to retreat from the TV business in the late 1940s. In fact, it was during the early 1950s that the rivalry between cinema and television intensified, with the Hollywood studios seeing television as an invading force fully responsible for displacing cinema as the principal pop culture industry in the postwar period. More significantly, in the absence of studio pressures, television began defining itself very differently from cinema. What follows is the story of television's efforts at self-definition, which was the true cause of Hollywood's anxieties about its rival medium. As Janet Wasko has suggested, it would be too simplistic to accuse Hollywood of an old-fashioned reluctance "to anticipate and accept new technological innovations, from the introduction of sound to the home video 'revolution.'"[22] Or, as Paul Young astutely points out, it would be naive to assume that Hollywood's anxious response to the rise of a rival medium was purely hysterical technophobia; after all, its "videophobic fantasy films ... could not have been intended merely as anti-TV propaganda."[23] Indeed, the source of Hollywood's real fears was that television was formulating new modes and pleasures of spectatorship that would only be available on the small screen. In other words, television was writing the narrative of its own identity in terms of immediacy and liveness as opposed to Hollywood's classical past-ness. As we shall see later in this chapter, this is a narrative that cinema would covertly but consistently counteract on the big screen.

In 1955, NBC news director Gary Simpson articulated what television was coming to mean for most viewers: "Mr. Public views that television set in his home as a 20th Century electronic monster that can transport him to a ball game, to Washington D.C., to the atomic bomb blast in Nevada – and do it *now*. . . . The miracle of television is actually Man's ability to see at a distance while the event is happening."[24] In the first half of the fifties, television had in fact come to resemble an "electronic monster," capable of beaming the world into one's living room – usually live, raw, and unedited. The grainy, black-and-white images of early television began to create a narrative about the medium's rising significance in American culture. But this was not a smooth story, for the fortunes of the new medium were in as much flux as the culture that gave birth to it. The sign "Please stand by, we are experiencing technical difficulties" too often interrupted programming and remains a fine reminder of the daunting cultural climate during television's early years. Although it had taken "infant steps" in the previous decade, television came of age and experienced "adolescent growing pains" in the 1950s.[25] While there are many moments in early television's history that proved significant in solidifying viewers' impressions of this new electronic medium, the coverage of the Kefauver Crime Committee hearings, the atomic bomb explosions at Yucca Flat, and the showdown between Joseph R. Mc-Carthy and Edward R. Murrow were particularly crucial in defining its role – and defining it differently from cinema. That is, television was linking itself to providing information, in stark opposition to Hollywood's emphasis on storytelling.

Television was growing up in a "witch-hunt atmosphere," with its "adolescence traumatized by phobias."[26] That witch-hunt atmosphere wreaked havoc on cinema, and as we saw in the previous chapter, many in Hollywood had to find ways to work around it. Television, on the other hand, learned to telecast that witch-hunt atmosphere and its phobias for profit. In 1951, stations around the country began carrying live the antics of the Senate Special Committee to Investigate Crime in Interstate Commerce, and the nation seemed to be gripped by Kefauver Fever.[27] Although the HUAC hearings of 1947 investigating alleged Communist infiltration of Hollywood are remembered as having inaugurated sensational postwar inquiries by Congress, they were not carried live on television. That circus-like atmosphere was covered only by newsreel companies and radio networks. The anti-Communist hearings that enthralled televisual audiences would come into focus later, but the star of 1951 was Estes Kefauver, a Tennessee senator who called for an investigation of organized crime around the nation. Kefauver contended that the Mafia had infiltrated mainstream American society, using a front of respectability to become virtually indistinguishable from average citizens while conducting illegal activities. In the hearings, he tried to capitalize on the growing public fear that the Mafia presented an alien conspiratorial threat, much like Communism, to bring down America, and television was happy to oblige. Knowing that the hearings would be broadcast live, Kefauver called a colorful cast of criminals to testify in cities around the country. As the *New York Times*'s TV critic Jack Gould put it, "The poker-faced Erickson, the saucily arrogant Adonis, the shy Costello and the jocose Virginia Hill might have been hired from Hollywood Central Casting Bureau."[28] The characters may have been cinematic, but the rigors of live transmission did not allow the hearings to unfold in the classical linear fashion of Hollywood storytelling. Kefauver's star witness in New York, for instance, was Frank Costello, nicknamed the "Prime Minister of the Underworld," who did not plead the Fifth. But his lawyers refused to let his face be broadcast on live TV, although "nothing was said about keeping the lens off the rest of his person, so millions watched in fascination as his fingers diddled with papers or poured water into a glass."[29] The telecast proved to be "strangely hypnotic."[30] The focus was no longer on the larger criminal narrative. In its immediacy, there was a compelling magnetism in Costello's performance. In its authenticity, there was a mesmerizing quality that proved even more appealing than most dramatic or improvisational series on TV at that time.

Even Raymond Chandler could not resist the charms of the Kefauver hearings. "I don't know whether you have a television set," he raved in a letter to his friend James Sandoe in 1952, "or whether having one you could have seen films of the Kefauver committee hearings. I saw part of those held in Los Angeles and found them fascinating. Obviously nothing that a mystery writer could dream up could be more fantastic than what actually goes on in the hoodlum empire which infests this country."[31] Chandler's commentary underscores early television's appeal, because what he finds fascinating is watching the story of crime in the United States unfold live, raw, and uncut. Moreover, his lament that no mystery writer could imagine better crime narratives might also be extended to Hollywood – although Hollywood did try. In the early 1950s, many films noirs focused on matters of law and order, and their tales appeared to have been grabbed right out of the televisual headlines. However, films like Joseph M. Newman's *711 Ocean Drive* (1950), Robert

Parrish's *The Mob* (1951), and Joseph Kane's *Hoodlum Empire* (1952), all contemporaries of the Kefauver committee hearings, were minor films and could not even come close to competing with the popularity of the real thing. Television began to establish itself in terms of spontaneity and authenticity, something Hollywood, even with the semi-documentary style of film noir, could not duplicate. TV made Kefauver, a little-known senator on a seemingly obscure assignment around the country, into a celebrity. But with twenty million viewers reportedly spellbound by the Costello performance, television itself emerged as a star.

After 1951, politicians on the make actively sought out television coverage, giving the new medium the authority to agitate power structures in the nation's capital. But before television broadcast the McCarthy hearings that shook the nation, and shortly thereafter made McCarthy himself tremble, America witnessed another explosion on TV, and this one sent shock waves from coast to coast. Although we mostly associate television in the 1950s with images of domestic bliss at best and crass consumerism at worst, having arrived on the national scene during the atomic age, TV was also allied with the dark legacy of technological developments. As Lynn Spigel has demonstrated, at a time when the notion of "technology out of control" was being promoted by science fiction, television "was often likened to a monster that threatened to wreak havoc on the family."[32] NBC vice president John F. Royal even asserted, "Television is the atomic bomb of the culture."[33] In fact, the fates of atomic energy and television seemed so intertwined that the terrors of the atomic bomb tests were carried live on television. In the previous decade, before the medium became a household commodity, television had aided in the initial postwar nuclear weapons tests conducted in Operation Crossroads on the islands of Bikini Atoll in 1946. Writing that year, Kingdon S. Tyler described how television had assisted by allowing visual access to the test site. Cameras in an observation plane transmitted images to military personnel onboard the *USS Mount McKinley*, where they were able to monitor the fallout in real time, including the fact that "the palm trees of Bikini Atoll were still standing after the atomic bomb exploded."[34] But this was the trial phase of the relationship between TV and the bomb, before commercial television was widely available to bring the blasts into American homes. By the 1950s, such experiments were telecast as made-for-TV events, "emphasizing television's unprecedented ability to provide live, democratic, and safe access to the spectacle of the atomic blast."[35] And there was no doubt about the electronic medium's capacity to put on a show. If the era's sci-fi cinema was concerned with what Susan Sontag has called "the aesthetics of destruction," then television would try to outdo it with the spectacle of the real.[36]

In April 1952, television networks worked with the Atomic Energy Commission to broadcast live atomic bomb tests from Yucca Flat, Nevada. As Nancy E. Bernhard notes, "Four cameras filmed from eleven miles away, and two filmed from a mountaintop forty miles away."[37] The result was that thirty-five million people were transfixed by the detonation live, even though the actual images themselves were less than spectacular. "Viewers squinted," Doherty reports, "to discern a tiny white spot in a wall of pitch black, unaware that the white pinhole centered in the blackness resulted from an optical malfunction: the orthicon tube in the pickup camera had blacked out under the blinding light of the blast."[38] Still, those imprecise images on small screens marked a new stage for the young medium, even though *Variety* panned the transmission as "A-Bomb in TV Fluff Fizzles Fission Vision." In spite of its low-grade quality or perhaps because of it, television, born at the same time as the bomb, seemed to have the unique capacity to represent its awesome energy. Bernhard notes that at the time of the blast "motion pictures were also shot in case the blast interfered with the direct relay."[39] But those motion pictures looked like an afterthought or merely a back-up plan. This was the moment when television began to replace the theatrical newsreel and, more significantly, started establishing liveness as its crucial and incomparable essence.

At the same time, television was being pulled in the opposite direction as well. Although beaming the world live into homes remained popular in the ratings, TV networks were redirecting their efforts. Commerce was beginning to handily win the battle with public service broadcasting. In the absence of Hollywood's involvement during its formative years, as William Boddy has shown, the TV business was being modeled on the radio industry and defined "simultaneously as itself a consumer product for the home and as an audio-visual showroom for advertisers' consumer goods."[40] And advertisers were far more likely to support game shows, soap operas, and situation comedies on regular schedules, without any interruptions except for their own commercials. This was especially true when the networks' lucrative daytime entertainment programs, like CBS's *The Guiding Light* and NBC's *The Big Payoff*, led to their turning profits. Still, even the profit-minded networks could not resist the magnetism of a Cold War drama that unfolded live in the nation's capital, featuring a massive clash of media-savvy personalities from politics, the military, and finally television itself.

When in 1950 a freshman and hitherto undistinguished senator from Wisconsin accused President Harry Truman's State Department of harboring Communists, there were no television cameras to capture the speech. In fact, to this day, we do not have a clear record of whether the speaker claimed the number of Communists to be 205 or 57. Barely a month after his Wheeling speech, the term McCarthyism was coined, and its signateur rose to prominence in U.S. politics. His meteoric rise, like Kefauver's, was fueled by television, especially after 1952, when Joseph R. McCarthy assumed leadership of the Senate Permanent Subcommittee on Investigations, with a seemingly open-ended mandate to probe Communist influence in the United States. In 1953, he held a number of hearings into the Voice of America, although these were not widely broadcast on television. A year later, he launched a TV-friendly investigation into the U.S. Army. Although this intergovernmental scuffle might have been completely banal, the presence of live cameras made this into what Doherty calls "a long-running, character-driven, political-*cum*-televisual show."[41] Indeed, the Army-McCarthy hearings have become a seminal moment in TV history, not because of high ratings or "the inherent significance of the event but because television coverage itself determined the meaning of the event."[42] The investigation began routinely enough, first into a supposed spy network at the Fort Monmouth laboratory, then moved on to the promotion of an alleged left-leaning dentist named Irving Peress, and finally climaxed with the showstopper moment with U.S. Army counsel Joseph N. Welch.

During this time, McCarthy also fought a parallel battle with the news media, in particular with Edward R. Murrow, who emerged as the moral voice of the era and inaugurated television's role as the ethical watchdog of American democracy. Before Welch was able to call out McCarthy for his lack of decency, Murrow confronted the McCarthy persona and its role in the Cold War, forever linking the two men in "America's collective memory of itself in 1954: one sinner, one saint, eternally at odds with each other."[43] The March 9 program of *See it Now*, a newsmagazine on CBS, consisted mostly of clips from McCarthy's previous appearances, particularly from congressional hearings, where close-up shots of the senator's large, sweaty face, appearing even more grotesque on the era's tiny television screen, make him look menacing as he badgers, harangues, and taunts witnesses. Finally, Murrow appears for his concluding argument, that the external threat of Communism had been exploited by McCarthy to create an internal monster to stifle the exercise of free speech, which Murrow was single-handedly defending, live on national television. "Purely as a theatrical feat," Doherty argues, "Murrow's talk is an act of showstopping oratory."[44] It is more than that, too, because Murrow's assault on McCarthy functions also as an attack on McCarthyism. It does not just bring down a man – that is fully accomplished within a few months – but it also injects a healthy dose of ethics into live TV drama, making television capable of shaping history, not merely reporting it.

By June 9, 1954, then, the TV audience had been primed to be sympathetic to the calm and sagacious Welch when confronted by the combative McCarthy. This showdown occurred on the thirtieth day of the thirty-six-day Army-McCarthy hearings, which were deemed so significant by Chairman Mundt that he even allowed the networks to find sponsors to help put on the show. The hearings had almost become a television miniseries, although it must be noted that they were broadcast live only on ABC and DuMont, with nightly recaps by CBS and NBC. Due to the growing reach of television, as many as twenty million viewers were supposed to be watching the hearings at any given time. They reached their high point on June 9, when McCarthy brought up an unrelated, alleged Communist sympathizer, Fred Fisher, a lawyer at Welch's law firm of Hale and Dorr, in order to divert attention from Welch's request that Roy Cohn, McCarthy's chief counsel, submit the names of 130 alleged Communists in the Defense Department "before the sun goes down." After some back and forth between the two giants,

and after several of Welch's attempts at trying to salvage the young lawyer's reputation, Welch launched his memorable, and perhaps memo-
rized, attack: "Until this moment, senator, I think I never gauged your
cruelty or recklessness." As if that weren't enough, Welch went in for the
kill: "Have you no sense of decency, sir, at long last?" And then again, for
dramatic emphasis, "Have you left no sense of decency?" Although Mc-
Carthy tried to interject, Welch waved him off, asking the chairman to
call the next witness. Then, after a moment's silence, the crowd erupted
in wild applause – one suspects this might have cued, like the "applause"
sign going off during live tapings of sitcoms, similar approval around
television sets nationwide. Interestingly, the multiple television cameras
captured McCarthy caught off guard, as he leaned over to Cohn to ask
what happened. "What happened," Doherty argues, "was that television,
whose coverage of McCarthy's news conferences, direct addresses, and
senate hearings, had lent him legitimacy and stature, had now become
the stage for his downfall."[45] In some ways, the iconic exchange in 1954
wasn't just between McCarthy and Welch, or even McCarthy and Murrow, but also between McCarthy and television. And that battle was
handily won by television.

So, in 1954, the year that *Them!* was released, Hollywood found itself
on the verge of being supplanted by a rival entertainment medium as the
principal postwar culture industry. It was no longer possible to ignore
television, or dismiss it by disparagingly calling it "free television," or
assume its inferiority, as Y. Frank Freeman, an executive for Paramount,
does in the opening epigraph. It was also in the year 1954 that NBC and
CBS first turned profits, and it was clear that the studio system would
have to adapt to this new reality in order to survive. Amid alarm on the
backlots, the major studios began collaborating with the networks: Columbia Pictures began producing two TV series, *The Adventures of Rin
Tin Tin* for ABC and *Father Knows Best* for CBS; David O. Selznick made
his television debut with a two-hour documentary celebration of electricity known as *Light's Diamond Jubilee,* which brought such big stars to
the small screen as Lauren Bacall, Joseph Cotten, Dorothy Dandridge,
and Debbie Reynolds; and Walt Disney brought *Disneyland,* an anthology series that included animated cartoons, access to the construction
of the amusement park, and even abridged-for-TV versions of recent

Disney films like *Alice in Wonderland* (1951) to ABC. These forays into television were not only popular but also profitable. But there remained a lingering sense of the end of an era.

RETELLING HISTORY

Writing in the late 1950s to his friend John Hay Whitney, Hollywood mogul David O. Selznick lamented the waning of a glorious institution. "Our old stomping ground, what is laughingly known as the motion picture industry," Selznick argued, "is very mixed up and unhappy. Whatever the weakness of the old and rugged pioneers, who are all disappearing from the scene almost simultaneously – what a hardy race they were! – their successors are pygmies by comparison."[46] He was mourning not only the fall of particular giants of what was soon becoming old Hollywood but also the decline of the studio system itself, which for Selznick represented an epic mode of storytelling. As he confessed to Lloyd Shearer, the reason George Cukor was fired while making *Gone with the Wind* was because he "lacked the big feel, the scope, the breadth of the production."[47] It wasn't that Hollywood had stopped making big pictures. Indeed, it wasn't the size of the pictures that had shrunk but the size of Hollywood itself in American culture, and it was succeeded by the small screen, which the old giants like Selznick regarded as a "pygmy" by comparison. What had appeared as a challenge in the late 1940s had become a crisis in the early 1950s. By the time Selznick was writing to his former partner, he seemed to be wistfully marking the passing of an era and a tradition.

Selznick's nostalgia for an older art form vanishing before his eyes resembles Walter Benjamin's elegy for the art of storytelling. In 1936, on the eve of another crisis, Benjamin wrote "The Storyteller" as a requiem for storytelling. Ostensibly about the works of novelist Nikolai Leskov, the essay touches upon several familiar Benjaminian themes: the transmission of experience, the relationship between distance and proximity, the role of death, the communicability of wisdom, and so on. Most significantly, however, Benjamin is interested here in the rise of what we now call the information age, which is focused on the dissemination of verifiable data rather than the narration of wise counsel. Quoting

Hippolyte de Villemessant, the influential founder of *Le Figaro* who famously lamented that to his readers "'an attic fire in the Latin Quarter
is more important than a revolution in Madrid,'" Benjamin grieves for
the passing of a craftsmanlike mode of transmitting the past that is being supplanted by the modern world's interest in trivial information.[48]
Storytelling represents an older way of exchanging and passing on experience from one generation to another. Its disappearance signifies "an
increasing atrophy of experience itself."[49] In the wake of storytelling,
Benjamin finds a crisis of transmission, and in the departed figure of the
storyteller, he discovers a historian capable of transmitting "the lore of
the past, as it best reveals itself to natives of a place," that would otherwise be forgotten.[50]

In attempting to describe the contours of storytelling, Benjamin
begins by distinguishing the story from other forms of communication,
especially information or reportage. The story, he contends, is born in
an artisanal milieu, where local craftsmen, armed with indigenous tales,
mingle with traveling journeymen, who bring their own chronicles of
faraway places. Therefore, the story depends on the storyteller's capacity
to listen, remember, and recall the narrative. What is important in the
story is not verifiability; in fact, audiences expect that stories will blend
with the storyteller's own life and be retold anew, from one generation
to the next. Thus, the story is not subject to corroboration. It receives its
authority from the audience's awareness of its distance, both in terms
of time and space, from themselves. The story is not about the audience's immediate, everyday life, although it does not lack immediacy.
By weaving and spinning the story into his own life, the storyteller "in
turn makes it the experience of those who are listening to his tale."[51]
Thus, the story becomes a part of the audience's life, in a way that information never can. Even though it is about subjects close to the audience's life – the Latin Quarter, for instance, rather than the revolution
in Madrid – information cannot be merged with the audience's lives. As
McCole argues, "modern forms of communication broadcast discrete
items of information, but the demands of 'freshness, brevity,' and prompt
consumption work against their assimilation."[52] Because it is subject to
verification, information provides merely a series of facts, whose "value
... does not survive the moment in which it was new."[53] In surrendering

itself to the present, information can convey that which is only relevant for the moment. Therefore, unlike the story, which is told and retold over the centuries – after all, "storytelling is always the art of repeating stories" – information cannot transmit the past and dies shortly after it is communicated.[54]

The story, on the other hand, lives on because it "does not expend itself. It preserves and concentrates its strength and is capable of releasing it even after a long time."[55] This is because the story is assembled differently from information. Reportage is based on the facility of exposition, explication, and explanation. Because it is presented for immediate consumption, information comes in digestible form. In fact, what Benjamin resents about modern communication is that "no event any longer comes to us without already being shot through with explanation."[56] The story, however, cannot be explained away in a single telling, since it is open to multiple interpretations. Thus, it "achieves an amplitude that information lacks."[57] A little later in the essay, Benjamin explores how a story attains that amplitude from the way it is compiled. Since it originates in the oral tradition, the story consists of a "slow piling one on top of the other of thin, transparent layers which constitutes the most appropriate picture of the way in which the perfect narrative is revealed through the layers of a variety of retellings."[58] In other words, the story is not rushed, and it cannot be abbreviated. Since it is crafted by generations of storytellers, all adding their own nuances, the story accumulates multiple layers that can be unfurled by each member of the audience endlessly. To use Benjamin's analogy of the seeds of grain in the pyramids, the story retains its "germinative power" and thus remains inexhaustible.[59]

Benjamin's fascination is not only with the story but also with the pursuit of storytelling. As Philip Simay notes, "What interests him is the pragmatics of narrative communication: the fact of telling stories, not the stories in themselves."[60] For the story, which stems from the oral tradition, is not just a product. It is, in fact, a social activity and, for Benjamin, an alternative way of narrating history. The storyteller differs from the traditional historian in that he is a chronicler of the past. "The historian," Benjamin argues, "is bound to explain in one way or another the happenings with which he deals."[61] But the storyteller is not concerned with explanations. His craft deals with chronicling how individual moments "are embedded in the great inscrutable course of the world."[62] This enables his audience to contemplate the open-ended nature of the chronicles. Because storytelling is not meant only to inform or even to entertain. Since it is handed down from one generation to the next, storytelling conveys the wisdom of the ages. That may "in one case, consist in a moral; in another, in some practical advice; in a third, in a proverb or maxim."[63] The purpose of storytelling is to offer its audience some form of counsel. But that counsel is not utilitarian; it is "less an answer to a question than a proposal concerning the continuation of a story which is just unfolding."[64] So it does not offer particular solutions to specific problems. Rather, storytelling implies a "critical recovery of the past," so that the story becomes a guide rather than an explanation or a resolution.[65]

The storyteller, then, appears as the voice of generations past, not as a single individual or author but a palimpsest of compound layers, experiences, and chronicles. Storytelling becomes "the means by which an individual relates to collective experience."[66] And it is in that sense that storytelling might be similar to genre-driven Hollywood cinema, which also emphasized telling and retelling tales. As David S. Ferris argues, "like cinema, storytelling also offers a collective experience. So too did the epic before such experience declined with the rise of the novel and, later, with the ascendancy of the newspaper."[67] To this list, we could certainly add television, which is also a private form of consumption that causes further decline in the collective "communicability of experience."[68] In fact, television might be said to only accelerate the crisis of transmission that Benjamin noticed in the 1930s, when TV was mostly a theoretical proposition. What is even more interesting is that in the 1950s, when Hollywood moguls like Selznick were feeling nostalgic about what then seemed like the dying medium of cinema, television was often being championed as the harbinger of a new information era, not as a medium for continuing cinema's narrative tradition. NBC's lead programmer and developer of such shows as *Today* and *The Tonight Show,* Pat Weaver, claimed that the network's "grand design" was "to get the people to watch the realism and to get caught by it, but the end would be that we would inform them, enrich then, enlighten them, to liberate them from tribal primitive belief patterns."[69] It is not hard to see that Weaver is aligning television with the transmission of current information – liveness, as we saw in the previous section, became television's calling card – and "tribal primitive belief patterns" or old stories with cinema. Cultural critic Gilbert Seldes was even more explicit in defending live TV and suggesting that the essence of television was in its communication of the present. The television audience, he argued, can "feel that what they see and hear is happening in the present and therefore more real than anything taken and cut and dried which has the feel of the past."[70]

It is precisely this shunning of the past that Benjamin had anticipated with the rise of new communication technologies when he agonized over the lost art of storytelling. In "Experience and Poverty," he asked, "Who still meets people who really know how to tell a story?"[71] Twenty years later, Hollywood studio bosses were ruefully asking a similar question. The question was, of course, highly self-indulgent, if not downright irrational, because the studios did not stop telling stories or making movies. Moreover, they began making inroads into network schedules. The move toward television began as an eccentric gesture, when in 1955, under financial pressure, Howard Hughes sold RKO's film library to a tire manufacturing company that owned an independent TV station for $25 million. But the TV show *Million Dollar Movie,* launched by the New York area station WOR, which telecast films from the RKO library (and others), became hugely popular, and RKO's sale prompted other major studios to begin releasing feature films to television, thus radically revising the divide between the two media. In fact, Douglas Gomery has called the availability of movies on the small screen the "most significant change in the way Americans viewed films during the latter half of the twentieth century."[72] By 1959, collaborating with television had become so lucrative that the electronic medium's old nemesis Jack Warner himself was arguing in favor of television. Many of the films shown on television emerged out of old studio vaults, now available for viewing after many years of dormancy. Thus, the new electronic medium was far from shunning the past. And storytelling in Hollywood was far from dead.

What, then, was the cause of so much fear and paranoia during the mid-1950s? The next section represents an attempt to tell that story – of the deep-seated anxieties of an empire feeling itself on the verge of ruin. Following the storyteller-historian, it narrates the battle between cinema and television, represented inadvertently yet poignantly in the era's sci-fi films, which recount time and again an epic struggle with a technologically superior enemy. Susan Sontag has argued that, even when they do not explicitly refer to the bomb, "science fiction films bear witness to this trauma, and, in a way, attempt to exorcise it."[73] Similarly, although most of the films analyzed below do not overtly address the fear of emerging media, we can see them, in unexpected cinephiliac moments, bearing witness to this terror, fictionalizing it, and, in many cases, profiting from those tales of trauma. In the story that follows, Hollywood presents itself as the old, sagacious storyteller, in contest with its imprudent media rival, which offers nothing more than cold, indifferent information and seems poised to supplant the dynamics of traditional storytelling. It envisions the death of the studio system via stories of individual or collective annihilation. In representing itself as the endangered species, Hollywood becomes allied with all that is wholesome, masculine, and American – and under threat from the alien Other. This alignment seems to work for Hollywood in two ways: on one hand, it is able to redefine television as the "foreign" medium of entertainment; on the other, it attempts to exorcise accusations, made recently and often on TV, that cinema is too closely associated with anti-American sentiments and representations. Even after the studios and networks begin working in collaboration, television remains the antagonist in Hollywood's cinematic representations of the media rivalry. For the battle was not merely over ratings or revenues or box-office receipts but over the very definition of cinema. What Hollywood wanted was not just economic superiority but also ontological supremacy. If, by privileging immediacy and information, television has written its own narrative across the cultural landscape of the fifties, cinema tries to rewrite that story on the big screen. It is noteworthy that the story of their enmity changes over time. True to the role of the sagacious storyteller, in the latter half of the decade, Hollywood begins contemplating lessons learned about living in a post-invasion media universe.

ONCE UPON A TIME IN HOLLYWOOD

The story begins with the discovery of an extraterrestrial monster that feeds on human blood. Near a remote research station at the north pole,

4.2. *The Thing from Another World* (dir. Howard Hawks, 1951).

USAF pilot Captain Patrick Hendry (Kenneth Tobey), Dr. Carrington (Robert Cornthwaite), and their crew find and inadvertently destroy what appears to be an alien flying saucer. At that time, their Geiger counter signals the presence of a large creature in "the shape of a man" buried in the ice. It is cut out of the ice and flown to the research station for observation, although a naive squad member accidently allows it to thaw. As one might expect, the Thing escapes and goes on a rampage, attacking its guard, killing two dogs, and draining a couple of the scientists, whose blood it uses to reproduce. Although it looks humanoid, the Thing is an advanced form of plant life, "an intellectual carrot," that can only be overpowered with bolts of high voltage electricity. After certain disagreement between the airman and the scientist, with the former electing to use force and the latter desiring to preserve and communicate with it, the creature's terrors become impossible to ignore or control. Eventually, the Thing is electrocuted (Figure 4.2).

This tale is narrated at the end of Howard Hawks's *The Thing from Another World* by Scotty (Douglas Spencer), a reporter and former war correspondent, who has followed the crew to the Arctic in search of a story. Since there are no television cameras, his disembodied voice relates the story of an epic battle into a microphone for the rest of the country to hear. His climactic broadcast begins on a note of decisive victory: "One of the world's greatest battles was fought and won today by the human race," Scotty narrates, recounting how "at the top of the world, a handful of American soldiers and civilians met [and defeated] the first invasion from another planet." But perhaps this tale, which was a significant Hawksian addition to John W. Campbell's story, is prematurely optimistic. Even though the lumbering giant resembling Frankenstein's monster does not look as intimidating, its discovery is merely the beginning of invasions, which, over the course of the fifties, will become more severe and come close to annihilating civilization as we know it. Noting the explosion of hostile alien sci-fi in the 1950s, Melvin E. Matthews argues that while Captain Hendry, whose name echoes the radical revolutionary, saves America this time by being able "to keep the threat of the Thing confined to a solitary Arctic base," others will not be so lucky when future gigantic monsters begin attacking the mainland.[74] Even Scotty seems to intuitively know this, thus urging his audience at the end to "keep watching the skies" for potential threats, almost in the same way that Hollywood would like its audiences to stay tuned for future versions of such tales of annihilation.

What is intriguing about *The Thing* is that it serves as a virtual activation of cinematic representations of the raging battle between mechanical and electronic media. The release of Hawks's film, as noted earlier, is the moment Mark Jancovich marks as "the year the aliens arrived," but it also denotes the beginning of Hollywood's cinematic response to an expanding broadcast culture, particularly in sci-fi films, where the alien conveniently doubles for the new televisual monster. Although most of them can hardly allow the depiction of an actual TV set, their filmic universe is bursting with the irrational dread, paranoia, and outrage generated by an alien force that threatens to destroy cinema as we know it. Of course, there are other types of fifties films, like Jack Arnold's noir *The Glass Web* (1953) or Elia Kazan's drama *A Face in the Crowd* (1957), that take on and present cinema's contempt for television more directly. But sci-fi films of the era provide a more complex portrayal of Hollywood's view of its media Other, which is not as threatening yet in *The Thing*. Hawks's extraterrestrial monster does not appear too frightening, and he does not inflict much damage. As Michael Pinsky argues, "As invasions go, the Thing's assault on Earth is pretty feeble."[75] Perhaps at the start of the decade it is still possible at RKO – RKO is the studio that had earlier attempted to beat back larger menaces by subjugating the monstrous gorilla in *King Kong* (Merian C. Cooper and Ernest Schoedsack, 1933), a film that would be profitably re-released a year later, even as Howard Hughes is already running it into the ground – to fantasize about overpowering the looming threat of television, to virtually kill the electronic medium with bolts of electricity. But as the small screen menace swells, the sci-fi films grow darker and more pessimistic, and the aliens become gigantic. Just as television was spreading throughout the country, and appeasement or containment were not viable options, vigilance, which is what the storyteller Scotty advocates at the end of *The Thing*, is no longer enough.

That is why when another monster, in Eugène Lourié's *The Beast from 20,000 Fathoms*, is detected, it cannot be restricted to the Arctic, where it has been brought to life by a nuclear detonation. *Beast* begins in the vein of Hawks's film, but this fiend is not as benign as the Thing, who was played by James Arness, more popularly known as Marshal Matt Dillon, the defender of law and order on the Western frontier in CBS's *Gunsmoke*. This thing is a gigantic rhedosaurus, brought to life by the heat of a nuclear blast after one hundred million years in hibernation. Even before the rhedosaurus comes alive and threatens civilization (and cinema itself), the film seems to hint at media rivalry. It opens with a team of military scientists preparing for Operation Experiment, and a voiceover narrates the preparations being made at the secret test site. After the countdown, the nuclear blast occurs as scheduled. Interestingly, the film switches from conventional shots of men in winter gear standing on a snow-capped set, likely on the backlot of Warner Bros. studio, to stock footage of the atomic blast. The wide-angle shots of an actual mushroom cloud, followed by those of tectonic shifts in the Arctic tundra, provide precisely the thrill that television did not deliver a year earlier, when, as mentioned before, the planned live broadcast of atomic blasts at Yucca Flat fizzled into merely a blip on the small screen. Although not live, *Beast* is able to transmit on the silver screen the atomic blast in its full splendor, thus showcasing what critic Charles A. Siepmann had called Hollywood's intrinsic advantage, "the inherent attractiveness of moving pictures on a full-sized screen."[76] The celluloid mushroom is indeed far superior to the miniature version.

Still, there is no way to defer the fear of the small screen, which rears its head right after the blast. In a spectacular cinephiliac moment, back at the research station, a crew member notices a bug on a small screen, while another voices the anxiety: "There's something strange on the radar screen." At first, it is considered a "foreign object," then there are doubts about its existence, followed by false reassurance that "maybe the shock tossed something in front of the antenna." Soon enough they all realize that it is a prehistoric monster, making its way south by following the Arctic current to New York. Although it is a prehistoric monster, awakened from the past, the rhedosaurus is very much a creature of the future. That is to say, the beast is likened to the atomic energy that gives birth to it, and the angst it causes is very similar to deep concerns about nuclear technology as well as, more subtly, about television, which became the entertainment medium of the atomic age.

In the postwar era, conflation of past and future anxieties was not uncommon. William L. Laurence's account of the dropping of atomic bombs on Hiroshima and Nagasaki, for instance, combines such anxieties by referring to the mushroom cloud as "a monstrous prehistoric creature."[77] This is because, while nuclear knowledge held out the potential for technological evolution, it also gave rise to fears of devolution through complete annihilation, something that sci-fi films portray time and again. "The dropping of the atomic bomb in 1945," Isaac Azimov argued, "made science fiction respectable."[78] But while science fiction may have gained in reputation, the standing of science itself came into question at this time. Early wholesale enthusiasm about atomic energy waned, replaced in the 1950s with doubts about the promise of technological progress. Mark Jancovich pushes this notion further, arguing that fifties sci-fi texts reflect American culture's "sense of ambivalence" about science, which "may save us at times, but it also creates a world which we can no longer recognise, a world in which giant ants or man-eating plants threaten to overwhelm us."[79] Thus, science itself came to be seen as regressive, or worse, destructive. Interestingly, similar doubts were being voiced about another technological advance, television. Writing in the same year as *Beast* was released, Fredric Wertham criticized threats posed by the popular media environment. Following Wertham's lead, television was tied by some critics directly to the bomb, deeming it "as serious as an invasion of the enemy in war time, with as far-reaching consequences as the atom bomb."[80] Thus, television as an embodiment of nuclear technology was beginning to be considered destructive, threatening to make humans virtually like dinosaurs. This is a fear that Hollywood hysterically reconstructed in its own struggle for survival against the new medium. So Lourié's *Beast* exploits these overlapping anxieties, in an effort to redefine the rival medium as something alien, destructive, and set on unsettling the social order.

When the beast arrives in New York, it seems to confirm the worst fears of physicist Tom Nesbitt (Paul Hubschmid as Paul Christian) about advanced technology. At the nuclear test site, Nesbitt had wondered aloud about atomic energy's potentially apocalyptic consequences, about inadvertently writing "the last chapter" of human history. As the creature storms through the city, destroying everything in its wake, his worries materialize in a nightmarish trail of destruction. The place is gripped by pandemonium, as residents run helter-skelter and find that there is no escaping this monster. Moreover, as Cyndy Hendershot notes, the creature "causes them to devolve, as panic reduces motivation to pure instinct."[81] When the beast descends on the city, making its way from block to block, there is no sense of mutual cooperation. A blind man is trampled by a crowd, and there is no one who stops to help. People flee randomly, and the civil defense authorities trying to bring down the beast using firepower appear mostly feckless. The invasion seems analogous to an actual atomic bomb attack. As the National Guard is called in, civilians go underground to seek shelter; even "Times Square, the heart of New York, has stopped beating." If New York is the beast's breeding ground, then all that New Yorkers can do is wait until their city is pummeled to resemble a prehistoric site. The beast, a material representation of technological expansion, has brought about a dystopian future. It is not too delicate a reminder to fifties audiences about the flaws of futuristic technologies that promise to alleviate stress but threaten to destroy life as we know it.

More significantly, as the military and scientific communities soon discover, the beast is a "giant germ carrier of a horrible, virulent disease" that contaminates everything in its path. As the soldiers march in formation through deserted streets, they begin collapsing as soon as they come in contact with the beast's blood, which was spilled when it was earlier shot by bazookas. The contaminated particles of blood in the air clearly resemble nuclear fallout or radiation sickness. The disease-ridden beast also embodies contemporary notions of Communism, which was commonly conceived as a dangerous infection. During the 1952 presidential campaign, for instance, Adlai Stevenson is said to have called it "a disease which may have killed more people in this world than cancer, tuberculosis, and heart disease combined." Like the supposedly insidious epidemic of Communism, the beast has the potential to infect everyone who comes in contact with it. But the contaminated beast also embodies another kind of disease, one that could reach into people's homes and make them sick. This new sickness, also the result of advanced technologies, was the disease of television. As Lynn Spigel observes, "Metaphors of disease were continually used to discuss television's unwelcome presence in domestic life."[82] Critics sounded the alarm about psychological as well as physical problems caused by television, like poor hygiene or inappropriate social behavior. Hollywood films were more than willing to play up these maladies in their overt and covert representations of TV. An earlier science fantasy film, Clifford Sanforth's *Murder by Television* (1935), intimates that televisual waves could be used literally for murder; that year's *The Glass Web* suggests that television might lead to blackmail and homicide. But fifties sci-fi films were more outrageous, choosing instead to align television with the destructive effects of Communism and radiation. In *Beast* the new medium is both brutal and harmful. It is also un-American.

That is why the film ends on the striking image of the smoldering remains of Coney Island. Once it is discovered that the rhedosaurus is a disease-carrying monster, it becomes impossible to destroy it using conventional weapons for fear of spreading the contagion while burning it

4.3. *The Beast from 20,000 Fathoms* (dir. Eugène Lourié, 1953).

or blowing it up. The only way to obliterate it without leaving any trace is to inject a radioactive isotope in it. The beast is finally cornered at Coney Island and annihilated when military sharpshooter Corporal Stone (Lee Van Cleef) climbs aboard the roller coaster and fires the isotope launcher into it. After much groaning and destruction of the entire roller coaster, the rhedosaurus dies (Figure 4.3). Vivian Sobchack has argued that, in addition to atomic force, it "signifies primeval origins, the primal sink and slime from which life first emerged." Or, alternatively, it represents "the fear of an avenging nature which has been disturbed by technology."[83] But the location of its ultimate destruction might offer a more specific clue. The rhedosaurus is defeated at Coney Island, which might stand in for Hollywood as an older but wholesome, all-American space of entertainment. Even in its death throes, the beast continues to destroy the Cyclone, the very symbol of early twentieth-century amusement that was waning in popularity – in large measure because of suburbanization and the rise of alternative modes of entertainment like television.

Therefore, we might say that Lourié's final sequence resurrects the old roller coaster nostalgically to further denounce the beast, which has fully become the embodiment of destructive new technologies and media.[84]

To this notion of the destructive beast, Gordon Douglas's *Them!* appends another pejorative dimension. If the beast is decidedly damaging, then the gigantic ants that germinate in the New Mexico desert and head toward Los Angeles are also monstrously feminine. The threat of rampaging ants is initially discovered when two state police officers encounter a catatonic girl walking around aimlessly in the desert while clutching a broken doll, then stumble upon a ransacked trailer, and finally find the local general store wrecked and its owner Gramps Johnson dead. While waiting for other officers to arrive on the scene of the crime, one of them is mysteriously killed. At this point, the massacring entity remains off-screen, heard as a high-pitched buzz but unseen. Sergeant Ben Peterson (James Whitmore) speculates that it might be a homicidal maniac, since "there's no money stolen, violent wreckage, just sugar taken." But that is a false lead, as evidenced by the presence of "enough formic acid in [the dead storekeeper's] body to kill twenty men." On an intertextual note, it is clear that this monster is more fierce than the ones we've seen before, for even FBI agent Robert Graham, played by James Arness, the oversized alien Thing himself, remains as flustered as the rest of the men. Help arrives in the form of two myrmecologists, Drs. Harold (Edmund Gwenn) and Pat (Joan Weldon) Medford, who are able to jolt the little girl out of her catatonic state by making her sniff some formic acid, at which point she screams hysterically, "Them! Them!" Until now the monster has remained faceless, nameless, and essentially undefined; intuiting that the scientists are letting on less than they understand, Robert demands "to know exactly what this 'it' is." While Harold is asking for patience, the monster is finally revealed as a gigantic ant, crawling out of the desert right behind the spot where his daughter Pat is kneeling over and exploring the creature's footprints. The monster, it turns out, is a harmless domestic insect now made colossally destructive by the effects of radiation, generated by early atomic bomb tests conducted in the desert. The Air Force joins the battle, and when the ants' nest is found, phosphorous is laid over the mound with bazookas, and its tunnels are destroyed with cyanide. But even setting the entire colony on fire is not a solution, for two queen ants have escaped and will presumably mate and create other nests, which, as Harold muses, could mean the end of the world.

The public at large will be notified later via the small screen to stay at home, and that televisual briefing will contain neither substantive details nor wise counsel. But, in stunning contrast to that later moment, when the New Mexico contingent arrives in Washington, D.C., the top-secret briefing is made authoritatively on a big screen for maximum impact. That larger frame is able to accommodate many more contextual details that clarify the meaning and significance of the monster that mankind is up against. As the film rolls, Harold narrates the story of the mating habits of ants. Finally, the monstrous problem is revealed in gendered terms. In a room full of male authority figures (and Pat), Harold concludes that "unless these queens are located and destroyed before they've established thriving colonies and can produce heaven alone knows how many more queen ants, man, as the dominant species of life on earth, will probably be extinct within a year." Douglas's film has been leading up to this dire declaration. The ants' threat is explicitly matriarchal.[85] As Vivian Sobchack intimates, they have been following "a process of erosion which will eat away all traces of Man."[86] More specifically, the queen ants' threat signifies what Barbara Creed calls the "monstrous-feminine," with its "voracious maw, the mysterious black hole that threatens to give birth to equally horrific offspring as well as threatening to incorporate everything in its path."[87] And they are out to destroy the rational, masculine civilization of America (Figure 4.4).

There was a pervasive fear of the feminine in the 1950s, perhaps exacerbated by the difficulties of assimilating into postwar civilian life. As James Gilbert suggests, there was a "growing chorus of complaints . . . that women were intruding into male institutions and feminizing American life." The notion of an imperiled masculinity was generated by a fear of "America's growing culture of domesticity" as well as "the self-aggrandizing power of Momism."[88] But this is not necessarily a novel fear. After all, no decade is truly immune from a perceived crisis of masculinity. What is intriguing about this crisis in the 1950s is that a majority of the blame was placed on emerging media, particularly television, which was seen increasingly as a feminizing venue. Initially, criticism of television was based on its evolution as a marketing agent in the mid-

4.4. *Them!* (dir. Gordon Douglas, 1954).

1950s economy. But the voices of censure did not focus only on its being representative of consumerist mass culture. Television came to be seen as an emasculating force, even as shows like *Leave it to Beaver* and *Father Knows Best* were being praised in some circles, as Mary Beth Haralovich points out, "for realigning family gender roles" and restoring the place of the father as the primary breadwinner and provider.[89] Among the most vocal critics was Philip Wylie, whose *Generation of Vipers* was revised in 1955 to include the destructive effects of television. Wylie's text tied the fear of technological apocalypse to the image of the domineering woman or "the destroying mother," who functions much like Goebbels by employing mass media to decimate the national culture.[90] For him, the devil was "literally reincarnated over TV," allied with science and ex-ploited by women.[91] Television, Wylie argued, was being used by women to emasculate the man and turn him into "her de-sexed, de-souled, de-cerebrated mate."[92]

There is a similar alignment of the domineering woman with television in a gorgeous cinephiliac moment in Nicholas Ray's *Rebel without a Cause* (1955), when Jim Stark (James Dean) returns home after the chickie run to find his father passively passed out in front of a flickering TV set. When his dictatorial mother descends the stairs to join them, the camera follows Jim's point of view and sees her upside down, the way he does, and becomes "a visual marker of a world turned upside down."[93] It soon rotates 180 degrees to right itself, but the skewed vision is directly linked with the static on the small screen, which remains central in most subsequent shots where the family argues over Jim's next move. The menacing blue static becomes symbolic of the damage TV has done and links it to the mother, whose overbearing, destructive manner is also emasculating and destroying the family and, by extension, civilization itself. Writing about another family melodrama from that year, Douglas Sirk's *All That Heaven Allows* (1955), which also uses television as a reflection of familial ills, Laura Mulvey argues that "at the moment of defeat, Hollywood could afford to point out the seeds of decay in its victorious rival's own chosen breeding ground."[94] Mulvey's metaphor is pregnant with implications of Hollywood's emasculation by television, whose feminine wiles are said to have given birth to a degenerate civilization.

In Douglas's *Them!*, the monstrous-feminine ants are likewise linked with the disastrous consequences of television. That is why the only way to guarantee the ants' annihilation is, as Harold advises the policeman and FBI agent when they begin firing their weapons, to "get the antennae!" At a time when the skyline of every town was dotted with skeletal metallic fingers pointing in all directions, it would be impossible to miss that televisual inference.[95] So when a queen ant is finally tracked down in the womb-like drains under the city of Los Angeles, it is not surprising that the televised broadcast does not calm fears but only exacerbates them, with the small screen appearing almost as terrifying as the gigantic ants themselves. Ultimately, the ants are destroyed along with the entire nest when "the phallic bazookas of the army incinerate the queen and her eggs."[96] Any possibility of future alien procreation is thereby prevented. As the camera zooms in on a dark hollow of the tunnel, the ants, like witches being burned at the stake, are burned alive (Figure 4.5).

4.5. *Them!* (dir. Gordon Douglas, 1954).

But at least as it relates to television, such finality or sense of victory over the alien Other is nothing more than wishful thinking by 1954. Even though the ants' tentacles could be set ablaze, television's cultural sway could not be suppressed. As we have already seen, amid television's growing prosperity, stability, and influence, the studios began seriously collaborating with the enemy. And the cinematic story of the relationship between the rival media began to change too. Until now, if television had written its own tale in terms of realism, liveness, and drama, assertively distinguishing its product from that on the big screen, Hollywood had responded – like Benjamin differentiating between storytelling and reportage – by reimagining television as an alien, destructive, diseased, emasculating Other. After the mid-1950s, it was no longer enough to narrate the big screen's paranoia about invasion or its (failed) attempts to slow its course. With many sci-fi films now set in a post-apocalyptic universe, the story begins to turn toward lessons learned about living in this new multimedia environment.

This new landscape may look familiar; it may even resemble old Hollywood. But there is something distinctly different about it. From Hollywood's point of view, it is as if a Norman Rockwell–style idyllic panorama has been turned into a noirish, paranoiac nightmare. This nightmarish new world is reflected in Don Siegel's *Invasion of the Body Snatchers,* where average citizens of the tranquil town of Santa Mira are replaced by emotionless replicas of their former selves. The transformation takes place as podded aliens take over human bodies, "cell for cell, atom for atom," while they sleep, only to wake up, as Dr. Miles Bennell (Kevin McCarthy) and his old flame Becky Driscoll (Dana Wynter) fearfully realize, "changed into something evil and inhuman." This invasion, however, is different from the ones we've seen before. There is no monstrous beast visibly clashing with humans in an effort to take over the world. Rather, the invasion is more like a conversion, which happens slowly and at first even appears to be a delusion, as people begin reporting that their family members or friends are not quite being themselves. Before they know it, Miles and Becky recognize that they might be the only people in town who have resisted conversion. They barricade themselves in his office and avoid falling asleep. The next day, however, their former friends Jack Belicec (King Donovan) and Dr. Kaufman (Larry Gates) arrive, both transformed, and try to convince them of the benefits of conversion. But a robotic transformation is unacceptable to Miles and Becky, who get away and, pursued by a mob of transformed pods, run up a hill and hide in an abandoned mine. When Miles leaves Becky to check on music playing in the distance, she falls asleep and is converted. So, being the only one who has not been transformed, Miles escapes and makes it to a nearby highway to Los Angeles. There, he looks directly into the camera and, in the film's iconic moment, declares the frightening inevitability of conversion: "You're next!" A dissolve returns us to the film's flashback narrative frame, where Miles is in a hospital recalling his story to doctors, who ultimately agree to call it an emergency and alert all authorities.

There is some disagreement about how this ending, which Don Siegel reportedly despised because he wanted the film to end with Miles's warning, should be interpreted. Sidney Perkowitz, for instance, sees in it "a glimmer of hope," since Miles's escape suggests that it might be possible to stall the transformation of humans into zombies.[97] But as Barry

Keith Grant suggests, the conclusion is in fact quite grim. There is no comfort in cautioning the authorities. Unlike earlier invasion films, *Invasion* does not promise the annihilation of the alien in the end. In fact, there isn't merely one alien entity; conversion has spread like wildfire throughout the town and, we may assume, the nation. How can it be restrained, Grant argues, when "it has spread much wider than the town of Santa Mira and may be nearer to the patrons in the theater than they think"?[98] If we see the film, as many critics do, as a symbolic critique of the perceived loss of personal freedom in the Soviet Union and how that reflects life under McCarthyist fascism, then perhaps there is still the possibility of stalling such a fate by opposing small-town conformity in America. There might even be hope of waking up from the nightmare, if we regard the film as a paranoid allegory of "an America that is being poisoned and transformed in its sleep in the safety of suburbia."[99]

But if we take Grant's argument more literally, we can read *Invasion* as a conversion narrative of a different kind, of Hollywood's reluctant but inevitable transition to television. Although Norma Desmond may have complained that "it's the pictures that got small," or Clark Gable may have objected to screening his old films on the small screen for fear of being in competition with himself, the shift to television was unavoidable. As Christine Becker demonstrates, by the mid-1950s, film stars like Ida Lupino and Ronald Reagan made successful transitions to television. Some appeared on variety shows, whereas others, from Donna Reed to Jack Benny to Alfred Hitchcock, became TV regulars with their own sitcoms or anthology series.[100] Still, this did not mean that such crossovers would receive friendly treatment in the movies. Siegel's film presents conversion as a horrifying inevitability.

In the film's most startling scene, which has far more cinephiliac potential than the one most commonly cited when Miles screams at motorists like a wild prophet of doom, Miles and Becky hide out in his office and watch their converted neighbors from a small window in alarm and disgust (Figure 4.6). Santa Mira looks like any cozy suburban neighborhood, with neighbors going about their business "just like [on] any Saturday morning." What is unnerving about *Invasion* is that the "transformed self is virtually indistinguishable from its original."[101] Yet, there is something markedly different about familiar folks like "Len Pearl-

4.6. *Invasion of the Body Snatchers* (dir. Don Siegel, 1956).

man, Bill Bittner, Jim Clark and his wife Shirley and their kids." What the ghastly view from their window reveals is that Santa Mira has been converted and has now become a distribution center for emotionless pods destined for nearby towns. Everyone in town uncannily resembles their old human selves, and yet there is something missing. Soon, Miles and Becky are discovered by Jack and Kaufman, who portray conversion as a solution to all of their problems. The pod transformation, Dr. Kaufman proposes, is like being "reborn into an untroubled world." This new world, Miles understands, is a place "where everyone's the same" and real emotions like love are impossible to experience. Interestingly, this new environment of Santa Mira is remarkably similar to the fictional world of many fifties television shows, where life is often simple and painless, and any problem can be resolved within thirty minutes (or less, if we allow for advertising).[102]

The notion that television presented "an untroubled world" and a false sense of contentment was already gaining ground. Borrowing a phrase from Herbert Gold, Todd Gitlin notes, fifties T V presented "happy people with happy problems."[103] Real life did not intrude much on such a happy place. *I Love Lucy,* for instance, one of the decade's most popular shows, fictionalized the stars' marriage by erasing any signs of trouble. The show, as Lori Landay argues, "was a bizarre public fantasy that recreated the Ball-Arnaz marriage along more traditional lines; not only is Ricky the star and Lucy the ordinary housewife who wants to be a star (in contrast to 'real life' in which Ball's career was more success-ful than Arnaz's), but each week the happy ending implied that the love between Ricky and Lucy was ideal and unchanging."[104] In contrast to this televisual fantasy, the Ball-Arnaz marriage in real life was strained and suffering. Although their professional relationship was successful, with their company Desilu even purchasing R KO in 1958, their marriage did not survive the real-life complexities of being a dual-career couple. At the end of the decade, only a day after filming the final episode of *The Lucy-Desi Comedy Hour,* the couple filed for divorce, which of course did not become a prominent storyline on their show. The show, like most television programs of the 1950s, ended happily.

In fact, it is because of the era's television shows that we remember the 1950s as the "good old days," that we think of the time with images of what Fredric Jameson calls "the happy family in the small town, of normalcy and nondeviant everyday life."[105] And it is precisely this kind of happiness that is being offered by the pod people in Siegel's film and resisted by Miles and Becky, whose bleak assessment of life after con-version as existence in "a world without love or grief or beauty" is a not too oblique critique of television. By exposing the superficiality of their former friends' contentment, *Invasion* portrays televisual happiness as a version of Herbert Marcuse's notion of false happiness, possible only through repression of the unpleasant. Ray Pratt has argued that *Invasion* demonstrates "the pressure on individuals of the era to conform – or suf-fer the consequences."[106] With its images of mostly homogeneous homes and families and suburbs, the small screen intensified and even natural-ized this type of conformity, which was already coming under fire. Also published in 1956, William H. Whyte's *The Organization Man* identifies a new world that is very similar to the one created by pods in *Invasion.* Whyte criticizes the spread of conformism throughout American society, where individual white-collar workers are being transformed into zombie-like, powerless conformists by a culture that encourages "belongingness" and "togetherness" for their own sake. Whyte observes the desire for forced consensus arising from all quarters, and he cites the following crucial example of how television is contributing to it. A bulletin from the Protestant Council of New York City encourages the mass media to promote conformity: "Subject matter should project love, joy, courage, hope, faith, trust in God, good will. Generally avoid condemnation, criticism, controversy."[107] By rejecting a fake world filled only with love, joy, and hope, and opting for a gritty world with real problems, Becky and Miles echo Whyte's condemnation of false consensus and exterior contentment. *Invasion* claims that only cinema is capable of portraying a gritty, realistic world, one that tackles tough issues rather than shying away from them. As Jackie Byars has argued, because TV took over as the family medium, cinema of the 1950s could afford "venturing into previously taboo areas" and portraying "controversial stories," thus rejecting television's claims of realism.[108] Moreover, *Invasion* was shown in widescreen SuperScope, whose anamorphic lens visually suggests that the widescreen technique is far better suited to narrating the full range of human emotions, in contrast to the cheerful but claustrophobic environment of the small screen. Thus, the film implies that, although conversion to television may now be inescapable, cinema continues to be institutionally superior to television.

Jack Arnold's *The Incredible Shrinking Man* (1957) takes the inevitability of transformation one step further, by envisioning Hollywood's place in a new media environment. In a sense, *Man* may be seen as the summative sci-fi film of the 1950s. Its three-part structure tells the familiar tale of the discovery of a monstrous anxiety, followed by attempts at overcoming it, and concluding in some kind of resolution. Shawn Rosenheim describes the three sections as "social allegory, adventure film, and apocalyptic essay."[109] As do most sci-fi films, *Man* begins "on a very ordinary summer day," when Robert Scott Carey (Grant Williams) and his wife Louise (Randy Stuart) are vacationing on a boat. But this ordinary trip becomes "strange, almost unbelievable" as a mist coming off the horizon engulfs Scott and covers him in a sparkling powder. Six months later, "on an equally ordinary day" in his suburban Los Angeles home, he discovers that his clothes are too big, and a visit to Dr. Bramson (William Schallert) reveals that he is ten pounds lighter and two inches shorter. Numerous tests later, Scott learns that the molecular structure of his cells has realigned due to exposure to both radiation and insecticide; the only plausible explanation, then, is that the mysterious mist that engulfed him on an ordinary summer day had been atomic. Thus begins Scott's existential battle with the world, which becomes more and more gargantuan as his shrinking process continues. Feeling like a freak, he wanders into a carnival and is temporarily revived by companionship offered by Clarice Bruce (April Kent). Scott also finds comfort in storytelling; as he works on his autobiography, he hopes that "it's the world that's changed, that [he's] the normal one." But such optimism doesn't last long. Although the shrinking process is temporarily arrested by the doctors, it picks up again, and soon Scott is so small that he must live in a dollhouse. After being attacked by his own cat, he winds up in the basement, where he fights, like Robinson Crusoe, for his life. His foes include a ravenous spider, his appetite, and his fear of dwindling to the point of nothingness. Eventually, he diminishes so far that he can walk out of the basement through a window grate. Thus freed, he contemplates the meaning of personhood and the relationship between "the infinitesimal and the infinite."

The issue of size lies at the heart of *Man*. Although it parallels the structure of most sci-fi films, it is unique in that it is the only one of the decade wherein the primary threat is not of a gigantic Other but of a diminished self. The world that Scott inhabits has not literally changed in size. It appears enormous because his own sense of self diminishes, which in turn magnifies his fears. As M. Keith Booker points out, his diminished size "suggests a very 1950s fear of being overwhelmed by forces larger than oneself, whether those forces involve something as spectacular as fear of being destroyed by a nuclear explosion or something as mundane as fear of loss of individual power and identity."[110] Just as his diminutive self amplifies his existential fears, it also magnifies his immediate foes. But although he finds some solace from his existential fears through storytelling, there is no way to overwhelm his real antagonists, including his pet cat, a household spider, or the pangs of hunger.

Interestingly, one of his enemies is the news media. As Scott shrinks to three feet, a mob of reporters and television trucks gather outside his

home, willing to do almost anything to report on the incredible shrinking man. Their coverage of him as a curiosity at best and monstrosity
at worst reduces him further and alienates him from Louise, who fails
at keeping them at bay. Further, their growing cultural sway is unmis-
takable. When Louise discovers Scott's bloody shirt and fears the cat
ate him, it does not take long for television newscasters to inaccurately
broadcast his death. Switching dispassionately from a humdrum piece
about a politician vowing to reduce taxes, the news reporter announces
"the passing of Robert Scott Carey." With his large talking head looking
menacing on the small screen, he smugly claims that "thus ends the life of
a man whose courage and will to survive lasted until the very end." Then,
just as detachedly, the news reporter moves on to sports. But, as it turns
out, news of Scott's death is premature. Even though he has been reduced
to the size of an atom, he still persists in fighting his battle and telling
the story of his struggle with monstrous adversaries. Television does not
pause to ponder his fate. Due to its rushed desire to go live, television is
not interested in thinking about "what it is about Carey that makes him
a human being at the size of an insect."[111] But Scott is interested in such
ontological questions of personhood, proportion, and balance. And so is
Hollywood. In fact, we can see how Hollywood aligns itself with Scott,
whose diminished size functions as a dreadful reminder of the studio
system's own weakened status in the realigned media universe.

Still, Scott perseveres, and so does Hollywood. Just as he questions
and ultimately relearns his place in the world, the studio system reor-
ganizes in the face of competition from television. This is why the concluding monologue in *Man* is so significant for understanding the realignment taking place in the culture industry. Scott defeats his most
formidable foe, the spider, which has transformed itself into "every unknown terror in the world, every fear fused into one hideous night-black
horror," by stabbing it with a needle until its tentacles shrivel up and the
creature dies. And then, he steps out of his basement and looks up at the
sky. With the crawl space vent that resembles a series of small screens
behind him, Scott contemplates his place in this new atomic age, even
more eager to narrate the story of his diminished status in it (Figure
4.7). The revelation Scott has is that no matter how diminished he may
become or feel, he still exists. There is a remarkable mixture of hopeful-

4.7. *The Incredible Shrinking Man* (dir. Jack Arnold, 1957).

ness and despair in this final epiphanic moment, as his desire to "mean something" collides with the realization that he remains only a fraction of his former self.

And such is the status of Hollywood too by the end of the 1950s. Although fears of annihilation by television may have been exaggerated, there is little doubt that its position in the mass cultural marketplace had weakened. Still, claims of Hollywood's death were just as premature as Scott's. Many historians trace the beginning of the end of the studio system to the 1948 Paramount decision, whose real consequence was that Hollywood could not participate in the nascent television industry, thus creating a gigantic rivalry between the two media throughout the 1950s. During this decade, Hollywood readjusted. While the old studio system of filmmaking, based on vertical integration and star-genre products, did not survive, Hollywood itself did. As was the case in sci-fi films of the decade, where nuclear science was simultaneously the destroyer and the savior, television turned out to be the problem as well as the solution. By supplying films and filmed programming to TV networks, as Michele Hilmes argues, "Hollywood appears to have been able to have its cake and eat it too."[112] In fact, ties between the two media became so firm that Los Angeles became the center for film and television production, and Hollywood came to signify the entertainment industry in general. More significantly, Hollywood's influence on television meant that the latter had to redefine itself, as liveness was quickly overtaken by previously filmed programming – a change that was mutually benefi-cial, since Hollywood could still assert its ontological superiority while television gained the economic advantage. As Richard Maltby notes, "Filmed material replaced live programming as the dominant televi-sion form. . . . By 1960, the major Hollywood studios were producing 40 percent of network programs, while 80 percent of that year's prime-time schedule was generated in Hollywood."[113] Although cinematic represen-tations of television continued to cast it as the reckless invader, instead of being the terrifying monster, television had unexpectedly enabled Hollywood to reimagine the pop culture landscape and strengthen the status of storytelling. While the movies would not remain the nation's prime culture industry – Douglas Gomery argues that by the end of the 1950s, "filmmaking was an ancillary business" – Hollywood itself would survive and thrive in the new environment.[114] More importantly, story-telling, not information, would become the norm in popular media. Like Scott Carey, Hollywood could confidently say that it "meant something." What it meant was no longer just the movies but a significant fraction of the new media universe.

CODA: AS SEEN ON TV

Several decades later, another technological monster rears its tentacles. Once again, old and new media collide. Once again, Hollywood equates eschatological fears, this time exacerbated by apocalyptic anxieties of the coming end of the millennium, with the dread of futuristic tech-nologies in the decade's films, which function as thinly veiled critiques of advanced digital technologies gearing up to destroy traditional me-chanical technologies. Just as television in the 1950s is portrayed as alien, destructive, emasculating, and inhuman, digital technology in the 1990s is coded as evil and becomes the source of scopic dread. Sci-fi films like James Cameron's *Terminator 2* (1991), Brett Leonard's *The Lawnmower Man* (1992), and Irwin Winkler's *The Net* (1995) especially create a terrifying discourse about emerging information technologies.

As Paul Arthur suggests, in these late twentieth-century films, advanced technology emerges as "an information-age avatar of uncontrollable, autonomous, inscrutable dread," threatening an all-too-human mechanical entertainment order that is "benign, user-friendly, and because prone to the ravages of time, redeemably mortal."[115] Moreover, they intensify the already pervasive millennial fears of cataclysmic destruction by aligning new media with the dreadfully overdetermined year 2000. Interestingly, just as the studios had simultaneously collaborated with and cinematically resisted television in the 1950s, these *fin de siècle* sci-fi films employ computer-generated imagery while decrying a soulless digital future. For instance, in the clash between two kinds of technology in *Terminator 2,* whose key effects are all created using computer graphics, the malevolent digital Other overpowers the older model. The Terminator (Arnold Schwarzenegger) has to sacrifice his life to protect the Connor clan in particular and humanity in general from a future technocratic nightmare. But he does win a moral victory, which "validates endangered institutions by conflating the Hollywood factory with vestiges of patriarchy and the nuclear family."[116] Once again, in the onscreen battle between old and new technologies, Hollywood bests its competition by positioning itself as a champion of wholesome, traditional entertainment.

Interestingly, although Hollywood locates a new adversary in the 1990s, it does not forget about the old one. Indeed, in its representation as a malevolent Other, the present enemy looks dreadfully similar to the former. This is not to suggest that Hollywood cinema, during the studio era or after its collapse, ever ceased to critique the technological upstart that tried to and succeeded in supplanting it as the leading mass culture industry. As Jon Nelson Wagner and Tracy Briga MacLean have recently demonstrated, since the proliferation of television, the newer medium has remained the subject of many technophobic films. From Kazan's *A Face in the Crowd* to Sidney Lumet's *Network* (1976) to Warren Beatty's *Bulworth* (1998), their text presents a comprehensive survey of Hollywood films that continue to represent television as a purveyor of social ills, dangerous because it can "distort reality, cause social disintegration, promote 'meaningless' violence, zombify, enslave, and reject history."[117] Behind the scenes, the story of their relationship might have changed. On the big screen, however, there has never been a truce between the original visual media rivals. Perhaps fittingly, then, when a new media challenger emerges, an old battle is reignited. While Hollywood's condemnation of electronic technology is primarily directed at digitization, it is also often hysterically redirected at its old adversary, television, which remains both ineffective and dangerous.

Many of these redirected attacks return to the moment and site of the original battle. Reversing Albert Robida's time travel fantasies by returning, whether literally or metaphorically, to fifties suburbia, films about television reaffirm cinema's ontological superiority in the age of digital reproduction. Peter Weir's *The Truman Show* (1998) and Gary Ross's *Pleasantville* (1998) both represent television as a pernicious force that can destroy the fabric of humanity. In both cases, individuals are trapped in the televisual suburbia of the 1950s. Truman Burbank (Jim Carrey), whose name evokes the first president who appeared on television regularly and yet remained bedeviled by controversies that played out on the small screen, has spent his entire life as a character on a TV show without knowing it. His small town of Seahaven is an elaborate set for a reality TV show where everyone but him is an actor, dutifully playing the role of wife, mother, friend, and so on. The film's retro look is reminiscent of *Invasion*'s post-apocalyptic suburbia, which was itself a critique of the fifties sitcom, where every problem is sentimentally resolved because reality can be manipulated to create a misleading sense of contentment. There is only one catch: there is no leaving this false utopia. When Truman finally learns of his entrapment, he decides to abandon the safety and comfort of his made-for-TV life to find his college girlfriend, a former extra on the show who is kicked off for truly falling in love with him. As Truman stands on the liminal edge of the artificially created TV world and the "real" world, Christof (Ed Harris), the show's mastermind, urges him to stay. But the star escapes, as the show's audience bursts into applause at Truman's having left the small-minded and simplistic TV world behind. Ironically, as Lynn Spigel notes, "Finally able to escape from his tortuous TV-land, Truman enters the 'real' world of Hollywood."[118] The door marked "exit" is really an entrance into the dream factory of Hollywood, with its promise of reversing the terrifyingly boring existence of the small screen by uniting lovers on the big screen.

Like *The Truman Show, Pleasantville* creates a romanticized, 50s-style
TV show that appears to be appealing but is in fact stultifying. In this sci-
fi fantasy, David (Tobey Maguire) and his sister Jennifer (Reese Wither-
spoon) are unwittingly teleported back to an old show similar to *Leave it
to Beaver* or *Father Knows Best*. They are now Bud and Mary Sue, living
in a suburban home as kids of the Parker family. Their televisual lives in
Pleasantville offer the perfect contrast to their cinematic lives in contemporary America. As the opening commercial for the show suggests,
TV-land is a "flashback to kinder, gentler times," while the cinematic
present is, as Greg Dickinson notes, "fractured, unsafe, and scary."[119] But
as David discovers over the course of his stay, the fake, black-and-white
suburb is also cold and stifling. He spends most of his time fighting the
small-minded conformity of life on the small screen, because "the ideal-
ized world of television [turns out] to be a false utopia that the hero must
escape."[120] Even after the town sheds its grey tones and turns to color,
a marker of moving beyond an overtly repressive existence, David, unlike Jennifer, abandons his TV role and returns to his "real" cinematic
character. As Alev Adil and Steve Kennedy argue, television appears
"as an autocratic anti-intellectual medium/technology that produces
undemocratic and dumbed-down viewing subjects."[121] Thus, in the renewed rivalry between old adversaries, the newer mode of dissemination
is once again disparaged and diminished. On the big screen, cinema
remains the place for "high art and individualism, offering opportunity
and free will," while television once again becomes an unimaginative,
uninhabitable, and ultimately undesirable space.[122]

The most powerful examination of cinema's contentious relationship with television (and, by proxy, with digital information technologies) occurs in Todd Haynes's films, which offer more than negative
appraisals of the new media.[123] They also enable us to return to Benjamin's notion of storytelling and consider cinema's ability to transmit
not information but experience. In *Safe* (1995), Carol White (Julianne
Moore) is a fifties-style suburban housewife who discovers that she suf-
fers from an inexplicable chemical disorder. Real and perceived toxins
in the atmosphere take their toll on her, recalling the pervasive fear of
contamination expressed in the fifties sci-fi films. She experiences per-
sistent coughing, dizziness, nose bleeds, and ultimately convulsions, and

she seeks desperately to understand her condition. Although the medical community appears fairly inept, in the information age, it is the notion of information itself that comes under attack in the film. As Marcia Landy points out, "background sounds of radio programmes and images from television talk shows warn of environmental hazards and of socially disruptive events revolving mostly around reports of rampant crime and failing familial relations."[124] But these pieces of information or the data that accompany them do not allay her anxieties or cure her disease. In fact, the relentless reporting on multiple crises only makes Carol feel worse, because these reports neither fully explain nor enlighten. Instead, they only heighten her state of frenzy and cause further alarm. They seem to confirm Gilles Deleuze's argument about information: "What makes information all-powerful (the newspapers, and then the radio, and then the television) is its very nullity, its radical ineffectiveness."[125] And, as Deleuze further argues, it is precisely information's ineffectiveness that makes it so dangerous. Following Deleuze, Haynes appears to be suggesting that information technologies are ill-equipped to explicate the maladies of late twentieth-century America. Only cinema can delve into Carol's condition. Rather than focusing on statistics or factual information, the film explores the full range of her (and our) crises through narration. Just as Benjamin's storyteller resists a lineup of facts and favors instead the transmission of experience, Haynes's film emphasizes the telling of the story over providing evidence of this or that diagnosis. Therefore, it closes open-endedly, without solving the mystery of Carol's ailment. A television broadcaster had earlier asked, "Are you allergic to the twentieth century?" Haynes does not provide an easy answer. In the film's hauntingly cinephiliac shot at the end, Carol retreats to a small, sterile igloo, looks into a mirror, and says, "I love you." There is still no explaining her disease. All she and Haynes can do is cinematically communicate it, transmit it, pass it on to her viewers.

This notion of cinema as transmitter of experience is also discernible in Haynes's *Far from Heaven* (2002). Set in 1957, this film tells the story of another suburban housewife, Cathy Whitaker (Julianne Moore), who is ostensibly happily married to Frank (Dennis Quaid), a television marketing executive. But their life as Mr. and Mrs. Magnatech is only a façade that begins to crumble as Frank, a closeted gay man, pursues his same-sex desire, and Cathy has an interracial relationship with her late gardener's son Raymond Deagan (Dennis Haysbert). The first crack in this façade appears in a crucial early scene, where Cathy is being interviewed for a puff piece in the *Weekly Gazette;* she is to be featured as Mrs. Magnatech, "the proud wife of a successful sales executive, planning the parties and posing at her husband's side on the advertisements." Posing next to her T V set as in the advertisement, Cathy shyly protests that she is like every other wife and mother and that she doesn't think she's "ever wanted anything . . ." Before she can finish articulating her desire, her voice trails off. Noticing Raymond in her backyard for the first time, she abandons her seat by the T V set and walks out to see who he is. This scene unironically echoes a moment in Sirk's *All That Heaven Allows,* when Cary Scott (Jane Wyman) is presented a television set by her adult children for forgoing her relationship with her gardener Ron (Rock Hudson), who, although white, is too far from her in age and social class. Television functions, as Lynne Joyrich argues, as "a typical 'media fix' to the problems inherent in her gender, race, and class position – consumer compensation in exchange for an active pursuit of her desire."[126] But the T V set is never turned on. Although the salesman informs her that "all you have to do is turn that dial," the only thing the small screen reflects is Cary's cheerless face. Television remains silent because it cannot mirror Cary's condition, much less provide any respite from it. Like Cary's, Cathy's T V set remains a piece of furniture – decorative, even informative when it reports on President Eisenhower's decision to send the 101st Airborne to Little Rock, but ultimately ineffective. Haynes's film argues that the information-driven medium cannot accomplish what cinematic storytelling can.

Why, we might ask, does Hollywood repeatedly revert to mediaphobic films, especially at a time when the convergence of mechanical, electronic, and digital media is underway? Why continue defending classical storytelling when, as David Bordwell argues, "crucial practices of storytelling [have] persisted, despite the demise of the studio system, the emergence of conglomerate control, and new methods of marketing and distribution"?[127] Why critique information and reportage when the real danger is from new modes of participatory spectatorship? Perhaps one way to respond to these questions may be found in the nature of storytelling itself. Drawing on Walter Benjamin, Philip Simay empha-sizes the connective role of storytelling when he argues that the story is "an answer found in the past to a question formulated in the present."[128] That is, because stories retain their "germinative power," they continue to resonate, and they offer wise counsel. And that is how cinephiliac moments occurring in these new mediaphobic tracts fit into the longer story that this chapter has been narrating about the epic struggle be-tween cinema and television. They demonstrate that, while we think of Hollywood as a rational industry, it consistently verges on the irrational and the excessive. By returning to this battle at a time when a new war is being fought with the mightier adversary of digital technology, they also offer lessons for Hollywood's survival in a new media universe. If *Man's* Scott Carey metaphorically shows how Hollywood can endure even after being reduced in stature following the primal realignment triggered by television, then *Far from Heaven's* Cathy Whitaker, who is in a sense channeling *All That Heaven Allows's* Cary Scott, instructs on the continuing resonance of storytelling, even in the hypertextual, interactive digital age.

If we toss away an older theory like an old dress or a used car, we lose an important part of a long conversation.

JAMES NAREMORE AND ADRIAN MARTIN,
"The Future of Academic Film Study"

Cinephilia can bring to light such "lost" movie fragments. . . . In doing so, film lovers may find renewed impetus to link the incandescent language of stray movie passages to everything that they already know, feel, and imagine about how movies work. With luck, some portion of the beauty and strangeness of these discoveries may unsettle the process of knowing, and place us once again, to our advantage, in the dark.

GEORGE TOLES, "Rescuing Fragments"

Conclusion

The Cinephiliac Return

FROM CINEPHILIA TO FILM STUDIES, OR FROM LOVER TO ASSASSIN

At a time when the disintegration of the studio system is all but inevitable, Frank O'Hara writes "To the Film Industry in Crisis," a tongue-in-cheek declaration of love for the movies. The poem extols the star system and hails the "glorious Silver Screen, tragic Technicolor, amorous / Cinemascope."[1] O'Hara's speaker appears as a classical cinephile, rebuffing "lean quarterlies and swarthy periodicals," experimental theater, and opera in favor of popular cinema, declaring "you, Motion Picture Industry, / it's you I love!"[2] Like his *Cahiers* contemporaries, O'Hara's cinephile loves not only the industry in general but also its inexplicably pleasurable moments. Like "Mae West / in a furry sled," or "Cornel Wilde coughing blood on the piano keys," or "Jean Harlow reclining and wiggling."[3] In the 1950s, such candid and unguarded assertions of ciné-love were entirely appropriate for a generation passionate about the movies. But only a decade later, cinephilia was discredited for being too invested in obsession, nostalgia, and fetishism. Expressions of love, as we recounted in the introduction, had to be replaced with a seriousness of tone and style appropriate to proper criticism. The film critic could no longer be a cinephile. Indeed, the critic had to become, to borrow a phrase from another O'Hara poem, "the assassin of / [the] orchards," deconstructing rather than applauding cinema's pleasures.[4]

Interestingly, the period around the late 1960s and early 1970s, when classical cinephilia lost currency, is generally assumed to be the moment when film studies was born, after critics made the transition to a more rigorously defined and theoretically informed field of inquiry. Until then, the story usually goes, film criticism was too concerned with the cinematic experience. Following a more critical understanding of the cinematic apparatus, a new discipline was born. Evaluating the "parallel histories" of cinema and psychoanalysis, for instance, Janet Bergstrom argues that film studies became "an academic discipline" when "psycho-analytic concepts [were introduced] into contemporary film theory."[5] Similarly, asking how film studies may be reinvented for the new century, Christine Gledhill and Linda Williams trace the beginnings of film as an "academic subject of study" and "the establishment of the discipline in the 1970s."[6] This claim makes sense, given the radical break with the past that this moment desires to mark. As political positions changed, continental theories, from Marxism to psychoanalysis to structuralism, began inflecting film criticism. As Peter Wollen claims in an exchange with Laura Mulvey, this is the time when writing on film began gravitat-ing away from Bazin, who had offered "ontology and language and then the influence of structuralism and semiotics opened up new directions and possibilities."[7] Encouraged by these new influences, which intro-duced a politically and theoretically sophisticated discourse, film studies became invigorated at this time.

But, as Lee Grieveson and Haidee Wasson have recently pointed out, the study of cinema has a much longer history. They argue that, while it makes for an interesting narrative, we cannot begin the history of film studies in the late 1960s. The study of cinema "was born in the early twentieth century as a political problem in conjunction with the social turbulence of the 1910s, 1920s, and 1930s."[8] Film study began ini-tially with a sociological emphasis, with critics focusing on the influence of the new medium on the public. At this early stage, the nascent field was implicitly linked with governance and control of modern audiences. Film courses, as Dana Polan shows, were first introduced in the interwar period at American universities, which were responding to changing educational and sociopolitical missions. Over the course of its first few decades, academic film study began moving away from this sociologi-cal approach and toward a humanities-based approach. This move was partly fuelled by the popularity of Great Books pedagogy in the 1920s and 30s, when educators in the United States argued for a broad, cross-disciplinary teaching of the Western liberal arts tradition. They took to cinema, "which they appreciated as a humanistic venture comparable in its own fashion to the deeper promise of canonic, high-culture liberal education."[9] However, by the late 1930s, sustained critique of popular culture was already getting underway, which delayed the comprehensive academic incorporation of film studies for almost another three decades. It was not until the late 1960s that film studies became the formalized academic discipline that we recognize today. But cinema was studied for several decades before that turn – and it was studied quite differently from our semiotics-influenced conception of film studies will allow. Therefore, the shorthand narrative tracing the birth of film studies to the late 1960s is inaccurate, or at least it is incomplete. It keeps being repeated because "the narrative that has film studies emerging into the 1960s is the story also of its emergence *out of* the 1950s," a decade that offers an opportune contrast to the politically vigorous and theoretically inflected film studies.[10]

Even so, this moment represents something of a major turning point. The academization of film studies was partly launched in response to rapidly rising enrollments and a growing youth culture looking for sites to challenge traditional education. Laura Mulvey has suggested that her own move toward a more critical stance was prompted by the fact that, after the intellectual and political shifts ushered in by May '68, "it was harder to combine a political allegiance to the Left and an allegiance to the culture of the United States."[11] To use O'Hara's terminology, it was harder to remain a lover when one was becoming an assassin. At the same time, a series of new journals, such as *Screen* in the United Kingdom, where Mulvey's groundbreaking "Visual Pleasure and Narrative Cinema" was first published in 1975, to *Wide Angle* and *Camera Obscura* in the United States, began to set the theoretical agenda for the study of cinema. Taking on directly questions of ideology – of gender and sexuality as well as race, ethnicity, and nationality – these journals unlocked new areas of inquiry, bolstered the field's political bona fides, and introduced a theoretical rigor that was ostensibly lacking until that point. Alongside new journals emerged new books on cinema. Mark Betz calls them "little books," which institutionalized the study of cinema further. These little books offered "specialized studies of . . . directors, national film movements, and genres." They "cemented the paradigms, methodologies, and critical terrain for the burgeoning academic discipline, and [they] were pressed into service as course texts by the first generation of film scholars trained in other disciplines."[12] Thus, cinema as a field of knowledge was reinvented. The era before the late 1960s now began being regarded as a diffuse film culture, while this became the new age of film as an academic discipline. So, what truly shifted in the late 1960s?

Geoffrey Nowell-Smith argues that what this moment really marks is the turn from aesthetics to semiotics. Writing about the theoretical revolution that took place at this time, Nowell-Smith contends that "philosophically it vaunted its materialism, in opposition to idealisms of every kind."[13] The semiotic tradition that began with Saussurean structural linguistics and the psychoanalytic tradition that was developed under the tutelage of Jacques Lacan were "quickly seized on by film theorists on the lookout for ways of completing the jigsaw society – ideology – individual."[14] In this system, priority was given to epistemological questions of meaning. There was no more room for questions of art or taste or pleasure. Indeed, Nowell-Smith suggests that this semiotic turn was, "at least in part, a reaction against the kind of aesthetics that dealt in concepts that were 'indeterminate' and could not be brought within a rational schema."[15] One of those concepts now chastised for its idealism was cinephilia. So, let us return for a moment to Christian Metz's redefinition of what it means to be a film theorist, a redefinition that involves a dire declaration of farewell to cinephilia. Metz invoked cinephilia in order to distinguish its ostensibly easy pleasures from the rigorous study of cinema. Writing at a time when the "love" of cinema became increasingly problematic, he exhorted film theorists to move past the naive and sometimes self-indulgent phase of film criticism, whose heyday is marked at *Cahiers* in the 1950s. That earlier discourse now led only to disillusionment. Malte Hagener and Marijke de Valck point out that, animated by "a deep feeling of loss and betrayal because the object of their love did not actually deserve their affection . . . the psycho-semiotics of the 1970s became a kind of inverted cinephilia, a disappointed love's labor's lost."[16] Instead of the thrilled and immersive responses of an earlier generation, Metz advocated a kind of scientific detachment between critic and screen. As George Toles points out, the new, more theoretical discourse "was eager to purge itself of the allegiances of childhood in order to don the lab coats of an earnest, disengaged maturity."[17] This new film theorist had to relinquish his gullible love for the movies, which now appeared ideologically suspect. Indeed, what is most striking about Metz's denunciation is his desire to "no longer be invaded by [the cinephile]," whom he considered childlike for being afflicted by "the thousand paralysing bonds of a tender unconditionality."[18] The new task of the critic was to keep cinephilia in check. In this incarnation, the critic would "not have lost sight of [the cinephile], but be keeping an eye on him," disallowing himself to regress into a film enthusiast or buff.[19] Only someone not susceptible to the trappings of the cinematic illusion was now capable of investigating cinema properly. To paraphrase Nowell-Smith, the shift in the late 1960s was really from cinephilia to film studies – and, at least for a time, the two seemed wholly incompatible and tragically irreconcilable.

The period from then until the 1990s, when cinephilia began reappearing in film discourse, may be considered the era of anti-cinephilia. Thomas Elsaesser considers this the era of disenchantment, when "cinephilia had been dragged out of its closet, the darkened womb-like auditorium, and revealed itself as a source of disappointment."[20] During this time, cinephilia became a love that dared not speak its name. Like Metz, Laura Mulvey called on theorists to disavow visual pleasure and build film theory at the burial site of this love. "It is said," she declared in "Visual Pleasure and Narrative Cinema," "that analysing pleasure, or beauty, destroys it. That is the intention of this article."[21] In those polemical years, love had to be shunned in favor of academic discipline. Or, drawing on O'Hara's formulation again, one had to convert from being a lover to becoming a killer. Cinephilia thus disappeared, as "love tainted by doubt and ambivalence, [became] ambivalence turning into disappointment, and disappointment, which demanded a public demonstration or exhorted confession of 'I love no more.'"[22] In the meantime, film studies turned from its celebration of grand theory toward cultural studies, new historicism, and cognitive psychology, and it opened up new avenues and historical periods of study. But Metz's and Mulvey's exhortation to destroy pleasure and to take up displeasure did not triumph. After several detours, cinephilia has emerged anew. What, then, does the recent resurgence of cinephilia indicate for the field? Beyond a nostalgic rumination like Susan Sontag's, which I traced in the introduction, what can this return in the direction of cinephilia offer? To put it somewhat differently, why cinephilia? And why now?

. . . AND HALFWAY BACK AGAIN

It is commonplace to observe that cinephilia has returned to film studies just when cinema appears in danger of mutating into something else. Contested as it is by digitization and new media, it appears that we have arrived at (to borrow the title of Jon Lewis's edited collection on 1990s American cinema) the end of cinema as we know it.[23] But new forms of filmmaking and film viewing aren't merely threats to the film industry. They have also been intuitively perceived as challenges to film studies – challenges that have prompted several soul-searching theses about the state of the field, its relation to media studies, and so on.[24] So, we need to think about the return to cinephilia within the context of new forms of spectatorship and reevaluate the mid-twentieth century concept of cinephilia for the early twenty-first century in relation to new media. Because if cinema is not what it used to be, even cinephilia is not what it used to be. Writing about the return in a striking piece about the fate of cinephilia, James Morrison argues that new cinephiles "appear to have repudiated a model of cinephilia as yearning intoxication, desirous and driven by appetites."[25] Contemporary cinephiles no longer pine, like Scottie in Hitchcock's *Vertigo*, for the lost love object. In an era of DVDs, YouTube, and instant streaming, the love object is never fully lost. Morrison cites Bernardo Bertolucci's *The Dreamers* (2003), about an American college student studying in Paris and frequenting the Cinémathèque Française during the student riots of 1968, as an ode to classical cinephilia. It is a film, he argues, that shows that the eroticism, narcissism, and voyeurism that so compelled the first generation of cinephiles are no longer possible. Classical cinephilia is impossible "*because* it was delectably imperfect, and is now irretrievably gone."[26] But, happily, in its place we seem to have a new kind of cinephilia. While this cinephilia is also invested in a project of recovering an alternative canon and the "advancement of cinema as cross-cultural communication, the lingua franca of the global age, these writers turn away from the model of cinephilia as proprietary desire."[27] The new cinephilia is not "conditioned on the unavailability of its object, an elusiveness that was what gave movies some of their mystic allure."[28] In this globalizing, digital environment, cinephilia is transformed. This new cinephilia is not an uncritical embrace of juvenile passions. In fact, this cinephiliac return is at least "a love of movies that is meticulous and sober," and it signifies more than mere obsession or fetishism or nostalgia.[29]

Jonathan Rosenbaum makes similar observations about cinephilia's return in *Goodbye Cinema, Hello Cinephilia.* He begins by remarking on the "strange paradox" that makes this current moment appear to be the best of times and the worst of times for cinema. Depending on whom you believe, "we're currently approaching the end of cinema as an art form and the end of film criticism as a serious activity," or "we're enjoying some form of exciting resurgence and renaissance in both areas."[30] Rosenbaum himself appears to identify mostly with the latter group, and he attributes that exciting resurgence to the ascent of cinephilia. Cinephilia, he argues, is not dead. It thrives online, where a new community of film lovers has turned to the task of recovering and rediscovering cinema. Rosenbaum is excited that "there are still cinephiles much younger than [him]self who are full of excitement about films made even before the glory days of Louis Feuillade and Yevgeni Bauer."[31] More than that, he is thrilled by the new possibilities offered by cinephilia, which can be more than a form of cultism. If cinephilia has indeed been transformed, then we need new ways of thinking about it. Rosenbaum argues that we should "start to think of cinephilia less as a specialized interest than as a certain kind of necessity – an activity making possible things that would otherwise be impossible."[32]

If we think about cinephilia as an activity rather than a concept, we might better understand what this cinephiliac (re)turn, however partial, implies for film studies. The initial quarrel with cinephilia was ignited by the fact that the libidinal attachment to the movies was hard to pin down theoretically and then sustained by the fact that, given its subjective nature, the love of cinema stood outside of critical practice. What we are seeing now is what Dale Hudson and Patricia Zimmerman advocate when asking historians to "remove the object from the monumentalizing position and open it to multiple vectors of recirculation for new connections and new meanings."[33] In other words, instead of trying to find an approach to cinephilia, we ought to be thinking of cinephilia as an approach. Cinephiliac historiography, as *Cinematic Flashes* has tried to demonstrate, is one such approach. It offers a new methodology for reengaging with film history, theory, and visual culture – without suppressing the initial, affective encounter with cinema. I have argued that this methodology is particularly suited for historicizing classical Hollywood, which is traditionally thought of in terms of a rational system with a standard way of filmmaking. What these chapters have demonstrated is that, if we begin with disruptive fragments, even classical Hollywood can appear less cohesive and more vibrant – because cinephiliac moments are productive interruptions in their otherwise standard narratives, and cinephiliac historiography can transform the love of such moments into an investigative practice that can reinvigorate film history. It does not eschew audiovisual pleasure but employs it for doing film studies in the twenty-first century.[34] To put it another way, here is what today's cinephilia enables: to take seriously one's attachment to the movies; to begin with, but not stop at, personal obsession; to generate productive encounters with alluring interruptions.

Writing about something as ostensibly trivial as George Washington's false teeth, Robert Darnton argues in his unconventional history of the Enlightenment that Washington's contemporaries "probably worried more about the pain in their gums than about the new constitution in 1787." Lest the reader think that Darnton is not serious, he emphasizes the point by adding, "they were an odd lot, if seen up close." "In fact," he concludes, "everything about the eighteenth century is strange, once you examine it in detail."[35] The same is true, I believe, of classical Hollywood cinema. Although it appears to be a standardized system, everything about the studio era is strange and unpredictable, once you examine it in detail. George Toles argues that cinephiles have always been intrigued by such seemingly minor elements. Because they have "always delighted in the serendipitous finding and elaboration of the overlooked moment, the 'corner of the eye' detail in film narratives."[36] Rather than merely fetishizing such moments, today's cinephilia, informed by the various turns in film theory, can investigate their appeal and use them to generate fresh theses about that genre or era or industry. For cinephilia points to new ways of understanding marginal moments and their place in film history at large. A cinephile-historian, as Toles puts it, "pursues the apparently incidental, throwaway element in order to discover, on closer inspection born of intuition or feeling, how the inconsequential is essential – a possible key to the whole design."[37] *Cinematic Flashes* has presented four case studies that demonstrate this method in action. But as Pop Liebel tells Scottie after narrating the tragic but unfamiliar tale of Carlotta's suicide in *Vertigo,* "there are many such stories." Mining other lost or forgotten movie fragments that interrupt their linear narratives might bring to light other such stories. Walter Benjamin has argued that "interruption is one of the fundamental methods of all form-giving."[38] Cinephilia as historiography enables a new kind of form-giving, by offering a way to expand upon the cinephiliac moment's audiovisual pleasure more productively. If cinephiliac moments act primarily as pleasurable disruptions, then cinephiliac historiography transforms interruption itself into a critical and historical practice. Therefore, by trying to find a balance between critical inquiry and audiovisual pleasure, today's cinephilia can begin to bridge the divide that has existed for so long in film studies between lover and assassin.

Notes

INTRODUCTION

1. Jean Epstein, "Magnification," in *French Film Theory and Criticism, 1907–1939*, ed. Richard Abel (Princeton: Princeton University Press, 1988), 236.

2. Jean Epstein, "The Senses I (b)," in Abel, *French Film Theory and Criticism*, 243.

3. Ibid.

4. André Breton, *Nadja*, trans. Richard Howard (New York: Grove Press, 1960), 19.

5. René Crevel, "Battlegrounds and Commonplaces," in *The Shadow and Its Shadow: Surrealist Writings on the Cinema*, ed. and trans. Paul Hammond (San Francisco: City Lights Books, 2000), 57.

6. Paul Willemen, *Looks and Frictions: Essays in Cultural Studies and Film Theory* (Bloomington: Indiana University Press, 1994), 231.

7. Mary Ann Doane, *The Emergence of Cinematic Time: Modernity, Contingency, the Archive* (Cambridge: Harvard University Press, 2002), 228. In fact, Doane argues that "because cinephilia has to do with excess in relation to systematicity, it is most appropriate for a cinema that is perceived as highly coded and commercialized." *Emergence*, 226.

8. Walter Benjamin, "On Some Motifs in Baudelaire," in *Illuminations: Essays and Reflections*, ed. Hannah Arendt, trans. Harry Zohn (New York: Schocken, 1968), 175.

9. Walter Benjamin, "Theses on the Philosophy of History," in Arendt, *Illuminations: Essays and Reflections*, 255.

10. Ibid., 262.

11. Walter Benjamin, "N [On the Theory of Knowledge, Theory of Progress]," *The Arcades Project*, trans. Howard Eiland and Kevin McLaughlin (Cambridge: Harvard University Press, 1999), 456. Hereafter all references to the *Arcades Project* are cited as *AP*, along with the title of the appropriate convolute.

12. Mark Betz, "Introduction," *Cinema Journal* 49, no. 2 (2010): 130.

13. Doane, *Emergence*, 228.

14. See Susan Sontag, "A Century of Cinema," in *Where the Stress Falls: Essays* (New York: Farrar, Straus and Giroux, 2001), 117–122. It should be noted that Sontag wrote a revised version of that piece for the *New York Times Magazine* in 1996; my citations here appear from the original, which was later published in her collection of essays, *Where the Stress Falls*.

15. Ibid., 118, 117.

16. Ibid., 120.

17. Ibid., 118.

18. Adrian Martin rightly cautions us to not limit historicizing cinephilia to its French incarnation, arguing that "every country that has had cinema may have

a history of cinephilia." Adrian Martin, "Cinephilia as War Machine," *Framework* 50, nos. 1, 2 (2009): 223. Without disputing his claim, this book associates classical cinephilia with the *Cahiers* version because that is where it fully flowered as a personal and intellectual discourse.

19. Roger Cardinal, "Pausing over Peripheral Detail," *Framework* 30–31 (1986): 114. This is not to suggest that *Cahiers* critics were interested only in Hollywood cinema. Of course they also championed such "masters" as F. W. Murnau, Sergei Eisenstein, Jean Renoir, Roberto Rossellini, and Carl Theodor Dreyer. I emphasize their polemical attraction to Hollywood films because their desire to uncover hidden, forgotten, or ignored gems led them to a cinema that was then widely regarded as unworthy of serious philosophical reflection.

20. François Truffaut, *The Films in My Life,* trans. Leonard Mayhew (New York: Da Capo, 1994), 70.

21. Jacques Rivette, "The Essential," in *Cahiers du Cinéma, the 1950s: Neo-Realism, Hollywood, New Wave,* ed. Jim Hillier, trans. Liz Heron (Cambridge: Harvard University Press, 1985), 133.

22. Ibid., 134.

23. Ibid., 133.

24. Doane, *Emergence,* 227.

25. James Morrison, "After the Revolution: On the Fate of Cinephilia," *Michigan Quarterly Review* 44, no. 3 (2005): 406.

26. David Kehr, "*Cahiers* Back in the Day," *Film Comment* 37, no. 5 (2001): 35.

27. Dudley Andrew, "The Core and the Flow of Film Studies," *Critical Inquiry* 35 (2009): 898.

28. *Cahiers du Cinéma* editors, "John Ford's *Young Mr. Lincoln,*" trans. Helen Lackner and Diana Matias, *Screen* 13, no. 3 (1972): 8.

29. Christian Metz, *The Imaginary Signifier: Psychoanalysis and the Cinema,* trans. Celia Britton, Annwyl Williams, Ben Brewster, and Alfred Guzzetti (Bloomington: Indiana University Press, 1977), 15.

30. Serge Daney, "Theorize/Terrorize: Godardian Pedagogy," in *Cahiers du Cinéma: Volume Four, 1973–1978: History, Ideology, Cultural Struggle,* ed. David Wilson, trans. Annwyl Williams (New York: Routledge, 2000), 120.

31. Laura Mulvey and Peter Wollen, "From Cinephilia to Film Studies," in *Inventing Film Studies,* ed. Lee Grieveson and Haidee Wasson (Durham: Duke University Press, 2008), 228.

32. Sontag, "Century," 120.

33. Ibid., 122.

34. Stanley Kauffmann, "A Lost Love," *The New Republic,* September 8–15, 1997, 28–29; David Denby, "The Moviegoers: Why Don't People Like the Right Movies Anymore?" *The New Yorker,* April 6, 1998, 94.

35. Willemen, *Looks,* 240.

36. Ibid., 235.

37. Antoine de Baecque, *La Cinéphilie: Invention d'un Regard, Histoire d'une Culture, 1944–1968* (Paris: Librairie Arthème Fayard, 2003).

38. Christian Keathley, *Cinephilia and History, or the Wind in the Trees* (Bloomington: Indiana University Press, 2006), 8.

39. Ibid., 9.

40. Jonathan Rosenbaum and Adrian Martin, eds., *Movie Mutations: The Changing Face of World Cinephilia* (London: BFI, 2003).

41. Marijke de Valck and Malte Hagener, "Down with Cinephilia? Long Live Cinephilia? and Other Videosyncratic Pleasures," in *Cinephilia: Movies, Love and Memory,* ed. de Valck and Hagener (Amsterdam: Amsterdam University Press, 2005), 14.

42. Ibid.

43. For detailed analyses of film viewing in a fully digitized culture, see Scott Balcerzak and Jason Sperb, eds., *Cinephilia in the Age of Digital Reproduction: Film,*

Pleasure and Digital Culture (London: Wallflower, 2008).

44. François Truffaut, "Foreword," in *Orson Welles: A Critical View,* trans. Jonathan Rosenbaum (New York: Harper & Row, 1978), 19.

45. Some of these debates have recently played out in the special dossiers of *Senses of Cinema, Framework,* and *Cinema Journal.*

46. Willemen, *Looks,* 227.

47. Peter Wollen, *Paris Hollywood: Writings on Film* (London: Verso, 2002), 5.

48. Ibid., 5, 6.

49. Ibid., 20.

50. Laura Mulvey, *Death 24 x a Second: Stillness and the Moving Image* (London: Reaktion Books, 2006), 8.

51. Ibid., 147.

52. Ibid., 160.

53. George Toles, "Rescuing Fragments: A New Task for Cinephilia," *Cinema Journal* 49, no. 2 (2010): 161.

54. Keathley, *Cinephilia and History,* 134.

55. Geoffrey O'Brien, *Castaways of the Image Planet: Movies, Show Business, Public Spectacle* (Washington, DC: Counterpoint, 2002), 132.

56. W. Benjamin, "Theses," 257.

57. Richard Wolin, *Walter Benjamin: An Aesthetic of Redemption* (Berkeley: University of California Press, 1994), 227.

58. Ibid., 232.

59. Vanessa R. Schwartz, "Walter Benjamin for Historians," *American Historical Review* 106 (2001): 1739.

60. W. Benjamin, "Theses," 263.

61. Ibid., 262.

62. Ibid.

63. Ibid., 255.

64. Schwartz, "Walter Benjamin," 1740.

65. Walter Benjamin, "The Work of Art in the Age of Mechanical Reproduction," in Arendt, *Illuminations: Essays and Reflections,* 226.

66. Ibid., 240.

67. W. Benjamin, "Theses," 262.

68. Stephanie Polsky, "Down the K. Hole: Walter Benjamin's Destructive Land-Surveying of History," in *Walter Benjamin and History,* ed. Andrew Benjamin (London: Continuum, 2005), 82.

69. Gerhard Richter, "A Matter of Distance: Benjamin's *One-Way Street* through *The Arcades,*" in *Walter Benjamin and the Arcades Project,* ed. Beatrice Hanssen (London: Continuum, 2006), 135.

70. Walter Benjamin, "One-Way Street," in *One-Way Street and Other Writings,* trans. Edmund Jephcott and Kingsley Shorter (London: New Left Books, 1979), 91.

71. Theodor Adorno, *Prisms,* trans. Shierry Weber Nicholsen and Samuel Weber (Cambridge: MIT Press, 1983), 233.

72. Susan Buck-Morss, *The Dialectics of Seeing: Walter Benjamin and the Arcades Project* (Cambridge: MIT Press, 1989), 217.

73. W. Benjamin, "M [The Flâneur]," in *AP,* 431.

74. Howard Eiland and Kevin McLaughlin, "Translators' Foreword," in *AP,* trans. Eiland and McLaughlin (Cambridge: Harvard University Press, 1999), xii.

75. Dimitris Vardoulakis, "The Subject of History: The Temporality of Praxis in Benjamin's Historiography," in *Walter Benjamin and History,* 125.

76. Schwartz, "Walter Benjamin," 1733. That is why elsewhere Schwartz dismisses the critique of the flâneur as someone who offers only a bourgeois male perspective, arguing instead that the "debate over the existence of the flâneuse or the working-class flâneur, for that matter, misses the point. The flâneur is not so much a person as flânerie is a positionality of power." Vanessa R. Schwartz, *Spectacular Realities: Early Mass Culture in Fin-de-Siècle Paris* (Berkeley: University of California Press, 1999), 10. I follow Schwartz's lead, using the masculine pronoun when refer-

ring to Benjaminian figures without assigning them any gendered implications.

77. Doane, *Emergence*, 227.

78. Kristin Thompson, "The Concept of Cinematic Excess," in *Film Theory and Criticism: Introductory Readings*, ed. Leo Braudy and Marshall Cohen (New York: Oxford University Press, 1999), 492.

79. Keathley, *Cinephilia and History*, 41.

80. Willemen, *Looks*, 277.

81. Richard Maltby, *Hollywood Cinema* (Oxford: Blackwell, 2003), 2.

82. Ibid.

83. W. Benjamin, "B [Fashion]," in *AP*, 69.

84. W. Benjamin, "Theses," 262.

85. Doane, *Emergence*, 228.

86. André Bazin, "On the *politique des auteurs*," in Hillier, ed., *Cahiers du Cinéma, the 1950s*, 258.

87. Roland Barthes, *S/Z: An Essay*, trans. Richard Miller (New York: Hill and Wang, 1974), 156.

88. David Bordwell, Janet Staiger, and Kristin Thompson, *The Classical Hollywood Cinema: Film Style and Mode of Production to 1960* (New York: Columbia University Press, 1985), 3–4.

89. Robert B. Ray, *A Certain Tendency of the Hollywood Cinema, 1930–1980* (Princeton: Princeton University Press, 1985), 33.

90. Thomas Schatz, *The Genius of the System: Hollywood Filmmaking in the Studio Era* (New York: Metropolitan, 1988), 8.

91. Ibid., 8–9.

92. Douglas Gomery, *The Hollywood Studio System: A History* (London: BFI, 2005); David Bordwell, *The Way Hollywood Tells It: Style and Story in Modern Movies* (Berkeley: University of California Press, 2006), 14. Of course, some challenges have been mounted to this generalized position in recent years. Rick Altman's inquiry, for instance, into "How classical was classical narrative?" disputes the Bordwell, Staiger, Thompson model. Rick Altman, "Dickens, Griffith, and Film Theory Today," in *Classical Hollywood Narrative: The Paradigm Wars*, ed. Jane Gaines (Durham: Duke University Press, 1992), 14.

93. Miriam Hansen, "The Mass Production of the Senses: Classical Cinema as Vernacular Modernism," in *Reinventing Film Studies*, ed. Christine Gledhill and Linda Williams (London: Arnold, 2000), 339.

94. Robert B. Ray, *How a Film Theory Got Lost and Other Mysteries in Cultural Studies* (Bloomington: Indiana University Press, 2001), 2.

95. Hansen, "Mass Production," 337.

96. F. Scott Fitzgerald, *The Love of the Last Tycoon*, ed. Matthew J. Bruccoli (Cambridge: Cambridge University Press, 1994), 3.

1. SONIC BOOMS

1. William K. Everson, *American Silent Film* (New York: Oxford University Press, 1978), 338.

2. Crosland's film was, of course, not the first with segments of synchronized sound. A year earlier, Crosland's *Don Juan* (1926) was released with synchronized sound effects and a musical soundtrack. There were others too, including sound newsreels of Charles Lindbergh's illustrious flight to Paris and return to New York. But *The Jazz Singer*, which also boasted synchronized dialogue sequences, was promoted as a media event and soon heralded the commercial dominance of the talkies.

3. A. Scott Berg, *Goldwyn: A Biography* (New York: Riverhead, 1998), 173.

4. Quoted in Mark A. Vieira, *Irving Thalberg: Boy Wonder to Producer Prince* (Berkeley: University of California Press, 2009), 78.

5. Aida Hozic, *Hollyworld: Space, Power, and Fantasy in the American Economy* (Ithaca: Cornell University Press, 2001), 68.

6. Douglas Gomery, *The Coming of Sound* (New York: Routledge, 2005), 3.

7. Marilyn Fabe, *Closely Watched Films: An Introduction to the Art of Narrative Film Technique* (Berkeley: University of California Press, 2004), 59.

8. Donald Crafton, *The Talkies: American Cinema's Transition to Sound, 1926–1931* (Berkeley: University of California Press, 1999), 532.

9. Scott Eyman, *The Speed of Sound: Hollywood and the Talkie Revolution, 1926–1930* (New York: Simon and Schuster, 1997), 162.

10. Bordwell, Staiger, and Thompson, *Classical Hollywood Cinema*, 301.

11. Gomery, *Coming of Sound*, 114.

12. Gerald Horne, *The Final Victim of the Blacklist: John Howard Lawson, Dean of the Hollywood Ten* (Berkeley: University of California Press, 2006), 51; James Lastra, *Sound Technology and the American Cinema: Perception, Representation, Modernity* (New York: Columbia University Press, 2000), 93.

13. Crafton, *The Talkies*, 532.

14. Ibid., 4.

15. Ibid., 532.

16. Everson, *American Silent Film*, 338.

17. Michel Chion, *Film, A Sound Art*, trans. Claudia Gorbman (New York: Columbia University Press, 2009), 36.

18. Aldous Huxley, *Brave New World and Brave New World Revisited* (New York: Harper Perennial, 2005), 225–226, 231.

19. Ibid., 199.

20. Ibid., 154.

21. Ibid., 155.

22. Ibid., 199.

23. Laura Frost, "Huxley's Feelies: The Cinema of Sensation in *Brave New World*," *Twentieth-Century Literature* 52 (2006): 457.

24. Aldous Huxley, *Complete Essays, Volume II: 1926–1929*, ed. Robert S. Baker and James Sexton (Chicago: Dee, 2000), 23.

25. Ernest Betts, *Heraclitus, or the Future of Films* (London: Kegan Paul, 1928), 86, 88.

26. Quoted in Tim Armstrong, *Modernity, Technology, and the Body: A Cultural Study* (Cambridge: Cambridge University Press, 1998), 231.

27. Frost, "Huxley's Feelies," 445.

28. Quoted in Bill Brown, *The Material Unconscious: American Amusement, Stephen Crane, and the Economies of Play* (Cambridge: Harvard University Press, 1996), 46.

29. Michael Immerso, *Coney Island: The People's Playground* (New Brunswick: Rutgers University Press, 2002), 3.

30. Armstrong, *Modernity*, 2, 3.

31. Georg Simmel, "The Metropolis and Mental Life," in *The Nineteenth-Century Visual Culture Reader*, ed. Vanessa R. Schwartz and Jeannene B. Przyblyski (New York: Routledge, 2004), 51.

32. Charles Dickens, *Dombey and Son* (London: Penguin, 2002), 79.

33. Wolfgang Schivelbusch, *The Railway Journey: The Industrialization of Time and Space in the 19th Century* (Berkeley: University of California Press, 1977), 130.

34. Henry Adams, *The Education of Henry Adams*, ed. Ira Nadel (Oxford: Oxford University Press, 1999), 412.

35. W. Benjamin, "On Some Motifs," 175.

36. Ben Singer, *Melodrama and Modernity: Early Sensational Cinema and Its Contexts* (New York: Columbia University Press, 2001), 26.

37. Tom Gunning, "An Aesthetic of Astonishment: Early Film and the (In)Credulous Spectator," in *Film Theory and Criticism*, ed. Leo Braudy and Marshall Cohen (New York: Oxford University Press, 2009), 736–750.

38. Quoted in Martin Loiperdinger, "Lumière's *Arrival of the Train*: Cinema's Founding Myth," *The Moving Image* 4, no. 1 (2004): 91.

39. Gunning, "Aesthetic of Astonishment," 737.

40. Miriam Hansen, *Babel and Babylon: Spectatorship in American Silent Film* (Cambridge: Harvard University Press, 1991), 25.

41. Ibid., 29.

42. W. Benjamin, "Work of Art," 250.

43. Quoted in Hansen, *Babel and Babylon*, 32.

44. Robert C. Allen, "The Movies in Vaudeville: Historical Context of the Movies as Popular Entertainment," in *The American Film Industry*, ed. Tino Balio (Madison: University of Wisconsin Press, 1985), 73; Lynne Kirby, *Parallel Tracks: The Railroad and Silent Cinema* (Durham: Duke University Press, 1997), 62.

45. Lee Grieveson and Peter Krämer, eds. *The Silent Cinema Reader* (New York: Routledge, 2003), 193.

46. Gunning, "Aesthetic of Astonishment," 744.

47. Of course, these moments have never disappeared and, as many film scholars would argue, they have gained renewed impetus in our current age of hyperindustralization and digitization. From time to time one hears of how sensational images result in a feeling of physical assault. In 1997, for instance, seven hundred Japanese children are supposed to have suffered seizures from a Pokémon cartoon.

48. Gunning, "Aesthetic of Astonishment," 744.

49. André Bazin, "The Evolution of the Language of Cinema," in *What Is Cinema? Vol. 1*, ed. and trans. Hugh Gray (Berkeley: University of California Press, 1967), 23.

50. Erwin Panofsky, "Style and Medium in Motion Pictures," in *Film Theory and Criticism*, ed. Leo Braudy and Marshall Cohen (New York: Oxford University Press, 2009), 251.

51. Gomery, *Coming of Sound*, 23.

52. Wolin, *Walter Benjamin*, 233.

53. Susan Buck-Morss, "The Flâneur, the Sandwichman and the Whore: The Politics of Loitering," in *Walter Benjamin*

and the Arcades Project, ed. Beatrice Hanssen (New York: Continuum, 2006), 40.

54. W. Benjamin, "O [Prostitution, Gambling]," *AP*, 498.

55. Ibid.

56. W. Benjamin, "O [Prostitution, Gambling]," *AP*, 513.

57. W. Benjamin, "M [The Flâneur]," *AP*, 417.

58. Howard Eiland, "Reception in Distraction," in *Walter Benjamin and Art*, ed. Andrew E. Benjamin (London: Continuum, 2005), 11.

59. W. Benjamin, "On Some Motifs," 177.

60. W. Benjamin, "O [Prostitution, Gambling]," *AP*, 513.

61. W. Benjamin, "Theses," 262.

62. Richard Barrios, *A Song in the Dark: The Birth of the Musical Film* (Oxford: Oxford University Press, 1995), 45.

63. Robert Spadoni, *Uncanny Bodies: The Coming of Sound Film and the Origins of the Horror Genre* (Berkeley: University of California Press, 2007), 24.

64. Fitzhugh Green, *The Film Finds Its Tongue* (New York: G. P. Putnam's, 1929), 12.

65. Mordaunt Hall, "Vitaphone Stirs as Talking Movie," *New York Times*, August 7, 1926, accessed June 23, 2010, http://select .nytimes.com/gst/abstract.html?res=FA0E16FC355B12738DDDAE0894D0405B868EF1D3&scp=1&sq=vitaphone+stirs+as+talking+movie&st=p.

66. Lastra, *Sound Technology*, 120.

67. Ibid.

68. The image of a horse also connects Hayes's automobile history to film history via Muybridge.

69. Crafton, *The Talkies*, 544.

70. John Belton, "Awkward Transitions: Hitchcock's *Blackmail* and the Dynamics of Early Film Sound," *Musical Quarterly* 83, no. 2 (1999): 228.

71. Julian Smith, "A Runaway Match: The Automobile in the American Film,

1900–1920," in *The Automobile and American Culture*, ed. David L. Lewis and Laurence Goldstein (Ann Arbor: University of Michigan Press, 1983), 182–183.

72. Quoted in Smith, "Runaway," 183.

73. Crafton, *The Talkies*, 172.

74. Belton, "Awkward Transitions," 236.

75. Crafton, *The Talkies*, 525.

76. Quoted in Crafton, *The Talkies*, 95.

77. Lotte Eisner, *Murnau* (Berkeley: University of California Press, 1973), 181.

78. Melinda Szaloky, "Sounding Images in Silent Film: Visual Acoustics in Murnau's *Sunrise*," *Cinema Journal* 41, no. 2 (2002): 127.

79. Ibid., 123.

80. Molly Haskell, "*Sunrise*," *Film Comment* 7, no. 2 (1971): 19.

81. Lauren Rabinovitz, "The Coney Island Comedies: Bodies and Slapstick at the Amusement Park and the Movies," in *American Cinema's Transitional Era: Audiences, Institutions, Practices*, ed. Charlie Keil and Shelley Stamp (Berkeley: University of California Press, 2004), 178.

82. Ian Conrich, "Before Sound: Universal, Silent Cinema, and the Last of the Horror-Spectaculars," in *The Horror Film*, ed. Stephen Prince (New Brunswick: Rutgers University Press, 2004), 54.

83. Spadoni, *Uncanny Bodies*, 55.

84. Quoted in Spadoni, *Uncanny Bodies*, 56.

85. Gaylyn Studlar, *This Mad Masquerade: Stardom and Masculinity in the Jazz Age* (New York: Columbia University Press, 1996), 200. Studlar cites Lon Chaney's films as the best examples of "freak shows" in the movies. Not coincidentally, Chaney was the first choice to play Gwynplaine, but he was unavailable.

86. Conrich, "Before Sound," 52.

87. Thomas Doherty, "This Is Where We Came in: The Audible Screen and the Voluble Audience of Early Sound Cinema," in *American Movie Audiences: From the Turn of the Century to the Early*

Sound Era, ed. Melvyn Stokes and Richard Maltby (London: BFI, 1999), 143.

88. Barrios, *Song in the Dark*, 42.

89. Quoted in Crafton, *The Talkies*, 175.

90. Eyman, *Speed of Sound*, 242.

91. Quoted in Barrios, *Song in the Dark*, 47.

92. Crafton, *The Talkies*, 169.

93. Belton, "Awkward Transitions," 236.

94. Review of *The Kiss*, *Variety* November 20, 1929.

95. Lucy Fischer, "Greta Garbo and Silent Cinema: The Actress as Art Deco Icon," *Camera Obscura* 48, no. 3 (2001): 102.

96. Melinda Szaloky, "'As You Desire Me': Reading the 'Divine Garbo' through Movement, Silence and the Sublime," *Film History* 18, no. 2 (2006): 201.

97. The struggle between Charles Guarry and Pierre Lassalle over Irene's affections may be read as a generational conflict, a familiar theme from the earliest sound films. Here, as in *Old San Francisco*, the old patriarch is killed.

98. Eyman, *Speed of Sound*, 343.

99. Christian Metz, "Aural Objects," trans. Georgia Gurrieri *Yale French Studies* 60 (1980): 29.

100. Ibid.

101. Eyman, *Speed of Sound*, 343.

102. Crafton, *The Talkies*, 313.

103. Laura Marcus, *The Tenth Muse: Writing about Cinema in the Modernist Period* (Oxford: Oxford University Press, 2007), 405.

104. Quoted in Spadoni, *Uncanny Bodies*, 30.

105. Spadoni, *Uncanny Bodies*, 60.

106. Sergei Eisenstein, *Film Form: Essays in Film Theory*, ed. and trans. Jay Leyda (San Diego: Harcourt Brace, 1949), 105.

107. Quoted in Marcus, *Tenth Muse*, 426.

108. Sergei Eisenstein, Vsevolod Pudovkin, and Grigori Alexandrov, "State-

ment on Sound," in *Film Form: Essays in Film Theory*, ed. and trans. Jay Leyda (San Diego: Harcourt, 1977), 258.

109. Gomery, *Coming of Sound*, 54.

110. Bryher, *The Heart to Artemis: A Writer's Memoirs* (New York: Harcourt, Brace & World, 1963), 246.

111. Gomery, *Coming of Sound*, 87.

112. Crafton, *The Talkies*, 178.

2. SHOW STOPPERS

1. James Harvey, *Romantic Comedy in Hollywood from Lubitsch to Sturges* (New York: Alfred A. Knopf, 1987), 354.

2. All references to the script are to the Release Dialogue Script, dated July 7, 1937, housed at the Margaret Herrick library in Beverly Hills, CA.

3. Andrew Horton, ed., *Three More Screenplays by Preston Sturges: The Power and the Glory, Easy Living, Remember the Night* (Berkeley: University of California Press, 1998), 169.

4. Thompson, "Cinematic Excess," 491.

5. Roland Barthes, *Image-Music-Text*, trans. Stephen Heath (New York: Hill and Wang, 1977), 53.

6. Louis Aragon, "On Décor," in *The Shadow and Its Shadow: Surrealist Writings on the Cinema*, ed. and trans. Paul Hammond (San Francisco: City Lights Books, 2000), 52.

7. Samuel Marx, *Mayer and Thalberg: The Make-Believe Saints* (New York: Random House, 1975), vii.

8. Tino Balio, *Grand Design: Hollywood as a Modern Business Enterprise, 1930–1939* (Berkeley: University of California Press, 1993), 16.

9. Schatz, *Genius of the System*, 70.

10. Jane M. Gaines, "Costume and Narrative: How Dress Tells the Woman's Story," in *Fabrications: Costume and the Female Body*, ed. Jane M. Gaines and Charlotte Herzog (New York: Routledge, 1990), 196.

11. Bernard F. Dick, *Anatomy of Film* (Boston: Bedford/St. Martin's, 2002); Elizabeth Kendall, *The Runaway Bride: Hollywood Romantic Comedy of the 1930s* (New York: Alfred A. Knopf, 1990); Sarah Berry, *Screen Style: Fashion and Femininity in 1930s Hollywood* (Minneapolis: University of Minnesota Press, 2000), 42.

12. René Clair, *Cinema Yesterday and Today*, ed. R. C. Dale, trans. Stanley Applebaum (New York: Dover, 1972), 195.

13. James Morrison, *Passport to Hollywood: Hollywood Films, European Directors* (Albany: SUNY Press, 1998), 1.

14. Ibid., 2

15. Jürgen Habermas, "Modernity – An Incomplete Project," in *The Anti-Aesthetic: Essays on Postmodern Culture*, ed. Hal Foster (New York: New Press, 1983), 6.

16. Ibid. Interestingly, Habermas argues that even modernists still preserve a relationship with the classical, because the term "classic" has always been used for that which survives over time. Not wanting to give that up, modernists assign that honor to works not because they carry the authority of a past epoch but because they were once modern.

17. Hansen, "Mass Production," 334.

18. Andrew Horton, *Laughing Out Loud: Writing the Comedy-Centered Screenplay* (Berkeley: University of California Press, 2000), 13.

19. Ibid., 67.

20. Harvey, *Romantic Comedy*, 365.

21. Dick, *Anatomy of Film*, 199.

22. Harvey, *Romantic Comedy*, 365.

23. Antonin Artaud, *The Theater and Its Double*, trans. Mary Caroline Richards (New York: Grove, 1958), 142.

24. Quoted in Anthony Slide, *Silent Topics: Essays on Undocumented Areas of Silent Film* (Lanham: Scarecrow, 2004), vi.

25. Michael Richardson, *Surrealism and Cinema* (New York: Berg, 2006), 61.

26. Hansen, "Mass Production," 335.

27. Jerome Delamater, "Busby Berkeley: An American Surrealist," *Wide Angle* 1 (1976): 24–29; Martin Rubin, *Showstoppers: Busby Berkeley and the Tradition of Spectacle* (New York: Columbia University Press, 1993); Robin Wood, *Sexual Politics and Narrative Film: Hollywood and Beyond* (New York: Columbia University Press, 1998).

28. Wood, *Sexual Politics,* 47.

29. Ibid.

30. Quoted in Lucy Fischer, *Designing Women: Cinema, Art Deco, and the Female Form* (New York: Columbia University Press, 2003), 102.

31. André Breton, *Mad Love,* trans. Mary Ann Caws (Lincoln: University of Nebraska Press, 1987), 88.

32. Margaret Cohen, *Profane Illumination: Walter Benjamin and the Paris of Surrealist Revolution* (Berkeley: University of California Press, 1995), 135.

33. Breton, *Mad Love,* 13.

34. Quoted in Cohen, *Profane Illumination,* 134–135.

35. Cohen, *Profane Illumination,* 135.

36. Fiona Bradley, *Surrealism* (Cambridge: Cambridge University Press, 1997), 12.

37. Quoted in Bradley, *Surrealism,* 19.

38. Ibid.

39. Katharine Conley, *Automatic Woman: The Representation of Women in Surrealism* (Lincoln: University of Nebraska Press, 1996), 113.

40. Breton, *Nadja,* 156.

41. Ibid., 19.

42. Ibid.

43. Ina Rae Hark, "Introduction: Movies and the 1930s," in *American Cinema of the 1930s: Themes and Variations,* ed. Ina Rae Hark (New Brunswick: Rutgers University Press, 2007), 1–2.

44. Paige Reynolds, "'Something for Nothing': Bank Night and the Refashioning of the American Dream," in *Hollywood in the Neighborhood: Historical Case Studies of Local Moviegoing,* ed. Kathryn Fuller-Seeley (Berkeley: University of California Press, 2008), 214.

45. Ibid.

46. Jacques Derrida, "My Chances/*Mes Chances:* A Rendezvous with Some Epicurean Stereophonies," in *Taking Chances: Derrida, Psychoanalysis, and Literature,* ed. Joseph H. Smith and William Kerrigan, trans. Irene Harvey and Avital Ronell (Baltimore: Johns Hopkins University Press, 1984), 1–32.

47. John Baxter, *Buñuel* (London: Fourth Estate, 1994), 193.

48. Carlo Salzani, *Constellations of Reading: Walter Benjamin in Figures of Actuality* (Bern: Peter Lang, 2009), 204.

49. W. Benjamin, "J [Baudelaire]," *AP,* 349.

50. Irving Wohlfarth, "Et Cetera?: The Historian as Chiffonier," *New German Critique* 39 (1986): 147.

51. Salzani, *Constellations,* 188.

52. Walter Benjamin, "Surrealism: The Last Snapshot of the European Intelligentsia," in *One-Way Street and Other Writings,* trans. Edmund Jephcott and Kingsley Shorter (London: New Left Books, 1979), 229.

53. W. Benjamin, "N [On the Theory of Knowledge, Theory of Progress]," *AP,* 461.

54. Ibid., 460.

55. Quoted in Barbara Vinken, "Eternity – A Frill on a Dress," *Fashion Theory* 1 (1997): 67.

56. Wohlfarth, "Et Cetera?," 154.

57. Ibid., 156.

58. Ibid.

59. Ibid., 155.

60. Peter Wollen, "Strike a Pose," *Sight and Sound* 5, no. 3 (1995): 14.

61. Ibid.

62. Coincidentally, Tristan Tzara made a similar gesture of gratitude when he adopted another symbolic date in 1921. Although his date of arrival in Paris from New York was July 22, he would forever tell

everyone that he arrived on Bastille Day, July 14.

63. Berry, *Screen Style,* xviii.

64. Vinken, "Eternity," 60.

65. Ibid., 63.

66. Horton, *Three More Screenplays,* 2–3.

67. James Curtis, *Between Flops: A Biography of Preston Sturges* (New York: Harcourt Brace Jovanovich, 1982), 110.

68. This tale is recounted by Cecil B. DeMille in his autobiography, which remained incomplete at the time of his death in 1959. It was put together from his drafts and notes posthumously by his associate Donald Hayne.

69. DeMille and his cohorts were not the first filmmakers to end up northwest of Los Angeles. D. W. Griffith had shot *In Old California* (1910) there. But *The Squaw Man* was the first feature film made in Hollywood, and it accelerated the development of a film community in the area soon thereafter. By 1915, the majority of films had moved production from the East Coast to the Los Angeles area, and Hollywood was born.

70. Quoted in David Chierichetti, *Mitchell Leisen: Hollywood Director* (Los Angeles: Photoventures, 1995), 20.

71. Chierichetti, *Mitchell Leisen,* 2.

72. Wollen, "Strike a Pose," 14.

73. Sumiko Higashi, *Cecil B. DeMille and American Culture: The Silent Era* (Berkeley: University of California Press, 1994), 142.

74. Quoted in Chierichetti, *Mitchell Leisen,* 22.

75. Howard Gutner, *Gowns by Adrian: The MGM Years, 1928–1941* (New York: Harry N. Abrams, 2001), 20.

76. Fischer, "Greta Garbo and Silent Cinema," 85.

77. Ibid., 85.

78. Jane Gaines, "On Wearing the Film: *Madam Satan* (1930)," in *Fashion Cultures: Theories, Explorations and Analy-* sis, ed. Stella Bruzzi and Pamela Church Gibson (London: Routledge, 2000), 171.

79. Barrios, *Song in the Dark,* 261.

80. Lois Banner, *Women in Modern America: A Brief History* (New York: Harcourt Brace Jovanovich, 1974), 197.

81. Richard Martin, *Fashion and Surrealism* (New York: Rizzoli, 1987), 11.

82. The appropriation of mannequins in Surrealist imagery dates back to 1919, when Man Ray's *Aviary* displayed a figure that is part armless mannequin, part bird cage, suggesting the constraints of the body.

83. Martin, *Fashion and Surrealism,* 50.

84. Quoted in Ulrich Lehmann, *Tigersprung: Fashion in Modernity* (Cambridge: MIT Press, 2000), 324.

85. Lehmann, *Tigersprung,* 325.

86. Herbert Blau, *Nothing in Itself: Complexions of Fashion* (Bloomington: Indiana University Press, 1999), 250.

87. Gaines, "Costume and Narrative," 193.

88. Ibid., 194.

89. Ibid., 195.

90. Joan Acocella, "Imagining Dance," in *Moving History/Dancing Cultures: A Dance History Reader,* ed. Ann Dils and Ann Cooper Albright (Middletown: Wesleyan University Press, 2001), 14.

91. Hansen, "Mass Production," 337.

92. Caroline Evans, "Yesterday's Emblems and Tomorrow's Commodities: The Return of the Repressed in Fashion Imagery Today," in *Fashion Cultures: Theories, Explorations and Analysis,* ed. Stella Bruzzi and Pamela Church Gibson (London: Routledge, 2000), 108.

93. Barrett C. Kiesling, *Talking Pictures: How They Are Made, How to Appreciate Them* (Atlanta: Johnson, 1937), 33.

94. Quoted in Ronald L. Davis, *The Glamour Factory: Inside Hollywood's Big Studio System* (Dallas: Southern Methodist University Press, 1993), 210.

95. Elizabeth Nielsen, "Handmaidens of the Glamour Culture: Costumers in the Hollywood Studio System," in Gaines and Herzog, *Fabrications*, 170.

96. Gutner, *Gowns by Adrian*, 12.

97. Ibid., 12–13.

98. *Letty Lynton* has been out of circulation since 1933. The film was pulled from distribution due to a plagiarism case that was filed against MGM. *Letty Lynton* was based on a historical incident, the 1857 trial of Madeleine Smith, an heiress accused of murdering her lover. That incident also formed the basis of Edward Sheldon's play, *Dishonored Lady*. MGM failed to purchase the rights to the play, but they made the film anyway. In Sheldon v. MGM, the studio was accused of copyright infringement, and the appellate court ruled against it. Traces of the film have been kept alive through George Hurrell's photographs of the dress.

99. Gilbert Adair, *Flickers: An Illustrated Celebration of 100 Years of Cinema* (London: Faber and Faber, 1995).

100. Quoted in Gutner, *Gowns by Adrian*, 116.

101. Jane Mulvagh, *Vogue: History of the 20th Century Fashion* (London: Viking, 1988), 112.

102. Quoted in Gutner, *Gowns by Adrian*, 118.

103. David Wallace, *Hollywoodland* (New York: St. Martin's, 2002), 111.

104. Kiesling, *Talking Pictures*, 94.

105. Charlotte Herzog and Jane Gaines, "'Puffed Sleeves Before Tea-Time': Joan Crawford, Adrian and Women Audiences," in *Stardom: Industry of Desire*, ed. Christine Gledhill (London: Routledge, 1991), 89.

106. Elizabeth Wilson, *Adorned in Dreams: Fashion and Modernity* (Berkeley: University of California Press, 1985), 171.

107. William Wiser, *The Twilight Years: Paris in the 1930s* (New York: Carroll and Graf, 2000), 141.

108. Piers Brendon, *The Dark Valley: A Panorama of the 1930s* (London: Jonathan Cape, 2000), 356.

109. Quoted in Martin, *Fashion and Surrealism*, 205.

110. Chanel actually fared much better with Jean Renoir, designing costumes for bourgeois life in France in *The Rules of the Game* (1939).

111. Ed Sikov, *Screwball: Hollywood's Madcap Romantic Comedies* (New York: Crown Publishers, 1989), 122.

112. Crevel, "Battlegrounds and Commonplaces," 57.

113. Sikov, *Screwball*, 19.

114. Hark, "Introduction," 1.

115. Ibid., 2.

3. SIGNATURE CRIMES

1. Most commentators briefly mention that, like most of Welles's films after *Citizen Kane*, *The Stranger* was not released as it was originally conceived by its director. The shooting script, schedules, and other documents housed in the Welles archive at the Lilly Library at Indiana University suggest that an extended Latin American sequence was planned, although it isn't clear if it was ever fully shot. Even if it was shot, as far as we know, no copy of it exists.

2. Clinton Heylin, *Despite the System: Orson Welles versus the Hollywood Studios* (Chicago: Chicago Review Press, 2005), 178.

3. Ibid.

4. Quoted in Orson Welles and Peter Bogdanovich, *This is Orson Welles*, ed. Jonathan Rosenbaum (New York: Da Capo, 1998), 186.

5. Natasha Fraser-Cavassoni, *Sam Spiegel: The Incredible Life and Times of Hollywood's Most Iconoclastic Producer, the Miracle Worker Who Went from Penniless Refugee to Show Biz Legend, and Made Possible* The African Queen, On the Waterfront, The Bridge on the River Kwai, *and*

Lawrence of Arabia (New York: Simon & Schuster, 2003), 96.

6. The Good Neighbor policy was adopted by the Roosevelt administration toward Latin America in an effort to protect U.S. political and financial interests in the region diplomatically and without military intervention. It was articulated by President Roosevelt in his 1933 inaugural address, which affirmed that the United States would serve as "the good neighbor – the neighbor who resolutely respects himself and, because he does so, respects the rights of others." It was reaffirmed later that year by Hull, serving as Roosevelt's secretary of state, and it was meant to act as a deterrence to German efforts at establishing a fascist stronghold in the Western hemisphere.

7. Jennifer E. Langdon, *Caught in the Crossfire: Adrian Scott and the Politics of Americanism in 1940s Hollywood* (New York: Columbia University Press, 2009), 100.

8. Barbara Leaming, *Orson Welles: A Biography* (New York: Viking, 1985), 312.

9. Heylin, *Despite the System,* 175.

10. Quoted in Leaming, *Orson Welles,* 312.

11. James Naremore, *The Magic World of Orson Welles* (Dallas: Southern Methodist University Press, 1989), 123.

12. Leaming, *Orson Welles,* 311.

13. Heylin, *Despite the System,* 170.

14. Ibid., 174.

15. For instance, like *Citizen Kane, The Stranger* was to begin at the end. Mary Rankin was to wake up at midnight, walk through a graveyard, and arrive at a New England clock tower for her "date with destiny," the working title of the film. A scream and a cutaway would reveal the climactic struggle, and then the narrative would commence in flashback. But that introduction was abandoned. Instead, the film begins at the beginning and unfolds as a straightforward, linear thriller.

16. Heylin, *Despite the System,* 190.

17. See Michael Burlingame's "New Light on the Bixby Letter" for a historical account of the reception of and controversies surrounding this letter. It must be noted that the controversies have only added to the mythology of this letter. Incidentally, while there has always been critical interest in this letter's authenticity, the debate seems to have reached fever pitch around the time of World War II, when several monographs were published on the subject, including Jacob Blanck's *The Lincoln Letter to Mrs. Bixby* (1941), David Rankin Barbee's *The Plain Truth about the Bixby Letter* (1945), and Sherman Day Wakefield's *Abraham Lincoln and the Bixby Letter* (1948). It is no wonder then that it makes a cameo appearance in Steven Spielberg's *Saving Private Ryan* (1998), when General George Marshall (Harve Presnell) is shown reading precisely this letter in order to justify saving Private Ryan. Michael Burlingame, "New Light on the Bixby Letter," *Journal of the Abraham Lincoln Association* 16 (1995): 59–72.

18. Quoted in Burlingame, "New Light," 64.

19. Michael North, "Authorship and Autography," *PMLA* 116 (2001): 1382.

20. Roland Barthes, *Camera Lucida: Reflections on Photography,* trans. Richard Howard (New York: Hill and Wang, 1981), 12.

21. North, "Authorship and Autography," 1380.

22. Martha Woodmansee, "On the Author Effect: Recovering Collectivity," in *The Construction of Authorship: Textual Appropriation in Law and Literature,* ed. Martha Woodmansee and Peter Jaszi (Durham: Duke University Press, 1994), 17.

23. Ibid.

24. Jacqueline Miller, *Poetic License: Authority and Authorship in Medieval and Renaissance Contexts* (New York: Oxford University Press, 1986), 121.

25. Woodmansee, "On the Author Effect," 18.

26. Ibid.

27. Mark Rose, "The Author as Proprietor: Donaldson v. Becket and the Genealogy of Modern Authorship," *Representations* 23 (1988): 56.

28. Quoted in Catherine Labio, *Origins and the Enlightenment: Aesthetic Epistemology from Descartes to Kant* (Ithaca: Cornell University Press, 2004), 84.

29. M. H. Abrams, *The Mirror and the Lamp: Romantic Theory and the Critical Tradition* (Oxford: Oxford University Press, 1953), 202.

30. William Wordsworth, *The Major Works including* The Prelude (Oxford: Oxford University Press, 1984), 659.

31. Helen Stoddart, "Auteurism and Film Authorship Theory," in *Approaches to Popular Film,* ed. Joanne Hollows and Mark Jancovich (Manchester: Manchester University Press, 1995), 40.

32. John Caughie, "Introduction," in *Theories of Authorship: A Reader,* ed. Caughie (London: Routledge, 1981), 12.

33. Abrams, *Mirror and the Lamp,* 228–229.

34. Jacques Rivette, "The Genius of Howard Hawks," in *Cahiers du Cinéma, the 1950s: Neo-Realism, Hollywood, New Wave,* ed. Jim Hillier, trans. Russell Campbell and Marvin Pister (Cambridge: Harvard University Press, 1985), 128.

35. William Routt, "L'Évidence" *Continuum* 5, no. 2 (1990): 42.

36. Andrew Sarris, "Notes on the Auteur Theory in 1962," in *The Primal Screen* (New York: Simon and Schuster, 1973), 50–51.

37. Liz Wells, *Photography: A Critical Introduction* (New York: Routledge, 1996), 22.

38. Quoted in Wells, *Photography,* 28.

39. North, "Authorship and Autography," 1382.

40. André Bazin, "The Ontology of the Photographic Image," in *What is Cinema?*

Vol. 1, ed. and trans. Hugh Gray (Berkeley: University of California Press, 1967), 13.

41. Ibid., 15.

42. Colin MacCabe, *The Eloquence of the Vulgar: Language, Cinema and the Politics of Culture* (London: BFI, 1999), 152.

43. André Bazin, *Orson Welles: A Critical View,* trans. Jonathan Rosenbaum (New York: Harper & Row, 1978), 33.

44. Ibid.

45. Bazin, "On the *politique des auteurs,*" 255.

46. Ibid., 250.

47. Ibid., 258.

48. Sarris, "Notes," 51.

49. Bazin, "On the *politique des auteurs,*" 258.

50. Roland Barthes, *Image-Music-Text,* trans. Stephen Heath (New York: Hill and Wang, 1977), 143.

51. Timothy Corrigan, *A Cinema Without Walls: Movies and Culture After Vietnam* (New Brunswick: Rutgers University Press, 1991), 102.

52. Thomas M. Leitch, "The Hitchcock Moment," *Hitchcock Annual* (1997–98): 34.

53. Bazin, "On the *politique des auteurs,*" 258.

54. Richard Macksey, "'The Glitter of the Infernal System': The Splendors and Miseries of Francis Coppola," *Bennington Review* 15 (1983): 2.

55. Peter Cowie, *The Cinema of Orson Welles* (New York: A. S. Barnes, 1973), 95; Leaming, *Orson Welles,* 315; Joseph McBride, *Orson Welles* (New York: Da Capo, 1996), 100; Naremore, *Magic World,* 125.

56. Robert Garis, *The Films of Orson Welles* (Cambridge: Cambridge University Press, 2004), 96.

57. Ibid., 97.

58. Quoted in André Bazin, Charles Bitsch, and Jean Domarchi, "Interview with Orson Welles (II)," in *Orson Welles: Interviews,* ed. Mark W. Estrin (Jackson: University of Mississippi Press, 2002), 74.

59. Peter Conrad, *Orson Welles: The Stories of His Life* (London: Faber and Faber, 2003), 223.

60. Quoted in Leslie Megahey, "Interview from *The Orson Welles Story*," in *Orson Welles: Interviews*, ed. Mark W. Estrin (Jackson: University of Mississippi Press, 2002), 189.

61. Quoted in Heylin, *Despite the System*, 171.

62. Edgar Allan Poe, "The Purloined Letter," in *The Complete Tales and Poems of Edgar Allan Poe* (New York: Vintage, 1975), 209.

63. Ibid., 211.

64. Ibid., 216.

65. Ibid., 221.

66. James V. Werner, "The Detective Gaze: Edgar A. Poe, the Flâneur, and the Physiognomy of Crime," *American Transcendental Quarterly* 15 (2001): 15.

67. W. Benjamin, *AP*, 8.

68. W. Benjamin, "R [Mirrors]," *AP*, 537.

69. W. Benjamin, "M [The Flâneur]," *AP*, 417.

70. Tom Gunning, "The Exterior as *Intérieur*: Benjamin's Optical Detective," *boundary 2* 30 (2003): 109–110.

71. Ibid., 110.

72. Walter Benjamin, "The *Flâneur*," in *Charles Baudelaire: A Lyric Poet in the Era of High Capitalism*, trans. Harry Zohn (London: Verso, 1997), 48.

73. Edgar Allan Poe, "The Man of the Crowd," in *The Complete Tales and Poems of Edgar Allan Poe* (New York: Vintage, 1975), 478.

74. Ibid., 481.

75. W. Benjamin, "The Flâneur," 41.

76. Gunning, "The Exterior as *Intérieur*," 127.

77. Lastra, *Sound Technology*, 2.

78. Jonathan Rosenbaum, "The Battle over Orson Welles," in *Essential Cinema: On the Necessity of Film Canons* (Baltimore: Johns Hopkins University Press, 2004), 376.

79. James Naremore, "Authorship and the Cultural Politics of Film Criticism," *Film Quarterly* 44, no. 1 (1990): 21.

80. Dudley Andrew, "The Unauthorized Auteur Today," in *Film Theory Goes to the Movies*, ed. Jim Collins, Hilary Radner, and Ava Preacher Collins (New York: Routledge, 1993), 83.

81. Jacques Derrida, *Signsponge*, trans. Richard Rand (New York: Columbia University Press, 1984), 56.

82. Peggy Kamuf, *Signature Pieces: On the Institution of Authorship* (Ithaca: Cornell University Press, 1988), 39, 13.

83. Adair, *Flickers*, 94–95.

84. Edgar Allan Poe, "The Murders in the Rue Morgue," in *The Complete Tales and Poems of Edgar Allan Poe* (New York: Vintage, 1975), 153.

85. Conrad, *Orson Welles*, 17.

86. Of course, trouble was brewing before Welles even got started. The first two projects he suggested, an adaptation of Joseph Conrad's *Heart of Darkness* and another based on Nicholas Blake's *The Smiler with the Knife*, were both rejected by RKO. Also, he was already developing a reputation for being unmanageable, because even before he began filming in Hollywood, Welles quit *The Campbell Playhouse* (formerly *The Mercury Theater on the Air*) due to artistic disputes with the show's sponsor.

87. Conrad, *Orson Welles*, 17.

88. Bazin, *Orson Welles*, 81.

89. Bordwell, Staiger, and Thompson, *Classical Hollywood Cinema*, 348.

90. Quoted in Christine Battersby, "From Gender and Genius," in *Aesthetics: The Big Questions*, ed. Carolyn Korsmeyer (Malden: Blackwell, 1998), 306.

91. Bordwell, Staiger, and Thompson, *Classical Hollywood Cinema*, 351–352.

92. Ibid., 341.

93. Ibid., 344.

94. Andrew Sinclair, *Spiegel: The Man Behind the Pictures* (Boston: Little, Brown and Company, 1987), 69.

95. Ibid., 1.

96. Ibid., 43.

97. Ibid., 44.

98. Abrams, *Mirror and the Lamp*, 226.

99. Otto Friedrich, *City of Nets: A Portrait of Hollywood in the 1940's* (New York: Harper & Row, 1986), 266.

100. Naremore, *Magic World*, 83.

101. Oscar Wilde, *The Picture of Dorian Gray* (New York: Tribeca, 2011), 85.

102. R. Barton Palmer, "The Politics of Genre in Welles' *The Stranger*," *Film Criticism* 9, no. 2 (1984–1985): 5.

103. Ibid., 6.

104. Naremore, *Magic World*, 124.

105. Truffaut, *Films*, 280.

106. Palmer, "Politics of Genre," 20.

107. Raymond Borde and Etienne Chaumeton, *A Panorama of American Film Noir, 1941–1953*, trans. Paul Hammond (San Francisco: City Lights Books, 2002), 147.

108. R. Barton Palmer, *Hollywood's Dark Cinema: The American Film Noir* (New York: Twayne, 1994), 126.

109. David Thomson, *Rosebud: The Story of Orson Welles* (New York: Alfred A. Knopf, 1996), 266.

110. David Everitt, *A Shadow of Red: Communism and the Blacklist in Radio and Television* (Chicago: Ivan R. Dee, 2007), 169.

111. Michael Freedland, *Hollywood on Trial: McCarthyism's War Against the Movies* (London: Robson, 2007), 9.

112. Quoted in Victor S. Navasky, *Naming Names* (New York: Hill and Wang, 1980), 369.

113. Larry Ceplair and Stephen Englund, *The Inquisition in Hollywood: Politics in the Film Community, 1930–60* (Champaign: University of Illinois Press, 2003), 202.

114. Quoted in Naremore, *Magic World*, 117.

115. Langdon, *Caught in the Crossfire*, xviii.

116. Ibid., 174.

117. Jean-Louis Comolli and Jean Narboni, "Cinema/Ideology/Criticism," in *Movies and Methods: Volume I*, ed. Bill Nichols (Berkeley: University of California Press, 1976), 27.

118. Naremore, *Magic World*, 123.

119. Quoted in Wheeler Winston Dixon, *The Early Film Criticism of François Truffaut* (Bloomington: Indiana University Press, 1993), 98.

120. Michael Anderegg, *Orson Welles, Shakespeare, and Popular Culture* (New York: Columbia University Press, 1999), 148.

121. Thomson, *Rosebud*, 17.

122. McBride, *Orson Welles*, 26.

123. Andreas Huyssen, *Other Cities, Other Worlds: Urban Imaginaries in a Globalizing Age* (Durham: Duke University Press, 2008), 263.

124. McBride, *Orson Welles*, 189.

125. Quoted in Joseph McBride, *What Ever Happened to Orson Welles? A Portrait of an Independent Career* (Lexington: University Press of Kentucky, 2006), 247.

126. Thomas Schatz, *Hollywood Genres: Formulas, Filmmaking, and the Studio System* (Boston: McGraw-Hill, 1981), 12.

127. Steven Heller, *The Swastika: Symbol Beyond Redemption?* (New York: Allworth, 2000), 61.

128. Malcolm Quinn, *The Swastika: Constructing the Symbol* (London: Routledge, 1994), 3.

129. Garis, *Films of Orson Welles*, 28.

130. We can assume that the association is purely coincidental, since Allen Smithee was not "born" until 1969, when the name was first used as a stand-in directorial credit for Robert Totten and Don Siegel's *Death of a Gunfighter* (1969), fourteen years after the initial release of *Mr. Arkadin*.

131. Jonathan E. Eburne, "The Cheerless Art of Industry: Marcel Duchamp and the Smithee Readymade," in *Directed by Allen Smithee*, ed. Jeremy Braddock and Stephen Hock (Minneapolis: University of Minnesota Press, 2001), 232–233.

132. Marcel Duchamp, *The Writings of Marcel Duchamp*, ed. Michel Sanouillet and Elmer Peterson (New York: Da Capo, 1973), 141.

133. Quoted in Bazin, Bitsch, and Domarchi, "Interview with Orson Welles (II)," 74.

134. Wheeler Winston Dixon, "Movies and Postwar Recovery," in *American Cinema of the 1940s: Themes and Variations*, ed. Dixon (New Brunswick: Rutgers University Press, 2006), 162.

4. APOCALYPTIC ANTENNAE

1. Mark Jancovich, "Re-examining the 1950s Invasion Narratives," in *Liquid Metal: The Science Fiction Film Reader*, ed. Sean Redmond (London: Wallflower, 2007), 327.

2. Eric Avila, "Dark City: White Flight and the Urban Science Fiction Film in Postwar America," in Redmond, ed., *Liquid Metal*, 89.

3. Peter Biskind, *Seeing Is Believing: How Hollywood Taught Us to Stop Worrying and Love the Fifties* (New York: Pantheon, 1983), 103.

4. Sean Redmond, "Science Fiction's Disaster Imagination," in Redmond, ed., *Liquid Metal*, 38.

5. This skepticism originates in part from the devastation caused by atomic power. Although initially considered the means to achieving utopian postwar existence, the bomb became the source of pervasive dread and distrust in technological advances. As early as 1946, Harold C. Urey, Nobel prize-winning atomic scientist, was dreading the future of nuclear warfare: "Not only may our own culture be destroyed by these weapons of mass destruction, but all civilizations as they exist in the world may be retarded and weakened for centuries to come." Harold C. Urey, "How Does it All Add Up?," in *One World or None*, ed. Dexter Masters and Katherine Way (New York: McGraw-Hill, 1946), 58.

6. Redmond, "Science Fiction's Disaster Imagination," 38.

7. David Seed, *American Science Fiction and the Cold War: Literature and Film* (Chicago: Fitzroy Dearborn, 1999), 1.

8. Biskind, *Seeing Is Believing*, 134.

9. Cyndy Hendershot, *Paranoia, the Bomb and 1950s Science Fiction Films* (Bowling Green: Bowling Green University Press, 1999), 83.

10. Eric Avila, *Popular Culture in the Age of White Flight: Fear and Fantasy in Suburban Los Angeles* (Berkeley: University of California Press, 2004), 93.

11. Harry Horner's *Red Planet Mars* (1952) similarly restricts most cosmic broadcasts to radio, even when it appears likely that the man of Mars might be the same as the man of Nazareth. However, Horner's film cannot resist the allure of a futuristic, flat-screen TV set.

12. Lynn Spigel, *Make Room for TV: Television and the Family Ideal in Postwar America* (Chicago: University of Chicago Press, 1992), 1.

13. The hysteria wasn't entirely unjustified. In terms of numbers, profits were indeed declining, and theaters were shutting down. Blair Davis cites a Sindlinger & Co. study showing that "from 1948 to 1952, 'in those areas where television reception was good, 23 percent of the theaters closed compared to only 9 percent of the theaters closing in areas where television was not available.'" Blair Davis, "Small Screen, Smaller Pictures: Television Broadcasting and B-Movies in the Early 1950s," *Historical Journal of Film, Radio and Television* 28, vo. 2 (2008): 220. Such numbers would only worsen over the course of the decade.

14. Thomas Doherty, *Cold War, Cool Medium: Television, McCarthyism, and American Culture* (New York: Columbia University Press, 2003), 4.

15. Albert Robida, *The Twentieth Century* (Middletown: Wesleyan University Press, 2004).

16. Maggie Jackson, *Distracted: The Erosion of Attention and the Coming Dark Age* (Amherst: Prometheus, 2008), 43.

17. Robida, *The Twentieth Century*, 52.

18. Paul Young, *The Cinema Dreams Its Rivals: Media Fantasy Films from Radio to the Internet* (Minneapolis: University of Minnesota Press, 2006), 172–173.

19. Christopher Anderson, "Television and Hollywood in the 1940s," in *Hollywood: Critical Concepts in Media and Cultural Studies,* ed. Thomas Schatz (New York: Routledge, 2004), 228.

20. Ibid., 236.

21. Douglas Gomery, "Failed Opportunities: The Integration of the US Motion Picture and Television Industries," in *American Television: New Directions in History and Theory,* ed. Nick Browne (London: Routledge, 1993), 33.

22. Janet Wasko, *Hollywood in the Information Age* (Austin: University of Texas Press, 1994), 8.

23. Young, *Cinema Dreams Its Rivals,* 139.

24. Quoted in Spigel, *Make Room for TV,* 99.

25. Doherty, *Cold War,* 3.

26. Erik Barnouw, *Tube of Plenty: The Evolution of American Television* (New York: Oxford University Press, 1990), 112.

27. There were other hearings that were telecast live, but they were available only to a limited audience in the Washington, D.C., area. In 1947, George Marshall testified before the Senate Foreign Relations Committee, and in 1948, the HUAC hearings into Alger Hiss, a former State Department official who was accused of being a Soviet spy, were both carried live.

28. Quoted in Lee Bernstein, *The Greatest Menace: Organized Crime in Cold War America* (Amherst: University of Massachusetts Press, 2002), 75.

29. Edward Robb Ellis, *The Epic of New York City: A Narrative History* (New York: Kondasha America, 1997), 574.

30. Doherty, *Cold War,* 112.

31. Quoted in Frank MacShane, ed., *Selected Letters of Raymond Chandler* (New York: Columbia University Press, 1981), 266.

32. Spigel, *Make Room for TV,* 47.

33. Quoted in Christopher Anderson, *Hollywood TV: The Studio System in the Fifties* (Austin: University of Texas Press, 1994), 93.

34. Kingdon S. Tyler, *Telecasting and Color* (New York: Harcourt, Brace, 1946), 200.

35. Anderson, *Hollywood TV,* 93.

36. Susan Sontag, "The Imagination of Disaster," in Redmond, ed., *Liquid Metal,* 41.

37. Nancy E. Bernhard, *U.S. Television News and Cold War Propaganda, 1947–1960* (New York: Cambridge University Press, 1999), 140.

38. Doherty, *Cold War,* 9.

39. Bernhard, *U.S. Television News,* 140.

40. William Boddy, *Fifties Television: The Industry and its Critics* (Urbana: University of Illinois Press, 1993), 20.

41. Doherty, *Cold War,* 189.

42. Ibid.

43. Gary R. Edgerton, *The Columbia History of American Television* (New York: Columbia University Press, 2007), 153.

44. Doherty, *Cold War,* 176.

45. Ibid., 204.

46. Quoted in Anderson, *Hollywood TV,* 1–2.

47. Quoted in Rudy Behlmer, ed., *Memo from David O. Selznick: The Creation of Gone with the Wind and Other Motion-Picture Classics – as Revealed in the Producer's Private Letters, Telegrams, Memorandums, and Autobiographical Remarks* (New York: Modern Library, 2000), 211.

48. Walter Benjamin, "The Storyteller: Reflections on the Works of Nikolai Leskov," in *Illuminations: Essays and Reflections,* ed. Hannah Arendt, trans.

Harry Zohn (New York: Schocken, 1968), 88–89.

49. John McCole, *Walter Benjamin and the Antinomies of Tradition* (Ithaca: Cornell University Press, 1993), 275.

50. W. Benjamin, "The Storyteller," 85.

51. Ibid., 87.

52. McCole, *Walter Benjamin*, 275–276.

53. W. Benjamin, "The Storyteller," 90.

54. Ibid., 91.

55. Ibid., 90.

56. Ibid., 89.

57. Ibid.

58. Ibid., 93.

59. Ibid., 90.

60. Philip Simay, "Tradition as Injunction: Benjamin and the Critique of Historicisms," in A. Benjamin, ed., *Walter Benjamin and History*, 139.

61. W. Benjamin, "The Storyteller," 96.

62. Ibid.

63. Ibid., 86.

64. Ibid.

65. Simay, "Tradition as Injunction," 140.

66. David S. Ferris, *The Cambridge Introduction to Walter Benjamin* (Cambridge: Cambridge University Press, 2008), 111.

67. Ibid., 112.

68. W. Benjamin, "The Storyteller," 86. Although Anna McCarthy has argued that television was very much present in public spaces, and that it was initially conceived in the 1940s as a public medium to complement its liveness, television has since become a household fixture. Anna McCarthy, *Ambient Television: Visual Culture and Public Space* (Durham: Duke University Press, 2001).

69. Quoted in Boddy, *Fifties Television*, 105.

70. Gilbert Seldes, *Writing for Television* (New York: Doubleday, 1952), 30.

71. Walter Benjamin, "Experience and Poverty," in *Walter Benjamin: Selected Writings, Volume 2, 1927–1934*, ed. Michael W. Jennings, Howard Eiland, and Gary

Smith (Cambridge: Harvard University Press, 1999), 731.

72. Douglas Gomery, *Shared Pleasures: A History of Movie Presentation in the United States* (Madison: University of Wisconsin Press, 1992), 247.

73. Sontag, "Imagination of Disaster," 44.

74. Melvin E. Matthews, *Hostile Aliens, Hollywood and Today's News: 1950s Science Fiction Films and 9/11* (New York: Algora, 2007), 23.

75. Michael Pinsky, *Future Present: Ethics and/as Science Fiction* (Madison: Fairleigh Dickinson University Press, 2003), 99.

76. Charles A. Siepmann, *Radio, Television, and Society* (New York: Oxford University Press, 1950), 347.

77. William L. Laurence, *Dawn over Zero: The Story of the Atomic Bomb* (New York: Alfred A. Knopf, 1953), 347.

78. Quoted in Seed, *American Science Fiction*, 8.

79. Jancovich, "Re-examining," 325.

80. Quoted in Spigel, *Make Room for TV*, 53.

81. Cyndy Hendershot, "Darwin and the Atom: Evolution/Devolution Fantasies in *The Beast from 20,000 Fathoms, Them!*, and *The Incredible Shrinking Man*," *Science Fiction Studies* 25 (1998): 321.

82. Lynn Spigel, *Welcome to the Dreamhouse: Popular Media and Postwar Suburbs* (Durham: Duke University Press, 2001), 37.

83. Vivian Sobchack, "The Virginity of Astronauts: Sex and the Science Fiction Film," in *Alien Zone: Cultural Theory and Contemporary Science Fiction Cinema*, ed. Annette Kuhn (London: Verso, 1990), 111.

84. There is a comparable condemnation of advanced technologies in Byron Haskin's *War of the Worlds* (1953), made in the same year as *Beast*. In Haskin's film, the alien invaders may be technologically advanced, but they are seen as cool, un-

sympathetic, non-human, and therefore morally inferior.

85. For a comprehensive analysis of how horror films explicitly project masculine fears on the female Other, see Barry Keith Grant's *The Dread of Difference: Gender and the Horror Film*, ed. Grant (Austin: University of Texas Press, 1996).

86. Vivian Sobchack, *Screening Space: The American Science Fiction Film* (New Brunswick: Rutgers University Press, 1999), 116–117.

87. Barbara Creed, *The Monstrous-Feminine: Film, Feminism, Psychoanalysis (New York: Routledge, 1993)*, 27.

88. James Gilbert, *Men in the Middle: Searching for Masculinity in the 1950s* (Chicago: University of Chicago Press, 2005), 217.

89. Mary Beth Haralovich, "Sitcoms and Suburbs: Positioning the 1950s Homemaker," *Quarterly Review of Film and Video* 11 (1989): 62.

90. Philip Wylie, *Generation of Vipers* (Champaign: Dalkey Archive, 1996), 215.

91. Ibid., 41.

92. Ibid., 214.

93. Jon Lewis, "Movies and Growing up . . . Absurd," in *American Cinema of the 1950s: Themes and Variations*, ed. Murray Pomerance (New Brunswick: Rutgers University Press, 2005), 147.

94. Laura Mulvey, *Visual and Other Pleasures* (New York: Palgrave Macmillan, 2009), 67.

95. *Them!* is not the only time the monster is visually linked to television. In Kurt Neumann's *Kronos* (1957), the robot's antennae look very similar to rabbit ears on a television set.

96. Avila, "Dark City," 94.

97. Sidney Perkowitz, *Hollywood Science: Movies, Science, & the End of the World* (New York: Columbia University Press, 2007), 23.

98. Barry Keith Grant, "Movies and the Crack of Doom," in *American Cinema of*

the 1950s: *Themes and Variations*, ed. Murray Pomerance (New Brunswick: Rutgers University Press, 2005), 174.

99. Hendershot, *Paranoia*, 49.

100. Christine Becker, *It's the Movies that Got Small: Hollywood Film Stars on 1950s Television* (Middletown: Wesleyan University Press, 2008).

101. Seed, *American Science Fiction*, 134.

102. This is not to suggest that there were only cheerful shows on television. But those that did interrogate the myth of small town contentment did not commence until the tail end of the decade – like *The Twilight Zone*, which first aired in October 1959.

103. Todd Gitlin, "Prime Time Ideology: The Hegemonic Process in Television Entertainment," in *Television: The Critical View*, ed. Horace Newcomb (Oxford: Oxford University Press, 2000), 584.

104. Lori Landay, *Madcaps, Screwballs, & Con Women: The Female Trickster in American Culture* (Philadelphia: University of Pennsylvania Press, 1998), 190.

105. Fredric Jameson, *Postmodernism, or, the Cultural Logic of Late Capitalism* (Durham: Duke University Press, 1991), 280.

106. Ray Pratt, *Projecting Paranoia: Conspiratorial Visions in American Film* (Lawrence: University Press of Kansas, 2001), 33.

107. William H. Whyte, *The Organization Man* (Philadelphia: University of Pennsylvania Press, 2002), 378.

108. Jackie Byars, *All That Hollywood Allows: Re-reading Gender in 1950s Melodrama* (Chapel Hill: University of North Carolina Press, 1991), 88. In fact, producer Walter Wanger had reportedly considered having Edward R. Murrow interview the film's protagonist, Miles Bennell, thereby aligning him with the one figure on television who was truly regarded as nonconformist.

109. Shawn Rosenheim, "Extraterrestrial: Science Fictions in *A Brief History of Time* and *The Incredible Shrinking Man*," *Film Quarterly* 48, no. 4 (1995): 18.

110. M. Keith Booker, *Monsters, Mushroom Clouds, and the Cold War: American Science Fiction and the Roots of Postmodernism, 1946–64* (Westport: Greenwood, 2001), 156.

111. Michael Tavel Clarke, *These Days of Large Things: The Culture of Size in America, 1865–1930* (Ann Arbor: University of Michigan Press, 2007), 242.

112. Michele Hilmes, *Hollywood and Broadcasting: From Radio to Cable* (Urbana: University of Illinois Press, 1990), 165.

113. Maltby, *Hollywood Cinema*, 172.

114. Douglas Gomery, "Toward a New Media Economics," in *Post-Theory: Reconstructing Film Studies*, ed. David Bordwell and Noël Carroll (Madison: University of Wisconsin Press, 1996), 409.

115. Paul Arthur, "The Last Four Things: History, Technology, Hollywood, Apocalypse," in *The End of Cinema as We Know It: American Film in the Nineties*, ed. Jon Lewis (New York: New York University Press, 2001), 342, 343.

116. Ibid., 346.

117. Jon Nelson Wagner and Tracy Biga MacLean, *Television at the Movies: Cinematic and Critical Responses to American Broadcasting* (New York: Continuum, 2008), 14.

118. Spigel, *Welcome to the Dreamhouse*, 393.

119. Greg Dickinson, "The *Pleasantville* Effect: Nostalgia and the Visual Framing of (White) Suburbia," *Western Journal of Communication* 70, no. 3 (2006): 221.

120. Spigel, *Welcome to the Dreamhouse*, 394.

121. Alev Adil and Steve Kennedy, "Technology on Screen: Projections, Paranoia, and Discursive Practice," in *Cyberculture and New Media*, ed. Francisco J. Ricardo (New York: Rodopi, 2009), 223.

122. Ibid.

123. I am not arguing that Haynes's films need to be read as science fiction. However, their focus on the role of television and the unhinged nature of their diegeses make them relevant here.

124. Marcia Landy, "Storytelling and Information in Todd Haynes's Films," in *The Cinema of Todd Haynes: All That Heaven Allows*, ed. James Morrison (London: Wallflower, 2007), 16.

125. Gilles Deleuze, *Cinema 2: The Time Image*, trans. Hugh Tomlinson and Robert Galeta (Minneapolis: University of Minnesota Press, 1989), 269.

126. Lynne Joyrich, *Re-Viewing Reception: Television, Gender, and Postmodern Culture* (Bloomington: Indiana University Press, 1996), 45.

127. Bordwell, *Way Hollywood Tells It*, 17.

128. Simay, "Tradition as Injunction," 140.

CONCLUSION

1. Frank O'Hara, "To the Film Industry in Crisis," in *Meditations in an Emergency* (New York: Grove Press, 1957), 3.

2. Ibid.

3. Ibid., 4.

4. Frank O'Hara, "The Critic," in *The Collected Poems of Frank O'Hara*, ed. Donald Allen (Berkeley: University of California Press, 1995), 48.

5. Janet Bergstrom, *Endless Night: Cinema and Psychoanalysis, Parallel Histories* (Berkeley: University of California Press, 1999), 2–3.

6. Christine Gledhill and Linda Williams, "Introduction," in Gledhill and Williams, *Reinventing Film Studies*, 1–3. Dudley Andrew is even more specific about the moment of birth, marking "the advent of academic film studies at the moment when Metz leapfrogged over Mitry as he

reviewed the latter's *Esthétique et psychologie du cinéma.*" Because, Andrew argues, this is the time when Metz replaces "his elder's humanism with a new structuralist vocabulary and method." Andrew, "The Core and the Flow," 896.

7. Mulvey and Wollen, "From Cinephilia to Film Studies," 227.

8. Lee Grieveson and Haidee Wasson, "The Academy and Motion Pictures," in Grieveson and Wasson, *Inventing Film Studies,* xvi.

9. Dana Polan, *Scenes of Instruction: The Beginnings of the U.S. Study of Film* (Berkeley: University of California Press, 2007), 14.

10. Ibid., 4.

11. Mulvey and Wollen, "From Cinephilia to Film Studies," 228.

12. Mark Betz, "Little Books," in Grieveson and Wasson, *Inventing Film Studies,* 324.

13. Geoffrey Nowell-Smith, "How Films Mean, or, From Aesthetics to Semiotics and Half-way Back Again," in Gledhill and Williams, *Reinventing Film Studies,* 8.

14. Ibid., 13.

15. Ibid., 16.

16. Malte Hagener and Marijke de Valck, "Cinephilia in Transition," in *Mind the Screen: Media Concepts According to Thomas Elsaesser,* ed. Jaap Kooijman, Patricia Pisters, and Wanda Strauven (Amsterdam: Amsterdam University Press, 2008), 22.

17. Toles, "Rescuing Fragments," 160.

18. Metz, *Imaginary Signifier,* 15.

19. Ibid.

20. Thomas Elsaesser, "Cinephilia or the Uses of Disenchantment," in de Valck and Hagener, *Cinephilia,* 32.

21. Mulvey, *Visual and Other Pleasures,* 16.

22. Elsaesser, "Cinephilia or the Uses of Disenchantment," 32.

23. Jon Lewis, ed., *The End of Cinema as We Know It: American Film in the Nineties* (New York: NYU Press, 2001).

24. In the last decade, books like Chuck Tryon's *Reinventing Cinema* and Henry Jenkins's *Convergence Culture* have tried to take stock of how the digital revolution has impacted film and film culture, while anthologies like Gledhill and Williams's *Reinventing Film Studies,* mentioned earlier, have attempted to assess how film studies might reformulate itself for the new millennium. At the same time, in a much-noted move, the Society of Cinema Studies, the largest professional organization in the field, changed its name to the Society of Cinema and Media Studies, and film programs like the one at UC Berkeley reinvented themselves as programs or departments in film and media. Chuck Tryon, *Reinventing Cinema: Movies in the Age of Media Convergence* (New Brunswick: Rutgers University Press, 2009); Henry Jenkins, *Convergence Culture: Where Old and New Media Collide* (New York: NYU Press, 2006).

25. Morrison, "After the Revolution," 412.

26. Ibid., 404.

27. Ibid., 412.

28. Ibid.

29. Ibid.

30. Jonathan Rosenbaum, *Goodbye Cinema, Hello Cinephilia: Film Culture in Transition* (Chicago: University of Chicago Press, 2010), ix.

31. Ibid., 7.

32. Ibid., 5.

33. Dale Hudson and Patricia Zimmerman, "Cinephilia, Technophilia and Collaborative Remix Zones," *Screen* 50, no. 1 (2009): 139.

34. Offering a similar proposal, and borrowing Dudley Andrew's paradigm of the three stages of film studies – where the first stage is the era when (primarily

European) intellectuals hailed cinema as a modern medium, the second stage is the institutionalization of film studies, and the third stage has been the move away from grand theory – Christian Keathley argues that his project works "to remobilize the first stage's cinephilic spirit in the service of the third stage's primary interests: film history and reception studies." By reinjecting the cinephiliac spirit into film studies, he merges the biographical, the historical, and the theoretical. Keathley, *Cinephilia and History*, 6.

35. Robert Darnton, *George Washington's False Teeth: An Unconventional Guide to the Eighteenth Century* (New York: W. W. Norton, 2003), ix.

36. Toles, "Rescuing Fragments," 161.

37. Ibid.

38. Walter Benjamin, *Understanding Brecht*, trans. Anna Bostock (London: New Left Books, 1977), 19.

Bibliography

Abrams, M. H. *The Mirror and the Lamp: Romantic Theory and the Critical Tradition*. Oxford: Oxford University Press, 1953.

Acocella, Joan. "Imagining Dance." In *Moving History/Dancing Cultures: A Dance History Reader*, edited by Ann Dils and Ann Cooper Albright, 12–16. Middletown: Wesleyan University Press, 2001.

Adair, Gilbert. *Flickers: An Illustrated Celebration of 100 Years of Cinema*. London: Faber and Faber, 1995.

Adams, Henry. *The Education of Henry Adams*. Edited by Ira Nadel. Oxford: Oxford University Press, 1999.

Adil, Alev, and Steve Kennedy. "Technology on Screen: Projections, Paranoia, and Discursive Practice." In *Cyberculture and New Media*, edited by Francisco J. Ricardo, 219–230. New York: Rodopi, 2009.

Adorno, Theodor. *Prisms*. Translated by Shierry Weber Nicholsen and Samuel Weber. Cambridge: MIT Press, 1983.

Allen, Robert C. "The Movies in Vaudeville: Historical Context of the Movies as Popular Entertainment." In *The American Film Industry*, edited by Tino Balio, 57–82. Madison: University of Wisconsin Press, 1985.

Altman, Rick. "Dickens, Griffith, and Film Theory Today." In *Classical Hollywood Narrative: The Paradigm Wars*, edited by Jane Gaines, 9–47. Durham: Duke University Press, 1992.

Anderegg, Michael. *Orson Welles, Shakespeare, and Popular Culture*. New York: Columbia University Press, 1999.

Anderson, Christopher. *Hollywood TV: The Studio System in the Fifties*. Austin: University of Texas Press, 1994.

———. "Television and Hollywood in the 1940s." In *Hollywood: Critical Concepts in Media and Cultural Studies*, edited by Thomas Schatz, 227–254. New York: Routledge, 2004.

Andrew, Dudley. "The Core and the Flow of Film Studies." *Critical Inquiry* 35 (2009): 879–915.

———. "The Unauthorized Auteur Today." In *Film Theory Goes to the Movies*, edited by Jim Collins, Hilary Radner, and Ava Preacher Collins, 77–85. New York: Routledge, 1993.

Aragon, Louis. "On Décor." In *The Shadow and Its Shadow: Surrealist Writings on the Cinema*, edited and translated by Paul Hammond, 50–54. San Francisco: City Lights Books, 2000.

Armstrong, Tim. *Modernity, Technology, and the Body: A Cultural Study*. Cambridge: Cambridge University Press, 1998.

Arnheim, Rudolf. *Film as Art*. Berkeley: University of California Press, 1969.

Artaud, Antonin. *The Theater and Its Double*. Translated by Mary Caroline Richards. New York: Grove, 1958.

Arthur, Paul. "The Last Four Things: History, Technology, Hollywood, Apocalypse." In Lewis, *The End of Cinema as We Know It*, 342–355.

Avila, Eric. "Dark City: White Flight and the Urban Science Fiction Film in Postwar America." In Redmond, *Liquid Metal*, 88–97.

———. *Popular Culture in the Age of White Flight: Fear and Fantasy in Suburban Los Angeles*. Berkeley: University of California Press, 2004.

Babington, Bruce, and Peter William Evans. *Blue Skies and Silver Linings: Aspects of the Hollywood Musical*. Manchester: Manchester University Press, 1985.

Balcerzak, Scott, and Jason Sperb, eds. *Cinephilia in the Age of Digital Reproduction: Film, Pleasure and Digital Culture*. London: Wallflower, 2008.

Balio, Tino. *Grand Design: Hollywood as a Modern Business Enterprise, 1930–1939*. Berkeley: University of California Press, 1993.

Banner, Lois. *Women in Modern America: A Brief History*. New York: Harcourt Brace Jovanovich, 1974.

Barnouw, Erik. *Tube of Plenty: The Evolution of American Television*. New York: Oxford University Press, 1990.

Barrios, Richard. *A Song in the Dark: The Birth of the Musical Film*. Oxford: Oxford University Press, 1995.

Barthes, Roland. *Camera Lucida: Reflections on Photography*. Translated by Richard Howard. New York: Hill and Wang, 1981.

———. *Image-Music-Text*. Translated by Stephen Heath. New York: Hill and Wang, 1977.

———. *S/Z: An Essay*. Translated by Richard Miller. New York: Hill and Wang, 1974.

Battersby, Christine. "From Gender and Genius." In *Aesthetics: The Big Questions*, edited by Carolyn Korsmeyer, 305–313. Malden: Blackwell, 1998.

Baxter, John. *Buñuel*. London: Fourth Estate, 1994.

Bazin, André. "The Evolution of the Language of Cinema." In *What Is Cinema?* Vol. 1. Edited and translated by Hugh Gray, 23–40. Berkeley: University of California Press, 1967.

———. "On the *politique des auteurs*." In Hillier, *Cahiers du Cinéma, the 1950s*, 248–259.

———. "The Ontology of the Photographic Image." In *What is Cinema? Vol. 1*.

———. *Orson Welles: A Critical View*. Translated by Jonathan Rosenbaum. New York: Harper & Row, 1978.

Bazin, André, Charles Bitsch, and Jean Domarchi. "Interview with Orson Welles (II)." In *Orson Welles: Interviews*. Edited by Mark W. Estrin, 48–76. Jackson: University of Mississippi Press, 2002.

Becker, Christine. *It's the Movies That Got Small: Hollywood Film Stars on 1950s Television*. Middletown: Wesleyan University Press, 2008.

Behlmer, Rudy, ed. *Memo from David O. Selznick: The Creation of* Gone with the Wind *and Other Motion-Picture Classics – as Revealed in the Producer's Private Letters, Telegrams, Memorandums, and Autobiographical Remarks*. New York: Modern Library, 2000.

Belton, John. "Awkward Transitions: Hitchcock's *Blackmail* and the Dynamics of Early Film Sound." *Musical Quarterly* 83, no. 2 (1999): 227–246.

Benjamin, Andrew, ed. *Walter Benjamin and History*. London: Continuum, 2005.

Benjamin, Walter. *The Arcades Project*. Translated by Howard Eiland and Kevin McLaughlin. Cambridge: Harvard University Press, 1999.

———. "Experience and Poverty." In *Walter Benjamin: Selected Writings, Vol. 2, 1927–1934*. Edited by Michael W. Jennings, Howard Eiland, and Gary Smith, 731–736. Cambridge: Harvard University Press, 1999.

———. "The *Flâneur*." In *Charles Baudelaire: A Lyric Poet in the Era of High Capitalism*, 35–66. Translated by Harry Zohn. London: Verso, 1997.

———. "On Some Motifs in Baudelaire." In *Illuminations: Essays and Reflections*. Edited by Hannah Arendt, 155–200. Translated by Harry Zohn. New York: Schocken, 1968.

———. "One-Way Street." In *One-Way Street and Other Writings*, 45–104. Translated by Edmund Jephcott and Kingsley Shorter. London: New Left Books, 1979.

———. "The Storyteller: Reflections on the Works of Nikolai Leskov." In *Illuminations*, 83–109.

———. "Surrealism: The Last Snapshot of the European Intelligentsia." In *One-Way Street and Other Writings*, 225–239.

———. "Theses on the Philosophy of History." In *Illuminations*, 253–264.

———. *Understanding Brecht*. Translated by Anna Bostock. London: New Left Books, 1977.

———. "The Work of Art in the Age of Mechanical Reproduction." In *Illuminations*, 217–251.

Berg, A. Scott. *Goldwyn: A Biography*. New York: Riverhead, 1998.

Bergstrom, Janet. *Endless Night: Cinema and Psychoanalysis, Parallel Histories*. Berkeley: University of California Press, 1999.

Bernhard, Nancy E. *U.S. Television News and Cold War Propaganda, 1947–1960*. New York: Cambridge University Press, 1999.

Bernstein, Lee. *The Greatest Menace: Organized Crime in Cold War America*. Amherst: University of Massachusetts Press, 2002.

Berry, Sarah. *Screen Style: Fashion and Femininity in 1930s Hollywood*. Minneapolis: University of Minnesota Press, 2000.

Betts, Ernest. *Heraclitus, or the Future of Films*. London: Kegan Paul, 1928.

Betz, Mark. "Introduction." *Cinema Journal* 49, no. 2 (2010): 130–132.

———. "Little Books." In Grieveson and Wasson, *Inventing Film Studies*, 319–354.

Biskind, Peter. *Seeing Is Believing: How Hollywood Taught Us to Stop Worrying and Love the Fifties*. New York: Pantheon, 1983.

Blau, Herbert. *Nothing in Itself: Complexions of Fashion*. Bloomington: Indiana University Press, 1999.

Boddy, William. *Fifties Television: The Industry and its Critics*. Urbana: University of Illinois Press, 1993.

Booker, M. Keith. *Monsters, Mushroom Clouds, and the Cold War: American Science Fiction and the Roots of Postmodernism, 1946–64*. Westport: Greenwood, 2001.

Borde, Raymond, and Etienne Chaumeton. *A Panorama of American Film Noir, 1941–1953*. Translated by Paul Hammond. San Francisco: City Lights Books, 2002.

Bordwell, David. *The Way Hollywood Tells It: Style and Story in Modern Movies*. Berkeley: University of California Press, 2006.

Bordwell, David, Janet Staiger, and Kristin Thompson. *The Classical Hollywood Cinema: Film Style and Mode of Production to 1960*. New York: Columbia University Press, 1985.

Bradley, Fiona. *Surrealism*. Cambridge: Cambridge University Press, 1997.

Braudy, Leo, and Marshall Cohen, eds. *Film Theory and Criticism*. 7th ed. New York: Oxford University Press, 2009.

Brendon, Piers. *The Dark Valley: A Pan-orama of the 1930s*. London: Jonathan Cape, 2000.

Breton, André. *Mad Love*. Translated by Mary Ann Caws. Lincoln: University of Nebraska Press, 1987.

———. *Nadja*. Translated by Richard Howard. New York: Grove Press, 1960.

Brown, Bill. *The Material Unconscious: American Amusement, Stephen Crane, and the Economies of Play*. Cambridge: Harvard University Press, 1996.

Bryher. *The Heart to Artemis: A Writer's Memoirs*. New York: Harcourt, Brace & World, 1963.

Buck-Morss, Susan. *The Dialectics of See-ing: Walter Benjamin and the Arcades Project*. Cambridge: MIT Press, 1989.

———. "The Flâneur, the Sandwichman and the Whore: The Politics of Loiter-ing." In *Walter Benjamin and the Arcades Project*, edited by Beatrice Hanssen, 33–65. New York: Continuum, 2006.

Burlingame, Michael. "New Light on the Bixby Letter." *Journal of the Abraham Lincoln Association* 16 (1995): 59–72.

Byars, Jackie. *All That Hollywood Allows: Re-reading Gender in 1950s Melodrama*. Chapel Hill: University of North Caro-lina Press, 1991.

Cahiers du Cinéma editors. "John Ford's *Young Mr. Lincoln*." Translated by Helen Lackner and Diana Matias. *Screen* 13, no. 3 (1972): 5–44.

Cardinal, Roger. "Pausing over Peripheral Detail." *Framework* 30–31 (1986): 112–133.

Caughie, John. "Introduction." In *Theories of Authorship: A Reader*, edited by John Caughie, 9–16. London: Routledge, 1981.

Ceplair, Larry, and Stephen Englund. *The Inquisition in Hollywood: Politics in the Film Community, 1930–60*. Champaign: University of Illinois Press, 2003.

Chierichetti, David. *Mitchell Leisen: Hol-lywood Director*. Los Angeles: Photoven-tures, 1995.

Chion, Michel. *Film, A Sound Art*. Trans-lated by Claudia Gorbman. New York: Columbia University Press, 2009.

Cixous, Hélène. "Fiction and Its Phan-toms: A Reading of Freud's *Das Un-heimliche* (The 'Uncanny')." *New Liter-ary History* 7, no. 3 (1976): 525–548.

Clair, René. *Cinema Yesterday and Today*. Edited by R. C. Dale. Translated by Stanley Applebaum. New York: Dover, 1972.

Clarke, Michael Tavel. *These Days of Large Things: The Culture of Size in America, 1865–1930*. Ann Arbor: University of Michigan Press, 2007.

Cohen, Margaret. *Profane Illumination: Walter Benjamin and the Paris of Surreal-ist Revolution*. Berkeley: University of California Press, 1995.

Comolli, Jean-Louis, and Jean Narboni. "Cinema/Ideology/Criticism." In *Mov-ies and Methods: Vol. 1*, edited by Bill Nichols, 22–30. Berkeley: University of California Press, 1976.

Conley, Katharine. *Automatic Woman: The Representation of Women in Surrealism*. Lincoln: University of Nebraska Press, 1996.

Conrad, Peter. *Orson Welles: The Stories of His Life*. London: Faber and Faber, 2003.

Conrich, Ian. "Before Sound: Universal, Silent Cinema, and the Last of the Horror-Spectaculars." In *The Horror Film*, edited by Stephen Prince, 40–57. New Brunswick: Rutgers University Press, 2004.

Corrigan, Timothy. *A Cinema Without Walls: Movies and Culture After Vietnam*. New Brunswick: Rutgers University Press, 1991.

Cowie, Peter. *The Cinema of Orson Welles*. New York: A. S. Barnes, 1973.

Crafton, Donald. *The Talkies: American Cinema's Transition to Sound, 1926–1931*. Berkeley: University of California Press, 1999.

Creed, Barbara. *The Monstrous-Feminine: Film, Feminism, Psychoanalysis.* New York: Routledge, 1993.

Crevel, René. "Battlegrounds and Commonplaces." In *The Shadow and Its Shadow: Surrealist Writings on the Cinema,* edited and translated by Paul Hammond, 57–58. San Francisco: City Lights Books, 2000.

Curtis, James. *Between Flops: A Biography of Preston Sturges.* New York: Harcourt Brace Jovanovich, 1982.

Daney, Serge. "Theorize/Terrorize: Godardian Pedagogy." In *Cahiers du Cinéma: Vol. 4, 1973–1978: History, Ideology, Cultural Struggle,* edited by David Wilson, 116–123. Translated by Annwyl Williams. New York: Routledge, 2000.

Darnton, Robert. *George Washington's False Teeth: An Unconventional Guide to the Eighteenth Century.* New York: W. W. Norton, 2003.

Davis, Blair. "Small Screen, Smaller Pictures: Television Broadcasting and B-Movies in the Early 1950s." *Historical Journal of Film, Radio and Television* 28, no. 2 (2008): 219–238.

Davis, Ronald L. *The Glamour Factory: Inside Hollywood's Big Studio System.* Dallas: Southern Methodist University Press, 1993.

De Baecque, Antoine. *La Cinéphilie: Invention d'un Regard, Histoire d'une Culture, 1944–1968.* Paris: Librairie Arthème Fayard, 2003.

Delamater, Jerome. "Busby Berkeley: An American Surrealist." *Wide Angle* 1 (1976): 24–29.

Deleuze, Gilles. *Cinema 2: The Time Image.* Translated by Hugh Tomlinson and Robert Galeta. Minneapolis: University of Minnesota Press, 1989.

Denby, David. "The Moviegoers: Why Don't People Like the Right Movies Anymore?" *The New Yorker,* April 6, 1998, 94–101.

Derrida, Jacques. "My Chances/*Mes Chances:* A Rendezvous with Some Epicurean Stereophonies." In *Taking Chances: Derrida, Psychoanalysis, and Literature,* edited by Joseph H. Smith and William Kerrigan, 1–32. Translated by Irene Harvey and Avital Ronell. Baltimore: Johns Hopkins University Press, 1984.

———. *Signsponge.* Translated by Richard Rand. New York: Columbia University Press, 1984.

De Valck, Marijke, and Malte Hagener, eds. *Cinephilia: Movies, Love and Memory.* Amsterdam: Amsterdam University Press, 2005.

———. "Down with Cinephilia? Long Live Cinephilia? and Other Videosyncratic Pleasures." In de Valck and Hagener, *Cinephilia: Movies, Love and Memory,* 11–24.

Dick, Bernard F. *Anatomy of Film.* Boston: Bedford/St. Martin's, 2002.

Dickens, Charles. *Dombey and Son.* London: Penguin, 2002.

Dickinson, Greg. "The Pleasantville Effect: Nostalgia and the Visual Framing of (White) Suburbia." *Western Journal of Communication* 70, no. 3 (2006): 212–233.

Dixon, Wheeler Winston. *The Early Film Criticism of François Truffaut.* Bloomington: Indiana University Press, 1993.

———. "Movies and Postwar Recovery." In *American Cinema of the 1940s: Themes and Variations,* edited by Wheeler Winston Dixon, 162–181. New Brunswick: Rutgers University Press, 2006.

Doane, Mary Ann. *The Emergence of Cinematic Time: Modernity, Contingency, the Archive.* Cambridge: Harvard University Press, 2002.

Doherty, Thomas. *Cold War, Cool Medium: Television, McCarthyism, and American Culture.* New York: Columbia University Press, 2003.

———. "This Is Where We Came in: The Audible Screen and the Voluble Audience of Early Sound Cinema." In *American Movie Audiences: From the Turn of the Century to the Early Sound Era,* edited by Melvyn Stokes and Richard Maltby, 143–163. London: BFI, 1999.

Duchamp, Marcel. *The Writings of Marcel Duchamp.* Edited by Michel Sanouillet and Elmer Peterson. New York: Da Capo, 1973.

Eburne, Jonathan E. "The Cheerless Art of Industry: Marcel Duchamp and the Smithee Readymade." In *Directed by Allen Smithee,* edited by Jeremy Braddock and Stephen Hock, 229–247. Minneapolis: University of Minnesota Press, 2001.

Edgerton, Gary R. *The Columbia History of American Television.* New York: Columbia University Press, 2007.

Eiland, Howard. "Reception in Distraction." In *Walter Benjamin and Art,* edited by Andrew E. Benjamin, 3–13. London: Continuum, 2005.

Eiland, Howard, and Kevin McLaughlin. "Translators' Foreword." In W. Benjamin, *The Arcades Project,* ix–xiv. Translated by Howard Eiland and Kevin McLaughlin. Cambridge: Harvard University Press, 1999.

Eisenstein, Sergei. *Film Form: Essays in Film Theory.* Edited and translated by Jay Leyda. San Diego: Harcourt Brace, 1949.

Eisenstein, Sergei, Vsevolod Pudovkin, and Grigori Alexandrov. "Statement on Sound." In *Film Form: Essays in Film Theory.* Edited and translated by Jay Leyda, 257–260. San Diego: Harcourt, 1977.

Eisner, Lotte. *Murnau.* Berkeley: University of California Press, 1973.

Ellis, Edward Robb. *The Epic of New York City: A Narrative History.* New York: Kondasha America, 1997.

Elsaesser, Thomas. "Cinephilia or the Uses of Disenchantment." In de Valck and Hagener, *Cinephilia: Movies, Love and Memory,* 27–43.

Epstein, Jean. "Magnification." In *French Film Theory and Criticism, 1907–1939,* edited by Richard Abel, 235–241. Princeton: Princeton University Press, 1988.

———. "The Senses I (b)." In Abel, *French Film Theory and Criticism, 1907–1939,* 241–246.

Evans, Caroline. "Yesterday's Emblems and Tomorrow's Commodities: The Return of the Repressed in Fashion Imagery Today." In *Fashion Cultures: Theories, Explorations and Analysis,* edited by Stella Bruzzi and Pamela Church Gibson, 93–113. London: Routledge, 2000.

Everitt, David. *A Shadow of Red: Communism and the Blacklist in Radio and Television.* Chicago: Ivan R. Dee, 2007.

Everson, William K. *American Silent Film.* New York: Oxford University Press, 1978.

Eyman, Scott. *The Speed of Sound: Hollywood and the Talkie Revolution, 1926–1930.* New York: Simon and Schuster, 1997.

Fabe, Marilyn. *Closely Watched Films: An Introduction to the Art of Narrative Film Technique.* Berkeley: University of California Press, 2004.

Ferris, David S. *The Cambridge Introduction to Walter Benjamin.* Cambridge: Cambridge University Press, 2008.

Fischer, Lucy. *Designing Women: Cinema, Art Deco, and the Female Form.* New York: Columbia University Press, 2003.

———. "Greta Garbo and Silent Cinema: The Actress as Art Deco Icon." *Camera Obscura* 48, no. 3 (2001): 83–110.

Fitzgerald, F. Scott. *The Love of the Last Tycoon.* Edited by Matthew J. Bruccoli. Cambridge: Cambridge University Press, 1994.

Fraser-Cavassoni, Natasha. *Sam Spiegel: The Incredible Life and Times of Hollywood's Most Iconoclastic Producer, the*

Miracle Worker Who Went from Penniless Refugee to Show Biz Legend, and Made Possible The African Queen, On the Waterfront, The Bridge on the River Kwai, and Lawrence of Arabia. New York: Simon & Schuster, 2003.

Freedland, Michael. Hollywood on Trial: McCarthyism's War Against the Movies. London: Robson, 2007.

Friedrich, Otto. City of Nets: A Portrait of Hollywood in the 1940's. New York: Harper & Row, 1986.

Frost, Laura. "Huxley's Feelies: The Cinema of Sensation in Brave New World." Twentieth-Century Literature 52 (2006): 443–473.

Gaines, Jane M. "Costume and Narrative: How Dress Tells the Woman's Story." In Fabrications: Costume and the Female Body, edited by Jane M. Gaines and Charlotte Herzog, 180–211. New York: Routledge, 1990.

———. "On Wearing the Film: Madam Satan (1930)." In Fashion Cultures: Theories, Explorations and Analysis, edited by Stella Bruzzi and Pamela Church Gibson, 159–177. London: Routledge, 2000.

Garis, Robert. The Films of Orson Welles. Cambridge: Cambridge University Press, 2004.

Gilbert, James. Men in the Middle: Searching for Masculinity in the 1950s. Chicago: University of Chicago Press, 2005.

Gitlin, Todd. "Prime Time Ideology: The Hegemonic Process in Television Entertainment." In Television: The Critical View, edited by Horace Newcomb, 574–594. Oxford: Oxford University Press, 2000.

Gledhill, Christine, and Linda Williams. "Introduction." In Reinventing Film Studies, edited by Christine Gledhill and Linda Williams, 1–4. London: Arnold, 2000.

Godard, Jean-Luc. Godard on Godard. Edited and translated by Tom Milne. New York: Da Capo, 1986.

Gomery, Douglas. The Coming of Sound. New York: Routledge, 2005.

———. "Failed Opportunities: The Integration of the US Motion Picture and Television Industries." In American Television: New Directions in History and Theory, edited by Nick Browne, 23–36. London: Routledge, 1993.

———. The Hollywood Studio System: A History. London: BFI, 2005.

———. Shared Pleasures: A History of Movie Presentation in the United States. Madison: University of Wisconsin Press, 1992.

———. "Toward a New Media Economics." In Post-Theory: Reconstructing Film Studies, edited by David Bordwell and Noël Carroll, 407–418. Madison: University of Wisconsin Press, 1996.

Grant, Barry Keith. "Introduction." In The Dread of Difference: Gender and the Horror Film, edited by Barry Keith Grant, 1–12. Austin: University of Texas Press, 1996.

———. "Movies and the Crack of Doom." In American Cinema of the 1950s: Themes and Variations, edited by Murray Pomerance, 155–176. New Brunswick: Rutgers University Press, 2005.

Green, Fitzhugh. The Film Finds Its Tongue. New York: G. P. Putnam's, 1929.

Grieveson, Lee, and Haidee Wasson. "The Academy and Motion Pictures." In Grieveson and Wasson, Inventing Film Studies, i–xxxii.

Grieveson, Lee, and Haidee Wasson, eds. Inventing Film Studies. Durham: Duke University Press, 2008.

Grieveson, Lee, and Peter Krämer, eds. The Silent Cinema Reader. New York: Routledge, 2003.

Gunning, Tom. "An Aesthetic of Astonishment: Early Film and the (In)Credulous Spectator." In Braudy and Cohen, Film Theory and Criticism, 736–750.

———. "The Exterior as Intérieur: Benjamin's Optical Detective." boundary 2 30 (2003): 105–130.

Gutner, Howard. *Gowns by Adrian: The MGM Years, 1928–1941.* New York: Harry N. Abrams, 2001.

———. "'Now You See It, Now You Don't': The Temporality of the Cinema of Attractions." In Grieveson and Krämer, *The Silent Cinema Reader,* 41–50.

Habermas, Jürgen. "Modernity – An Incomplete Project." In *The Anti-Aesthetic: Essays on Postmodern Culture,* edited by Hal Foster, 3–15. New York: New Press, 1983.

Hagener, Malte, and Marijke de Valck. "Cinephilia in Transition." In *Mind the Screen: Media Concepts According to Thomas Elsaesser,* edited by Jaap Kooijman, Patricia Pisters, and Wanda Strauven, 19–31. Amsterdam: Amsterdam University Press, 2008.

Hansen, Miriam. *Babel and Babylon: Spectatorship in American Silent Film.* Cambridge: Harvard University Press, 1991.

———. "The Mass Production of the Senses: Classical Cinema as Vernacular Modernism." In Gledhill and Williams, *Reinventing Film Studies,* 332–350.

Haralovich, Mary Beth. "Sitcoms and Suburbs: Positioning the 1950s Homemaker." *Quarterly Review of Film and Video* 11 (1989): 61–83.

Hark, Ina Rae. "Introduction: Movies and the 1930s." In *American Cinema of the 1930s: Themes and Variations,* edited by Ina Rae Hark, 1–24. New Brunswick: Rutgers University Press, 2007.

Harvey, James. *Romantic Comedy in Hollywood from Lubitsch to Sturges.* New York: Alfred A. Knopf, 1987.

Haskell, Molly. "Sunrise." *Film Comment* 7, no. 2 (1971): 16–19.

Heller, Steven. *The Swastika: Symbol Beyond Redemption?* New York: Allworth, 2000.

Hendershot, Cyndy. "Darwin and the Atom: Evolution/Devolution Fantasies in *The Beast from 20,000 Fathoms, Them!,* and *The Incredible Shrinking Man.*" *Science Fiction Studies* 25 (1998): 319–335.

———. *Paranoia, the Bomb and 1950s Science Fiction Films.* Bowling Green: Bowling Green University Press, 1999.

Herzog, Charlotte Cornelia, and Jane Marie Gaines. "'Puffed Sleeves Before Tea-Time': Joan Crawford, Adrian and Women Audiences." In *Stardom: Industry of Desire,* edited by Christine Gledhill, 74–91. London: Routledge, 1991.

Heylin, Clinton. *Despite the System: Orson Welles versus the Hollywood Studios.* Chicago: Chicago Review Press, 2005.

Higashi, Sumiko. *Cecil B. DeMille and American Culture: The Silent Era.* Berkeley: University of California Press, 1994.

Hillier, James, ed. *Cahiers du Cinéma, the 1950s: Neo-Realism, Hollywood, New Wave.* Vol. 1. Cambridge: Harvard University Press, 1985.

Hilmes, Michele. *Hollywood and Broadcasting: From Radio to Cable.* Urbana: University of Illinois Press, 1990.

Horne, Gerald. *The Final Victim of the Blacklist: John Howard Lawson, Dean of the Hollywood Ten.* Berkeley: University of California Press, 2006.

Horton, Andrew. *Laughing Out Loud: Writing the Comedy-Centered Screenplay.* Berkeley: University of California Press, 2000.

Horton, Andrew, ed. *Three More Screenplays by Preston Sturges:* The Power and the Glory, Easy Living, Remember the Night. Berkeley: University of California Press, 1998.

Hozic, Aida. *Hollyworld: Space, Power, and Fantasy in the American Economy.* Ithaca: Cornell University Press, 2001.

Hudson, Dale, and Patricia Zimmerman. "Cinephilia, Technophilia and Collaborative Remix Zones." *Screen* 50, no. 1 (2009): 135–146.

Huxley, Aldous. *Brave New World and Brave New World Revisited.* New York: Harper Perennial, 2005.

———. *Complete Essays, Volume II: 1926–1929.* Edited by Robert S. Baker and James Sexton. Chicago: Dee, 2000.

Huyssen, Andreas. *Other Cities, Other Worlds: Urban Imaginaries in a Globalizing Age.* Durham: Duke University Press, 2008.

Immerso, Michael. *Coney Island: The People's Playground.* New Brunswick: Rutgers University Press, 2002.

Jackson, Maggie. *Distracted: The Erosion of Attention and the Coming Dark Age.* Amherst: Prometheus, 2008.

Jameson, Fredric. *Postmodernism, or, the Cultural Logic of Late Capitalism.* Durham: Duke University Press, 1991.

Jancovich, Mark. "Re-examining the 1950s Invasion Narratives." In Redmond, *Liquid Metal,* 325–336.

Jenkins, Henry. *Convergence Culture: Where Old and New Media Collide.* New York: NYU Press, 2006.

Joyrich, Lynne. *Re-Viewing Reception: Television, Gender, and Postmodern Culture.* Bloomington: Indiana University Press, 1996.

Kamuf, Peggy. *Signature Pieces: On the Institution of Authorship.* Ithaca: Cornell University Press, 1988.

Kauffmann, Stanley. "A Lost Love," *The New Republic,* September 8–15, 1997, 28–29.

Keathley, Christian. *Cinephilia and History, or the Wind in the Trees.* Bloomington: Indiana University Press, 2006.

Kehr, David. *"Cahiers* Back in the Day." *Film Comment* 37, no. 5 (2001): 30–35.

Kendall, Elizabeth. *The Runaway Bride: Hollywood Romantic Comedy of the 1930s.* New York: Alfred A. Knopf, 1990.

Kiesling, Barrett C. *Talking Pictures: How They Are Made, How to Appreciate Them.* Atlanta: Johnson, 1937.

Kirby, Lynne. *Parallel Tracks: The Railroad and Silent Cinema.* Durham: Duke University Press, 1997.

Labio, Catherine. *Origins and the Enlightenment: Aesthetic Epistemology from Descartes to Kant.* Ithaca: Cornell University Press, 2004.

Landay, Lori. *Madcaps, Screwballs, and Con Women: The Female Trickster in American Culture.* Philadelphia: University of Pennsylvania Press, 1998.

Landy, Marcia. "Storytelling and Information in Todd Haynes's Films." In *The Cinema of Todd Haynes: All That Heaven Allows,* edited by James Morrison, 7–24. London: Wallflower, 2007.

Langdon, Jennifer E. *Caught in the Crossfire: Adrian Scott and the Politics of Americanism in 1940s Hollywood.* New York: Columbia University Press, 2009.

Lastra, James. *Sound Technology and the American Cinema: Perception, Representation, Modernity.* New York: Columbia University Press, 2000.

Laurence, William L. *Dawn over Zero: The Story of the Atomic Bomb.* New York: Alfred A. Knopf, 1953.

Leaming, Barbara. *Orson Welles: A Biography.* New York: Viking, 1985.

Lehmann, Ulrich. *Tigersprung: Fashion in Modernity.* Cambridge: MIT Press, 2000.

Leitch, Thomas M. "The Hitchcock Moment." *Hitchcock Annual* (1997–98): 19–39.

Lewis, Jon, ed. *The End of Cinema as We Know It: American Film in the Nineties.* New York: NYU Press, 2001.

———. "Movies and Growing up . . . Absurd." In *American Cinema of the 1950s: Themes and Variations,* edited by Murray Pomerance, 134–154. New Brunswick: Rutgers University Press, 2005.

Loiperdinger, Martin. "Lumière's *Arrival of the Train:* Cinema's Founding Myth." *The Moving Image* 4, no. 1 (2004): 89–118.

Luhmann, Niklas. *Observations on Modernity.* Translated by William Whobrey. Stanford: Stanford University Press, 1998.

MacCabe, Colin. *The Eloquence of the Vulgar: Language, Cinema and the Politics of Culture.* London: BFI, 1999.

Macksey, Richard. "'The Glitter of the Infernal System': The Splendors and Miseries of Francis Coppola." *Bennington Review* 15 (1983): 2–16.

MacShane, Frank, ed. *Selected Letters of Raymond Chandler.* New York: Columbia University Press, 1981.

Maltby, Richard. *Hollywood Cinema.* Oxford: Blackwell, 2003.

Marcus, Laura. *The Tenth Muse: Writing about Cinema in the Modernist Period.* Oxford: Oxford University Press, 2007.

Martin, Adrian. "Cinephilia as War Machine." *Framework* 50, nos.1, 2 (2009): 221–225.

Martin, Richard. *Fashion and Surrealism.* New York: Rizzoli, 1987.

Marx, Samuel. *Mayer and Thalberg: The Make-Believe Saints.* New York: Random House, 1975.

Matthews, Melvin E. *Hostile Aliens, Hollywood and Today's News: 1950s Science Fiction Films and 9/11.* New York: Algora, 2007.

McBride, Joseph. *Orson Welles.* New York: Da Capo, 1996.

——. *What Ever Happened to Orson Welles? A Portrait of an Independent Career.* Lexington: University Press of Kentucky, 2006.

McCarthy, Anna. *Ambient Television: Visual Culture and Public Space.* Durham: Duke University Press, 2001.

McCole, John. *Walter Benjamin and the Antinomies of Tradition.* Ithaca: Cornell University Press, 1993.

Megahey, Leslie. "Interview from *The Orson Welles Story*." In *Orson Welles: Interviews.* Edited by Mark W. Estrin, 177–209. Jackson: University of Mississippi Press, 2002.

Metz, Christian. "Aural Objects." Translated by Georgia Gurrieri. *Yale French Studies* 60 (1980): 24–32.

——. *The Imaginary Signifier: Psychoanalysis and the Cinema.* Translated by Celia Britton, Annwyl Williams, Ben Brewster, and Alfred Guzzetti. Bloomington: Indiana University Press, 1977.

Miller, Jacqueline. *Poetic License: Authority and Authorship in Medieval and Renaissance Contexts.* New York: Oxford University Press, 1986.

Morrison, James. "After the Revolution: On the Fate of Cinephilia." *Michigan Quarterly Review* 44, no. 3 (2005): 393–413.

——. *Passport to Hollywood: Hollywood Films, European Directors.* Albany: SUNY Press, 1998.

Mulvagh, Jane. *Vogue: History of the 20th Century Fashion.* London: Viking, 1988.

Mulvey, Laura. *Death 24 x a Second: Stillness and the Moving Image.* London: Reaktion Books, 2006.

——. *Visual and Other Pleasures.* New York: Palgrave Macmillan, 2009.

Mulvey, Laura, and Peter Wollen. "From Cinephilia to Film Studies." In Grieveson and Wasson, *Inventing Film Studies,* 217–232.

Naremore, James. "Authorship and the Cultural Politics of Film Criticism." *Film Quarterly* 44, no. 1 (1990): 14–23.

——. *The Magic World of Orson Welles.* Dallas: Southern Methodist University Press, 1989.

Naremore, James, and Adrian Martin. "The Future of Academic Film Study." In *Movie Mutations: The Changing Face of World Cinephilia,* edited by Jonathan Rosenbaum and Adrian Martin, 119–132. London: BFI, 2003.

Navasky, Victor S. *Naming Names.* New York: Hill and Wang, 1980.

Nielsen, Elizabeth. "Handmaidens of the Glamour Culture: Costumers in the Hollywood Studio System." In *Fabrications: Costume and the Female Body,* edited by Jane Gaines and Charlotte Herzog, 160–179. New York: Routledge, 1990.

North, Michael. "Authorship and Autography." *PMLA* 116 (2001): 1377–1385.

Nowell-Smith, Geoffrey. "How Films Mean, or, From Aesthetics to Semiotics and Half-way Back Again." In Gledhill and Williams, *Reinventing Film Studies*, 8–17.

O'Brien, Geoffrey. *Castaways of the Image Planet: Movies, Show Business, Public Spectacle.* Washington, DC: Counterpoint, 2002.

O'Hara, Frank. "The Critic." In *The Selected Poems of Frank O'Hara.* Edited by Donald Allen, 48. Berkeley: University of California Press, 1995.

———. "To the Film Industry in Crisis." In *Meditations in an Emergency,* 3–5. New York: Grove Press, 1957.

Palmer, R. Barton. *Hollywood's Dark Cinema: The American Film Noir.* New York: Twayne, 1994.

———. "The Politics of Genre in Welles' *The Stranger.*" *Film Criticism* 9, no. 2 (1984–1985): 2–14.

Panofsky, Erwin. "Style and Medium in Motion Pictures." In Braudy and Cohen, *Film Theory and Criticism,* 247–261.

Perkowitz, Sidney. *Hollywood Science: Movies, Science, and the End of the World.* New York: Columbia University Press, 2007.

Pinsky, Michael. *Future Present: Ethics and/as Science Fiction.* Madison: Fairleigh Dickinson University Press, 2003.

Poe, Edgar Allan. "The Man of the Crowd." In *The Complete Tales and Poems of Edgar Allan Poe,* 475–481. New York: Vintage, 1975.

———. "The Murders in the Rue Morgue." In *The Complete Tales and Poems of Edgar Allan Poe,* 141–168.

———. "The Purloined Letter." In *The Complete Tales and Poems of Edgar Allan Poe,* 208–222.

Polan, Dana. *Scenes of Instruction: The Beginnings of the U.S. Study of Film.*

Berkeley: University of California Press, 2007.

Polsky, Stephanie. "Down the K. Hole: Walter Benjamin's Destructive Land-Surveying of History." In A. Benjamin, *Walter Benjamin and History,* 69–87.

Pratt, Ray. *Projecting Paranoia: Conspiratorial Visions in American Film.* Lawrence: University Press of Kansas, 2001.

Quinn, Malcolm. *The Swastika: Constructing the Symbol.* London: Routledge, 1994.

Rabinovitz, Lauren. "The Coney Island Comedies: Bodies and Slapstick at the Amusement Park and the Movies." In *American Cinema's Transitional Era: Audiences, Institutions, Practices,* edited by Charlie Keil and Shelley Stamp, 171–190. Berkeley: University of California Press, 2004.

Ray, Robert B. *A Certain Tendency of the Hollywood Cinema, 1930–1980.* Princeton: Princeton University Press, 1985.

———. *How a Film Theory Got Lost and Other Mysteries in Cultural Studies.* Bloomington: Indiana University Press, 2001.

Redmond, Sean, ed. *Liquid Metal: The Science Fiction Film Reader.* London: Wallflower, 2007.

———. "Science Fiction's Disaster Imagination." In Redmond, *Liquid Metal,* 38–39.

Reynolds, Paige. "'Something for Nothing': Bank Night and the Refashioning of the American Dream." In *Hollywood in the Neighborhood: Historical Case Studies of Local Moviegoing,* edited by Kathryn Fuller-Seeley, 208–232. Berkeley: University of California Press, 2008.

Richardson, Michael. *Surrealism and Cinema.* New York: Berg, 2006.

Richter, Gerhard. "A Matter of Distance: Benjamin's *One-Way Street* through *The Arcades.*" In *Walter Benjamin and the Arcades Project,* edited by Beatrice

Hanssen, 132–156. London: Continuum, 2006.

Rivette, Jacques. "The Essential." In Hillier, *Cahiers du Cinéma, the 1950s*, 132–135. Translated by Liz Heron.

——. "The Genius of Howard Hawks." In Hillier, *Cahiers du Cinéma, the 1950s*, 126–131. Translated by Russell Campbell and Marvin Pister.

Robida, Albert. *The Twentieth Century*. Middletown: Wesleyan University Press, 2004.

Rose, Mark. "The Author as Proprietor: Donaldson v. Becket and the Genealogy of Modern Authorship." *Representations* 23 (1988): 51–85.

Rosenbaum, Jonathan. "The Battle over Orson Welles." In *Essential Cinema: On the Necessity of Film Canons*, 376–385. Baltimore: Johns Hopkins University Press, 2004.

——. *Goodbye Cinema, Hello Cinephilia: Film Culture in Transition*. Chicago: University of Chicago Press, 2010.

Rosenbaum, Jonathan, and Adrian Martin, eds. *Movie Mutations: The Changing Face of World Cinephilia*. London: BFI, 2003.

Rosenheim, Shawn. "Extraterrestrial: Science Fictions in *A Brief History of Time* and *The Incredible Shrinking Man*." *Film Quarterly* 48, no. 4 (1995): 15–21.

Routt, William. "L'Évidence." *Continuum* 5, no. 2 (1990): 40–67.

Rubin, Martin. *Showstoppers: Busby Berkeley and the Tradition of Spectacle*. New York: Columbia University Press, 1993.

Salzani, Carlo. *Constellations of Reading: Walter Benjamin in Figures of Actuality*. Bern: Peter Lang, 2009.

Sarris, Andrew. "Notes on the Auteur Theory in 1962." In *The Primal Screen*, 38–53. New York: Simon and Schuster, 1973.

——. *"You Ain't Heard Nothin' Yet": The American Talking Film, History and Memory, 1927–1949*. Oxford: Oxford University Press, 1998.

Schatz, Thomas. *The Genius of the System: Hollywood Filmmaking in the Studio Era*. New York: Metropolitan, 1988.

——. *Hollywood Genres: Formulas, Filmmaking, and the Studio System*. Boston: McGraw-Hill, 1981.

Schivelbusch, Wolfgang. *The Railway Journey: The Industrialization of Time and Space in the 19th Century*. Berkeley: University of California Press, 1977.

Schrecker, Ellen. *The Age of McCarthyism: A Brief History with Documents*. New York: Bedford/St. Martin's, 2002.

Schwartz, Vanessa R. *Spectacular Realities: Early Mass Culture in Fin-de-Siècle Paris*. Berkeley: University of California Press, 1999.

——. "Walter Benjamin for Historians." *American Historical Review* 106 (2001): 1721–1743.

Seed, David. *American Science Fiction and the Cold War: Literature and Film*. Chicago: Fitzroy Dearborn, 1999.

Seldes, Gilbert. *Writing for Television*. New York: Doubleday, 1952.

Siepmann, Charles A. *Radio, Television, and Society*. New York: Oxford University Press, 1950.

Sikov, Ed. *Screwball: Hollywood's Madcap Romantic Comedies*. New York: Crown Publishers, 1989.

Simay, Philip. "Tradition as Injunction: Benjamin and the Critique of Historicisms." In A. Benjamin, *Walter Benjamin and History*, 137–155.

Simmel, Georg. "The Metropolis and Mental Life." In *The Nineteenth-Century Visual Culture Reader*, edited by Vanessa R. Schwartz and Jeannene B. Przyblyski, 51–55. New York: Routledge, 2004.

Sinclair, Andrew. *Spiegel: The Man Behind the Pictures*. Boston: Little, Brown, 1987.

Singer, Ben. *Melodrama and Modernity: Early Sensational Cinema and Its Contexts*. New York: Columbia University Press, 2001.

Slide, Anthony. *Silent Topics: Essays on Undocumented Areas of Silent Film*. Lanham: Scarecrow, 2004.

Smith, Julian. "A Runaway Match: The Automobile in the American Film, 1900–1920." In *The Automobile and American Culture*, edited by David L. Lewis and Laurence Goldstein, 179–192. Ann Arbor: University of Michigan Press, 1983.

Smoodin, Eric. "The History of Film History." In *Looking Past the Screen: Case Studies in American Film History and Method*, edited by Jon Lewis and Eric Smoodin, 1–33. Durham: Duke University Press, 2007.

Sobchack, Vivian. *Screening Space: The American Science Fiction Film*. New Brunswick: Rutgers University Press, 1999.

———. "The Virginity of Astronauts: Sex and the Science Fiction Film." In *Alien Zone: Cultural Theory and Contemporary Science Fiction Cinema*, edited by Annette Kuhn, 103–115. London: Verso, 1990.

Sontag, Susan. "A Century of Cinema." In *Where the Stress Falls: Essays*, 117–122. New York: Farrar, Straus and Giroux, 2001.

———. "The Imagination of Disaster." In Redmond, *Liquid Metal*, 40–47.

Spadoni, Robert. *Uncanny Bodies: The Coming of Sound Film and the Origins of the Horror Genre*. Berkeley: University of California Press, 2007.

Spigel, Lynn. *Make Room for T V: Television and the Family Ideal in Postwar America*. Chicago: University of Chicago Press, 1992.

———. *Welcome to the Dreamhouse: Popular Media and Postwar Suburbs*. Durham: Duke University Press, 2001.

Stoddart, Helen. "Auteurism and Film Authorship Theory." In *Approaches to Popular Film*, edited by Joanne Hollows and Mark Jancovich, 37–57. Manchester: Manchester University Press, 1995.

Studlar, Gaylyn. "'The Perfect Lover'?: Valentino and Ethnic Masculinity in the 1920s." In Grieveson and Krämer, *The Silent Cinema Reader*, 290–304.

———. *This Mad Masquerade: Stardom and Masculinity in the Jazz Age*. New York: Columbia University Press, 1996.

Sturges, Preston. *Preston Sturges by Preston Sturges*. Edited by Sandy Sturges. New York: Touchstone, 1990.

Szaloky, Melinda. "'As You Desire Me': Reading the 'Divine Garbo' through Movement, Silence and the Sublime." *Film History* 18, no. 2 (2006): 196–208.

———. "Sounding Images in Silent Film: Visual Acoustics in Murnau's *Sunrise*." *Cinema Journal* 41, no. 2 (2002): 109–131.

Thompson, Kristin. "The Concept of Cinematic Excess." In *Film Theory and Criticism: Introductory Readings*, edited by Leo Braudy and Marshall Cohen, 487–498. New York: Oxford University Press, 1999.

Thomson, David. *Rosebud: The Story of Orson Welles*. New York: Alfred A. Knopf, 1996.

Toles, George. "Rescuing Fragments: A New Task for Cinephilia." *Cinema Journal* 49, no. 2 (2010): 159–166.

Truffaut, François. *The Films in My Life*. Translated by Leonard Mayhew. New York: Da Capo, 1994.

———. "Foreword." In *Orson Welles: A Critical View*, 1–27. Translated by Jonathan Rosenbaum. New York: Harper & Row, 1978.

Tyler, Kingdon S. *Telecasting and Color*. New York: Harcourt, Brace and Company, 1946.

Tryon, Chuck. *Reinventing Cinema: Movies in the Age of Media Convergence*. New Brunswick: Rutgers University Press, 2009.

Urey, Harold C. "How Does it All Add Up?" In *One World or None*, edited by

Dexter Masters and Katherine Way,
53–58. New York: McGraw-Hill, 1946.

Vardoulakis, Dimitris. "The Subject of
History: The Temporality of Praxis
in Benjamin's Historiography." In A.
Benjamin, *Walter Benjamin and History*,
118–136.

Vieira, Mark A. *Irving Thalberg: Boy Wonder to Producer Prince*. Berkeley: University of California Press, 2009.

Vinken, Barbara. "Eternity – A Frill on a
Dress." *Fashion Theory* 1 (1997): 59–68.

Wagner, Jon Nelson, and Tracy Briga
MacLean. *Television at the Movies: Cinematic and Critical Responses to American
Broadcasting*. New York: Continuum,
2008.

Wallace, David. *Hollywoodland*. New York:
St. Martin's, 2002.

Wasko, Janet. *Hollywood in the Information
Age*. Austin: University of Texas Press,
1994.

Welles, Orson, and Peter Bogdanovich.
This is Orson Welles. Edited by Jonathan
Rosenbaum. New York: Da Capo, 1998.

Wells, Liz. *Photography: A Critical Introduction*. New York: Routledge, 1996.

Werner, James V. "The Detective Gaze:
Edgar A. Poe, the Flâneur, and the
Physiognomy of Crime." *American
Transcendental Quarterly* 15 (2001): 5–21.

Whyte, William H. *The Organization Man*.
Philadelphia: University of Pennsylvania Press, 2002.

Wilde, Oscar. *The Picture of Dorian Gray*.
New York: Tribeca, 2011.

Willemen, Paul. *Looks and Frictions: Essays in Cultural Studies and Film Theory*.
Bloomington: Indiana University Press,
1994.

Wilson, Elizabeth. *Adorned in Dreams:
Fashion and Modernity*. Berkeley: University of California Press, 1985.

Winokur, Mark. *American Laughter: Im-
migrants, Ethnicity, and 1930s Hollywood
Film Comedy*. New York: Palgrave Macmillan, 1996.

Wiser, William. *The Twilight Years: Paris in
the 1930s*. New York: Carroll and Graf,
2000.

Wohlfarth, Irving. "Et Cetera?: The Historian as Chiffonier." *New German Critique* 39 (1986): 142–168.

Wolin, Richard. *Walter Benjamin: An Aesthetic of Redemption*. Berkeley: University of California Press, 1994.

Wollen, Peter. *Paris Hollywood: Writings on
Film*. London: Verso, 2002.

———. "Strike a Pose." *Sight and Sound* 5,
no. 3 (1995): 10–15.

Wood, Robin. *Sexual Politics and Narrative
Film: Hollywood and Beyond*. New York:
Columbia University Press, 1998.

Woodmansee, Martha. "On the Author
Effect: Recovering Collectivity." In *The
Construction of Authorship: Textual Ap-
propriation in Law and Literature*, edited
by Martha Woodmansee and Peter
Jaszi, 15–28. Durham: Duke University
Press, 1994.

Wordsworth, William. *The Major Works
Including* The Prelude. Oxford: Oxford
University Press, 1984.

Wylie, Philip. *Generation of Vipers*. Champaign: Dalkey Archive, 1996.

Young, Paul. *The Cinema Dreams Its
Rivals: Media Fantasy Films from
Radio to the Internet*. Minneapolis:
University of Minnesota Press,
2006.

Index

Page numbers in italics refer to illustrations.

ABC, 175, 176, 177

Abrams, M. H., 122, 123–124, 145

Adair, Gilbert, 105, 138

Adorno, Theodor, 22

Adrian, Gilbert, 104–106, 108

Aesthetic of astonishment, 44–45, 48

L'Age d'Or, 73, 81

Allen, Woody, 85

Allen Smithee phenomenon, 130, 157, 235n130

All That Heaven Allows, 193, 208, 209

American Society of Cinematographers, 144

Anderegg, Michael, 152

Andrew, Dudley, 9, 136

Angel Face, 7–8

Aragon, Louis, 81, 101

Artaud, Antonin, 86

Arthur, Paul, 204

Auteurism: commercialization of, 10, 128; death of, 127; as defined at *Cahiers du Cinéma,* 7, 123–128 (see also *La politique des auteurs*); and signature experiment, 137–138, 155–156

Authorship, 120–123; and *auctor,* 120–121; and Romanticism, 121–123, 141

Azimov, Isaac, 186

Babington, Bruce, and Peter William Evans, 76

Baecque, Antoine de, 12

Balio, Tino, 81–82

Barrios, Richard, 100

Barthes, Roland, 13, 16, 28, 78, 120, 127

Basler, Roy, 120

Battle of the Sexes, The, 67

Bazin, André, 28, 48–49, 125–128, 129, 141, 156

Beast from 20,000 Fathoms, The, 162, 164, 185–190, *189*

Becker, Christine, 196

Belton, John, 59, 61, 68

Benjamin, Walter, xiv, 4, 13, 19–23, *24,* 25, 76, 96, 194, 219; and detective or detection, 27, 133–135; and flâneur or flânerie, 22–23, 50–51, 134–135; and gambler or gambling, 26, 49–51; and historical materialism, 5, 20–23; and modernity, 5, 20–21, 46, 50, 133; and photography, 21; and ragpicker or ragpicking, 26, 92–94, 96; and storyteller or storytelling, 27, 177–181, 207, 209

Bergstrom, Janet, 212

Bernhard, Nancy E., 173

Berry, Sarah, 82, 95

Betz, Mark, 213–214

Biskind, Peter, 163

Bixby letter, 119–120, 232n17

Blackmail, 68, 72

Blood of a Poet, 100–101

Boddy, William, 173–174

Booker, M. Keith, 200

Bordwell, David, 29, 208

Bordwell, David, Janet Staiger, and Kristin Thompson, 28, 37, 141, 143–144

Bradley, Fiona, 88
Brave New World, 39–40
Breathless, 7, 12
Breton, André, 2, 87–89
Broadway Melody, The, 40, 52, 68
Bryher, 74
Buck-Morss, Susan, 22, 50
Bulworth, 204
Byars, Jackie, 199

Cahiers du Cinéma, 6–9, 12, 24, 123–128, 151, 211, 214, 222n19
Cardinal, Roger, 6
Cat and the Canary, The, 65
CBS, 174, 175, 176, 185
Chance: in classical Hollywood, 90–91, 96–98, 108, 110; in Surrealism, 87–89, 93
Chandler, Raymond, 171
Chanel, Coco, 107–108
Chierichetti, David, 98
China Seas, 82
Chion, Michel, 38
Cinephilia: classical, 3, 6–8, 24; critique of, 3, 8–10, 214–215; definition of, 16–17; and excess, 4, 24, 80; and new media, 13–14, 17, 216–217; and Nouvelle Vague, 6, 12; opposition to, 10; rebirth of, 5–6, 11–14, 215–217; transformation of, 17, 217–219. *See also* Cinephiliac historiography
Cinephiliac historiography, 4, 17, 23–26, 29–30, 218–219
Cinephiliac moments, 5, 23–24, 25–26, 30, 33–34, 78–80, 113, 161–162, 218–219
Citizen Kane, 113, 129, 139, 140–142, *142,* 146
Clair, René, 83
Clash by Night, 15
Classical Hollywood: alternative history of, 26, 29–30, 74–75, 108–110, 154, 157–158, 194, 202–203, 218–219; critique of, 8, 28; moments in, 2, 4, 25–26; and relation to contemporary Hollywood, 208–209; in traditional film history, 4, 25, 28–29, 37–39, 81–82, 84, 118–119, 137, 144, 162–166
Cobra, 99
Cohen, Margaret, 87, 88
Comolli, Jean-Louis, and Jean Narboni, 151

Conley, Katharine, 88
Conrad, Peter, 130
Conversion to sound, 26, 35–36, 49, 51–52; as gamble, 38–39, 52–53, 53–72; Hollywood's version of, 36; in media history, 37–39; opposition to, 41
Cornered, 117, 150
Corrigan, Timothy, 128
Cowie, Peter, 129
Crafton, Donald, 36, 38, 58, 60, 74
Crawford, Joan, 105, 106
Creed, Barbara, 191
Crevel, René, 2–3, 108–109
Crossfire, 150
Crowther, Bosley, 160
Cukor, George, 177
Curtis, James, 97

Dada, 88
Dali, Salvador, 83, 86, 87, 107
Daney, Serge, 9–10
Darnton, Robert, 218
Dead End, 144
Delamater, Jerome, 86
Deleuze, Gilles, 207
DeMille, Cecil B., 83, 86, 97–98, 99
Denby, David, 11
Derrida, Jacques, 91, 136
Deserter, 73
Detour, 15
Dickinson, Greg, 206
Disney, Walt, 176–177
Doane, Mary Ann, 4, 6, 24
Doherty, Thomas, 66, 166, 173, 175, 176
Dombey and Son, 43
Don Juan, 52, 61, 224n2
Double Life, A, 144
Dreamers, The, 216
Duchamp, Marcel, 157

Early cinema, 42, 44–47, 56, 57, 59, 64, 66
Easy Living, 26, 77–80, *78, 79,* 82, 84–85, 90–91, 95, 96–97, 107, 108–109
Eburne, Jonathan E., 157
Eiland, Howard, and Kevin McLaughlin, 23
Eisenstein, Sergei, 73

Eisner, Lotte, 60–61
Elsaesser, Thomas, 215
Emerson, Ralph Waldo, 123
Epstein, Jean, 2, 13
Evans, Caroline, 104
Everitt, David, 149
Everson, William K., 32, 35, 38
Eyman, Scott, 37, 70, 71

Face in the Crowd, A, 165, 184–185, 204
Fantômas, 81
Far from Heaven, 207–208, 209
Fashion, 96; and classical Hollywood, 82, 99–100, 102–106, 107–108; and Surrealism, 100–102, 106–108
Father Knows Best, 176, 192, 206
FCC freeze, 168–169
Ferris, David S., 180
F for Fake, 113, 140, 153–154, 155
First Auto, The, 35, 56–61, 57, 58, 60
Fischer, Lucy, 69
Fitzgerald, F. Scott, 30
Five-cornered agreement, 68
Forty Guns, 7
42nd Street, 90
Fox, William, 61, 74
Freeman, Y. Frank, 160, 176
Friedrich, Otto, 145
Frost, Laura, 40, 41

Gable, Clark, 196
Gaines, Jane M., 99–100, 102
Garis, Robert, 112, 130, 156
Garland, Judy, 1–2
Gilbert, James, 191
Gitlin, Todd, 198
Glass Web, The, 184–185, 188
Gledhill, Christine, and Linda Williams, 212
Godard, Jean-Luc, 6–7
Goldwyn, Samuel, 35, 95, 97–98
Gomery, Douglas, 29, 36, 37, 74, 169, 181, 203
Gone with the Wind, 4, 168, 177
Good Neighbor policy in Latin America, 117, 232n6
Grant, Barry Keith, 195–196

Great Depression, 89; and film, 81–82, 90, 95, 102
Grieveson, Lee, and Haidee Wasson, 212
Griffith, D. W., 35
Gunning, Tom, 44–45, 48, 134, 135

Habermas, Jürgen, 84, 228n16
Hagener, Malte, and Marijke de Valck, 214
Hall, Mordaunt, 54, 65
Hansen, Miriam, 29–30, 45, 46, 46–47, 84, 86, 103–104
Haralovich, Mary Beth, 192
Hark, Ina Rae, 90, 109–110
Harvey, James, 78, 85–86
Haskell, Molly, 64
Hawks, Howard, 123, 124, 128
Hay, John, 120
Hays, Will, 53, 56
Hearts of Age, The, 152–153
Heller, Steven, 154
Hendershot, Cyndy, 164, 187
Heylin, Clinton, 118, 119
Higashi, Sumiko, 99
Hilmes, Michele, 202
Hitchcock, Alfred, 15, 107, 128, 139, 196
"Hitler Drawing Faulty Swastikas," 155
Holmes, Oliver Wendell, 125
"Homage to Mack Sennett," 101–102
Honor of His House, The, 2
Horton, Andrew, 85
House Un-American Activities Committee, 137, 149, 170
Howard, Frances, 35
How It Feels to Be Run Over, 46
Hudson, Dale, and Patricia Zimmerman, 217–218
Hughes, Howard, 181, 185
Huxley, Aldous, 41
Huyssen, Andreas, 153

I Love Lucy, 198
Impressionists, 2
Incredible Shrinking Man, The, 199–202, 202, 209
Invasion of the Body Snatchers, 162, 195–199, 197, 205
It Happened One Night, 78

It's All True, 118
Ivan, the Terrible, 80

Jack the Kisser, 47
Jameson, Fredric, 198
Jancovich, Mark, 163, 184, 186–187
Jazz Singer, The, 35, 37, 51, 52, 54, 55
Joyce, James, 73
Joyrich, Lynne, 208

Kauffman, Stanley, 11
Keathley, Christian, 12–13, 17, 241n34
Kennedy, Joseph P., 95
Kiesling, Barrett C., 104, 106
King Kong, 185
Kiss, The, 26, 33–35, 34, 38, 68–72, 70, 71, 99
Kracauer, Siegfried, 5, 94

Lady from Shanghai, The, 113
Laemmle, Carl, 65, 67, 68, 90
Landay, Lori, 198
Landy, Marcia, 207
Langdon, Jennifer E., 117, 150
Lasky, Jesse, 90, 97–98
Lastra, James, 37, 55–56, 135
Laurence, William L., 186
Lawnmower Man, The, 203
Leaming, Barbara, 117, 129
Leave It to Beaver, 192, 206
Leisen, Mitchell, 15, 98–99, 104, 108
Leitch, Thomas M., 128
Letty Lynton, 105–106, 231n98
Lights of New York, 52, 67
Lincoln, Abraham, 119–120
Loew, Marcus, 95
Luhmann, Niklas, xiv

MacCabe, Colin, 126
Madam Satan, 99–100
Magnificent Ambersons, The, 118, 139
Maltby, Richard, 25, 29, 203
Man Who Laughs, The, 64–67
Martin, Adrian, 221n18
Martin, Richard, 100, 101, 107
Marx Brothers, 83, 86
Materialist film historiography. *See* Cine-
    philiac historiography

Matthews, Melvin E., 184
Mayer, Louis B., 68, 91, 94, 95
McBride, Joseph, 129, 152, 153
McCarthy, Joseph R., 149, 174–176
McCole, John, 178
Metz, Christian, 9, 70–71, 214–215
MGM, 68, 91, 94, 105
Midnight, 108
Mighty Tumble, A, 46
Miller, Jacqueline, 121
Modernism, 84
Modernity, 42–44, 133. *See also* Benjamin,
    Walter
Morrison, James, 9, 83–84, 216
Motion Picture Producers and Distribu-
    tors of America, 168
Movietone, 61, 65, 74
Mr. Arkadin, 155–156
Mulvagh, Jane, 105–106
Mulvey, Laura, 10, 17, 193, 213, 215
Murder by Television, 188
Murrow, Edward R., 174–175
My Man Godfrey, 78

Naremore, James, 118, 129, 136, 147
Naremore, James, and Adrian Martin, 210
NBC, 168, 169, 172, 174, 175, 176, 180
Net, The, 203
Network, 204
Next Voice You Hear, The, 164
Nielsen, Elizabeth, 104
Nims, Ernest, 117, 118
Nobody's Baby, 102–103
North, Michael, 120, 125
Nowell-Smith, Geoffrey, 214

O'Brien, Geoffrey, 19
O'Hara, Frank, 211, 212, 215
Old San Francisco, 54–56, 54, 55, 59, 61, 70

Palmer, R. Barton, 146
Paramount decision, 168, 202
Perkowitz, Sidney, 195
Photogénie, 2, 13, 16
Pinsky, Michael, 185
Pleasantville, 206
Poe, Edgar Allan, 131–133, 134–135, 138

Poiret, Paul, 105, 107
Polan, Dana, 212
La politique des auteurs, 7, 124–128
Poor Little Rich Girl, The, 48
Pratt, Ray, 198
Proto-McCarthyism, 27, 150
Psycho, 4

Quinn, Malcolm, 154–155

Railroad Smashup, 46, 47
Rankin, John, 149–150
Ray, Man, 86, 230n82
Ray, Robert B., 28, 29
Rebel without a Cause, 193
Red Channels, 149
Redmond, Sean, 163
Richardson, Michael, 86
Rivette, Jacques, 7–8, 124
R K O, 118, 140, 145, 181, 185, 198
Robida, Albert, 166–167, 205
Rose, Mark, 122
Rosenbaum, Jonathan, 217
Rosenbaum, Jonathan, and Adrian Martin, 13–14
Rosenheim, Shawn, 199
Rounding Up the Yeggmen, 47
Routt, William, 124
Rubin, Martin, 86

Safe, 206–207
Salzani, Carlo, 92
Sarris, Andrew, 124–125
Scarface, 7
Schatz, Thomas, 28–29, 82
Schiaparelli, Elsa, 106–108
Schivelbusch, Wolfgang, 43
Schwartz, Vanessa, 20, 23, 223n76
Sci-fi films, 162–163, 165–166, 173, 182–203, 203–204
Seed, David, 163
Seldes, Gilbert, 181
"Self-Portrait," 101
Selznick, David O., 176, 177
Seven Year Itch, The, 165
Shadow of a Doubt, 146–147
Shall We Dance, 103–104, 103

Siepmann, Charles A., 186
Sikov, Ed, 108, 109
Simay, Philip, 179, 209
Simmel, Georg, 5
Sinclair, Andrew, 144
Singer, Ben, 44
Singing Fool, The, 36, 52
Singin' in the Rain, 36, 52
Sobchack, Vivian, 189, 191
Sontag, Susan, 6, 10–11, 173, 182, 216
Spadoni, Robert, 32, 52, 65
Spiegel, Sam, 117, 144–145
Spigel, Lynn, 165, 172, 189, 205
Star Is Born, A, 1–2, 2, 3
Stoddart, Helen, 123
Stranger, The, 27, 113–119, 114, 115, 128–131, 138–139, 142–143, 143, 144–155, 157–158
Studio system. *See* Classical Hollywood
Studlar, Gaylyn, 48, 65, 227n85
Sturges, Preston, 78, 96–97
Sullivan's Travels, 92
Sunrise, 61–64, 63
Sunset Boulevard, 165, 167, 196
Surrealism, 26, 86–89, 93, 100–102, 106–107, 108
Surrealists, 2, 80–81, 93, 125. *See also* Surrealism
Swing Time, 90
Szaloky, Melinda, 62

Television: and advertising, 173–174; and atomic bomb testing, 172–173; and film stars, 176, 196; growth of, 164–166, 168–170; Hollywood's critique of, 184–185, 187–189, 191–193, 197–199, 200–201, 203–209; and Kefauver Crime Committee hearings, 170–172; and McCarthy, 174–176
Ten Commandments, The, 165
Terminator 2, 203, 204
Thalberg, Irving, 35, 68, 81, 90
Them!, 27, 161–164, 162, 165, 190–193, 192, 194
Thing from Another World, The, 163, 182–185, 183
Third Man, The, 116
Thompson, Kristin, 24, 80

Thomson, David, 148, 152
Through the Haverstraw Tunnel, 46
Toland, Gregg, 141, 144
Toles, George, 17, 210, 215, 218, 219
Tolstoy, Leo, 112, 127, 129
Torrent, The, 99
Trouble with Harry, The, 152
Truffaut, François, 7, 15, 127, 152, 153
Truman Show, The, 205
Tual, Denise, 91
TV Guide, 164

Uncle Josh at the Moving Picture Show, 45, 72
Universal, 65, 67

Valck, Marijke de, and Malte Hagener, 14
Vardoulakis, Dimitris, 23
Vertigo, 18, 19, 216, 219
Virginian, The, 72
Vitaphone, 35, 49, 54, 56, 68, 74

Waldorf Statement, 137
Wallace, David, 106
Warner, Jack, 164, 165, 181
Warner, Sam, 49, 61, 74
Warner Bros., 35, 49, 56, 67, 68, 74, 164, 185
War of the Worlds, 140, 152

Wasko, Janet, 169
Welch, Joseph N., 175–176
Welles, Orson, 15, 117, 118–119, 128, 130, 137–138, 150; as signature, 136, 139–143, 146, 152–154, 157–158
Wells, H. G., 140
Wells, Liz, 125
Werner, James V., 133
Wertham, Fredric, 187
West, Mae, 107
Whyte, William H., 198–199
Why We Fight, 150
Wilde, Oscar, 146
Willemen, Paul, 4, 11–12, 16
Wilson, Elizabeth, 106
Wohlfarth, Irving, 92–94
Wolin, Richard, 20
Wollen, Peter, 16–17, 94–95, 212
Women, The, 102
Wood, Robin, 86–87
Woodmansee, Martha, 121
Wordsworth, William, 122–123
Wylie, Philip, 192

Young, Edward, 122, 141
Young, Paul, 167, 169

Zukor, Adolph, 68, 95, 97–98

RASHNA WADIA RICHARDS is Assistant Professor and Director of Film Studies at Rhodes College. Her areas of specialization include film history, critical theory, and transnational cultural studies. She has published on film theory as well as American, French, and Bollywood cinemas in *Framework, Film Criticism, Quarterly Review of Film and Video, Criticism,* and *Arizona Quarterly.*